Y0-CDD-130

POStroaD

Post Road publishes twice yearly and accepts unsolicited poetry, fiction, and nonfiction submissions. Complete submission guidelines are available at www.postroadmag.com.

Subscriptions: Individuals, $18/year; Institutions, $34/year; outside the U.S. please add $6/year for postage.

Post Road is a nonprofit 501(c)(3) corporation published by Post Road Magazine, Inc. in partnership with the Boston College Department of English. All donations are tax-deductible.

Distributed by:

Ingram Periodicals, Inc., LaVergne, TN

Printed by:

BookMasters, Mansfield, OH

Post Road was founded in New York City in 1999 by Jaime Clarke and David Ryan with the following core editors: Rebecca Boyd, Susan Breen, Hillary Chute, Mark Conway, Pete Hausler, Kristina Lucenko (1999-2003), Anne McCarty and Michael Rosovsky.

Editors Emeritus include Sean Burke (1999-2001), Jaime Clarke (1999-2008), Mary Cotton, as Publisher and Managing Editor (2004-2008), Erin Falkevitz (2005-2006), Alden Jones (2002-2005), Fiona Maazel (2001-2002), Marcus McGraw (2003-2004), Catherine Parnell, as Managing Editor (2003), Samantha Pitchel (2006-2008), and Ricco Villanueva Siasoco, as Managing Editor (2009-2010).

Cover Art:
Rosaire Appel, "bearings"

Copyright © 2016 Post Road

ISBN: 978-0-9849463-9-6

POST roaD

Publisher
Post Road Magazine, Inc.
in partnership with the
Boston College Department
of English

Art Editor
Susan Breen

Criticism Editor
Hillary Chute

Fiction Editors
Rebecca Boyd
Mary Cotton
David Ryan

Guest Editor
Christopher Boucher

Nonfiction Editors
Josephine Bergin
Pete Hausler

Poetry Editors
Mark Conway
Anne McCarty
Nicolette Nicola
Jeffrey Shotts
Lissa Warren

Recommendations Editors
Elizabeth Bologna
Annie Hartnett
Tim Huggins
Nelly Reifler

Theatre Editor
David Ryan

Layout and Design
Josephine Bergin

Web Designer
David Ryan

Managing Editor
Christopher Boucher

Assistant Managing Editors
James Boyman
Christina Freitas

Copyeditor
Valerie Duff-Strautmann

Interns
Kwesi Aaron
Rachel Aldrich
Kaitlin Astrella
Olivia Bono
Maria Jose Cordova
Bailey Flynn
Jakub Frankowicz
Christopher Kabacinski
Eileen Kao
Catherine Malcynsky
Caitlin Mason
Erin McGarvey
Anna Olcott
Ermol Clearfoster Sheppard
Katia Tanner
Ross Tetzloff

Readers
Lauren Bell
Stephanie Bergman
Cara Boulton
Charlie Clements
Sara Danver
Katelyn Eelman
Brendan Flanagan
Catherine Gellene
Melissa Hanan
Lindsey Hanlon
Allison Kolar
Caitlin Lahsaiezadeh
Meaghan Leahy
Sarah MacDonald
Ilana Masad
Matthew Mazzari
Marie McGrath
Matthew Messer
Joanne Nelson
Megyn Norbut
Laura Smith
Bailey Spencer
Hannah Taylor
Cedar Warman
Natasha Yglesias
Christine Zhao
Michele Zimmerman

Table of Contents

Contributor Notes

Jeffrey Alfier won the 2014 Kithara Book Prize for his poetry collection, *Idyll for a Vanishing River* (2013). He is also author of *The Wolf Yearling* (2013), *The Storm Petrel* (2014) and *The Red Stag at Carrbridge* (2016). He is founder and co-editor of Blue Horse Press and *San Pedro River Review*.

Rosaire Appel is an ex-fiction writer who abandoned words for images. She explores the betweens of reading / looking / listening. She makes books (commercially printed, hand-made, and recycled), ink drawings, digital drawings, abstract comics, and short animations. Her subject is visual language. She develops combinations and sequences which remain open to interpretation, keeping the relationship between the viewer and the work active rather than passive. Her website is www.rosaireappel.com.

Emily Barton's first two novels, *Brookland* and *The Testament Of Yves Gundron*, were both named *New York Times* Notable Books of the Year. Her third novel, *The Book of Esther*, came out in June. She has received grants from the Guggenheim Foundation, the National Endowment for the Arts, and the Sustainable Arts Foundation. She can be found on Twitter @embleybarton.

W.B. Belcher is the author of *Lay Down Your Weary Tune*, published by Other Press in early 2016. When not writing, Belcher is the Director of External Affairs at The Hyde Collection, an art museum and historic house in Glens Falls, New York. He lives on the border of New York and Vermont with his wife and two kids.

Loren Britton holds a BFA from SUNY Purchase and is currently enrolled in the MFA program at Yale. In January 2015, Britton presented a solo exhibition titled Physical Sun at Studio Kura in Fukuoka, Japan. Britton is half of the curatorial team for Improvised Showboat with Zachary Keeting, and Britton loves looking at and making juicy paintings. Artist website: lorenbritton.com.

Susan Carr is an MFA graduate from the School of the Museum of Fine Arts Boston and Tufts University. Susan is presently working to expand the idea of painting and curatorial practice. She is very interested in indigenous cultures, magic, and raw brute art. Susan also uses found objects in her work, which she feels give the work a sense of chance and possibility. You can find her surfing the Internet, at the ocean and in her studio. For more of her work: instagram.com/susancarr88.

Suzanne Cope is the author of *Small Batch: Pickles, Cheese, Chocolate, Spirits and the Return of Artisanal Food* and has written essays and articles for *The New York Times*, *The Atlantic*, *Washington Post*, and *Lucky Peach*, among other publications. She teaches writing at Manhattan College and University of Arkansas Monticello MFA Program. She lives in Brooklyn, NY.

Theodore Dawes lives in Irvine, California. This is his first published story.

Ezra Dan Feldman is a PhD student in English at Cornell University and the author of *Habitat of Stones*, a collection of poems. His dissertation, "Real Possibilities: Speculative Metafiction and the Poetics of Speculative Selves," focusing on works by Margaret Atwood, Lydia Davis, Tom McCarthy, Colson Whitehead, and Don DeLillo, will investigate the form and significance of fictional characters presented as possible, hypothetical, or projected—and yet unreal. Ezra's writing has most recently appeared in *Newfound, Hayden's Ferry Review*, and *The Carolina Quarterly*.

Kirby Gann is the author of three novels; his most recent, *Ghosting*, was named a Best Book of the Year by *Publishers Weekly* and *flavorpill*. Having served eighteen years as managing editor at Sarabande Books, he is now a freelance editor and book designer, while also on faculty at the brief-residency MFA Program at Spalding University.

Brad Geer is a native of Kansas who recently returned from a stint working at McMurdo Station, Antarctica. He is a teacher, instructional designer, and writer. His work has also been featured in *The Mondegreen*.

Holly George-Warren is the author of more than a dozen books, including *Public Cowboy #1: The Life and Times of Gene Autry* and *A Man Called Destruction: The Life and Music of Alex Chilton, from Box Tops to Big Star to Backdoor Man*. A two-time Grammy nominee and ASCAP-Deems Taylor Award recipient, she is currently writing a biography of Janis Joplin, to be published by Simon & Schuster in 2017.

Jaclyn Gilbert holds an MFA from Sarah Lawrence College. She teaches writing at Pace University and Westchester Community College and is at work on her first novel.

Connie Goldman utilizes the vocabulary of reductive art to visually articulate her intellectual and emotional responses to the world. Her use of essential means describes natural phenomena and the contradictory forces of stasis and flux. Goldman exhibits internationally and her work is featured in many museum collections. Her website is conniegoldman.com.

Becky Hagenston's first story collection, *A Gram of Mars*, won the Mary McCarthy Prize; her second collection, *Strange Weather*, won the Spokane Prize. Her third collection, *Scavengers*, won the Permafrost Book Prize and is forthcoming in 2016 from University of Alaska Press. Twice the recipient of an O. Henry Award, she is an associate professor of English at Mississippi State University.

Alan Hanson is a writer from California. He's written for *Cosmopolitan*, *McSweeney's*, and *The Hairpin*, among others.

David Huddle is from Ivanhoe, Virginia, and he taught at the University of Vermont for thirty-eight years. His fiction, poetry, and essays have appeared in *The American Scholar, Esquire, The New Yorker, Harper's*, and *Green Mountains Review*. In 2012, his novel *Nothing Can Make Me Do This* won the Library of Virginia Award for Fiction, and his collection *Black Snake at the Family Reunion* won the 2013 Pen New England Award for Poetry. His most recent book is a collection of poems, *Dream Sender*, published in September 2015 by LSU Press.

Noé Jimenez is a painter living and working in New Haven, CT. Starting with old family photographs, he assembles a structure by collaging and shaping the cut outs as a surface for paintings. The work comes out reading as sculpture first and a picture plane second, and so Jimenez explores personal narratives with color and flat space. Under the skin of paint on a textured 35mm print, the colors of both photography and painting are used to create the forms and abstracted imagery of his assembled canvases.

Josh Kalscheur is the 2015-16 Halls Emerging Artist Fellow. His book, *Tidal* (Four Way Books), was the winner of the 2013 Levis Prize in Poetry and was published in Spring 2015. Individual poems have been published in *Boston Review*, *The Iowa Review* and *Slate* among others.

Sarah Kennedy lives in Philadelphia and teaches at Rutgers University Camden. She previously worked as a lexicographer, a travel writer, a waitress, a bartender, and an amusement park ride operator. She holds a BA from Harvard and an MFA from Rutgers-Camden. Her work appears in *Chautauqua Magazine*, *Under the Sun*, *Some Call it Ballin'*, and *Hidden City Philadelphia*.

Lania Knight's first book, *Three Cubic Feet*, was a finalist for the 2012 Lambda Literary Award in Debut Fiction. Her stories, essays, and interviews have been published in *The Missouri Review*, *PANK*, *Fourth Genre*, *The Rumpus*, *Jabberwock Review*, *Midwestern Gothic*, and elsewhere. New work is forthcoming in *Quiddity* and *Queen Mob's Teahouse*. Lania was a Resident Writing Fellow at Vermont Studio Center for July 2015. She currently teaches as a Senior Lecturer in Creative Writing at University of Gloucestershire in the UK. Read more about her at www.laniaknight.com.

Stacy Leeman exhibits widely throughout the nation. She is represented by the Sharon Weiss Gallery in Columbus, Ohio, where her next solo exhibition will be shown in 2016. Leeman has a BA in Studio Art from Oberlin and an MFA from Rutgers. Her work can be found at stacyleeman.com.

Bonny Leibowitz is an artist working in mixed media with recent exhibitions at Art Cube Gallery, Laguna Beach, CA; Cohn Drennan Contemporary, Dallas, TX; and The Museum of Art, Wichita Falls, TX. Notable group exhibitions have been held in New York, Baltimore, and London. She co-curated "Family Ties" with Julie Torres of New York. Artist website: bonnyleibowitz.com.

Meg Lipke has had numerous solo and group exhibitions. She received a BA from the University of Vermont and an MFA from Cornell University. She lives and works in Brooklyn and Ghent, NY. She often treats her paper, canvas or panel as if she were working with fabric. Artist website: meglipke.com.

Stephen B. MacInnis lives and works in Charlottetown, Prince Edward Island, Canada, where he was born and raised. A painter, for the past several years he has been working on a long-term project entitled Long Series, a series of over 1,500, 12 x 12 inch mixed media paintings. It's his plan to complete 10,000 paintings in this series. The Long Series is primarily mixed media on paper. Within the series the exploration of drawing, painting, collage, and unusual materials such as tape, objects, and found papers are exploited. The use of accident, contrivance, simulation, and collaboration with other artists and the public have also been utilized. The project explores the effects of a long-term project on the development of a personal iconography.
Artist website: sbmacinnis.wordpress.com.

Jana Martin's books include the collection *Russian Lover and Other Stories* and *Smoke Gets in Your Eyes*. Her fiction and nonfiction has appeared in publications from *The New York Times* and *Cosmopolitan* to the *Mississippi Review*, *Glimmer Train*, *Five Points*, and *New World Writing*. She is a contributing editor for *The Weeklings* and the SUNY New Paltz Writer in Residence for Spring 2016. A veteran of numerous punk bands and a former denizen of the spoken word scene, she now lives in the Hudson Valley.

Carrie Messenger lives in West Virginia. Her fiction has appeared most recently in *Fairy Tale Review*, *The Florida Review*, and *The Literary Review*. Her translations from Romanian have appeared in *Circumference*, *The Review of Contemporary Fiction*, and *Words Without Borders*.

Lincoln Michel is the author of the story collection *Upright Beasts* and the co-editor of the science flash fiction anthology *Gigantic Worlds*. His work has appeared in *Tin House*, *Granta*, *The New York Times*, *NOON*, *The Believer*, and elsewhere. He is the editor-in-chief of electricliterature.com and the co-editor of *Gigantic* magazine. You can find him online at lincolnmichel.com and @ thelincoln.

Steve Monroe has written seven one-act plays, four ten-minute plays, three full-length plays, two original screenplays (co-written a third), a couple of short stories, and a novel. He is currently working on his first detective novel. He lives in Brooklyn, NY with his wife and three sons.

Andrew Morgan is a professor, poet, editor, and volunteer whose work can be found in magazines such as *Conduit*, *Verse*, *Slope*, *Stride*, *Fairy Tale Review*, *Country Music*, *GlitterPony*, *Pleiades* (as part of a "Younger American Poets" feature), and is included in the anthology *Disco Prairie Aid and Pleasure Club*. He is the recipient of a Slovenian Writer's Association Fellowship which sponsored a month long writing residency in the country's capital city of Ljubljana. He has served as the Juniper Fellow at the University of Massachusetts Amherst where he facilitated the Visiting Writers Program, and he has worked as an editorial assistant for *Verse Magazine*, and an assistant managing editor for Verse Press. He is currently an Associate Professor of Creative Writing at New England College. His first book, *Month of Big Hands*, was published by Natural History Press in 2013.

Laura Moriarty is former long-time director of the R&F workshop program and The Gallery at R&F. Her honors include two grants from the Pollock-Krasner Foundation, a Radius Award from the Aldrich Contemporary Art Museum, a MARK Award from the New York Foundation for the Arts, and most recently, a Projects Grant from United States Artists. Laura has participated in numerous artist residencies including The Vermont Studio Center, The Frans Masereel Center in Belgium and The Ucross Foundation in Wyoming. She has exhibited extensively at venues including the OK Harris Works of Art, International Print Center New York, The Islip Art Museum, The Nicolaysen Art Museum and Discovery Center, and The Jyväskylä Art Museum. She is the author of *Table of Contents*, an artist's book published in 2012. Artist website: lauramoriarty.com.

Lauri Lynnxe Murphy's work focuses on environmental issues by exploring the meaning embedded in materiality, utilizing everything from snail trails to honeycomb to industrial waste. She received her undergraduate degree in painting from the Metropolitan State College of Denver and earned her MFA at The Ohio State University in 2012. Artist website: lynnxe.com.

Jason Ockert is the author of *Wasp Box*, a novel, and two collections of short stories: *Neighbors of Nothing* and *Rabbit Punches*. Winner of the Dzanc Short Story Collection Contest, the Atlantic Monthly Fiction Contest, and the Mary Roberts Rinehart Award, he was also a finalist for the Shirley Jackson Award and the Million Writers Award. His work has appeared in journals and anthologies including *New Stories from the South*, *Best American Mystery Stories*, *Oxford American*, *The Iowa Review*, *One Story*, *Post Road*, and *McSweeney's*. He teaches writing at Coastal Carolina University.

Angela Palm is the author of *Riverine: A Memoir from Anywhere but Here*, winner of the 2014 Graywolf Press Nonfiction Prize. The book was published by Graywolf Press in August 2016. Palm owns Ink + Lead Literary Services and is the editor of *Please Do Not Remove*, a book featuring work by Vermont writers. Her work has appeared in or is forthcoming in *Brevity*, *DIAGRAM*, *Paper Darts*, *Midwestern Gothic*, *Sundog Lit*, *Essay Daily*, and elsewhere.

Ricardo Paniagua was born in Dallas, TX, in 1981. Ricardo left the educational system his sophomore year in high school and is self-informed. Now approaching ten years of serious practice, his work finds itself included amongst academically trained professionals and on institutional platforms throughout Texas and more recently abroad. While engaging in the ongoing dialogue that is "contemporary art," he has been known to evolve multiple bodies of work concurrently. Recurrent in his work are themes ranging from pure abstraction to exquisitely precise geometric design, at times experimental and/or conceptual. Having a rigorous work ethic and eye for detail that can be traced back to a lineage of master tile artisans, Paniagua utilizes articulated craftsmanship in much of his recent work.

Paola Peroni was born and raised in Rome. Her fiction has appeared in the *Bellevue Literary Review*, *Alaska Quarterly Review*, *The Antioch Review*, *Mississippi Review*, *Fence*, *The Common*, and other publications. She has worked as a screenwriter in Los Angeles for many years. She now lives in New York City and works as a psychoanalyst in private practice.

Wendy Rawlings is the author of a novel, *The Agnostics*, and a collection of short stories, *Come Back Irish*. Her work has appeared recently or is forthcoming in *AGNI*, *Creative Nonfiction*, *The Cincinnati Review*, and the 2016 Pushcart Prize anthology.

Jason Rohlf, born in 1970, is a native of Milwaukee, Wisconsin. He has resided with his family in Brooklyn, New York for the past sixteen years. While exhibiting nationally, Jason has also created a public work in glass for the MTA's Arts for Transit program. About his Shop Rag Project, he writes, "Like a recalled memory, a once obscure thing, hidden elements from the piece's past will form an essential role on the surface, often as relief, while the most hard-fought details will likely earn a swift opaque top coat as a result of each day's fits and starts. By conveying an urban palimpsest, many of the most thoughtful moments occur as these conflicting efforts achieve harmony and then begin to recede, resulting in the melding of competing ideas." Artist website: geoform.net/artists/jason-rohlf.

Suzanne Roszak's poetry has appeared or is forthcoming in *Crab Orchard Review*, *Ecotone*, *Hayden's Ferry Review*, *Redivider*, and *ZYZZYVA*. Her first full-length manuscript, *After the Wake*, was a finalist for the Brittingham and Pollak Poetry Prizes, the *Crab Orchard Review* First Book Award, and the Akron Poetry Prize. Suzanne received her MFA in poetry from University of California, Irvine in 2015.

Joanna Ruocco is an assistant professor of creative writing in the English Department at Wake Forest University. She has published several books, including *Another Governess/The Least Blacksmith: A Diptych*, which won the FC2 Catherine Doctorow Innovative Fiction Prize (judged by Ben Marcus), and most recently, *Dan* (Dorothy, a publishing project). Ruocco also works pseudonymously as Alessandra Shahbaz (*Ghazal in the Moonlight, Midnight Flame*) and Toni Jones (*No Secrets in Spandex*). Her stories have appeared in numerous journals including *NOON, Conjunctions, The Black Warrior Review, Caketrain*, and *The Brooklyn Rail*.

Ethan Rutherford's fiction has appeared in *Ploughshares, One Story, American Short Fiction*, and *The Best American Short Stories*. His first book, *The Peripatetic Coffin and Other Stories*, was a finalist for the *Los Angeles Times* Art Seidenbaum Award, received honorable mention for the PEN/Hemingway Award, and was the winner of a Minnesota Book Award. Born in Seattle, Washington, he now lives in Hartford, Connecticut, and teaches at Trinity College.

Susan Still Scott is an artist living and working in New Lebanon, NY. She has exhibited throughout the United States in galleries and museums, and on multiple occasions in Europe. She has received noteworthy residency fellowships from Yaddo and the MacDowell Colony. More information can be found at susanstillscott.com.

Suzan Shutan's work straddles two and three dimensions. Rooted in Post Minimalism, she explores life processes through materials, pattern, and color. She received a BFA from Cal Arts and MFA from Rutgers University. Her work has been shown throughout the United States, Latin America, and Europe, and is in various collections and publications. Artist website: www.suzanshutan.com.

Remy Smidt is a 21-year-old writer from Phoenix, Arizona.

Julie Torres is a Brooklyn-based painter and curator, organizing community focused projects and frequent collaborations with likeminded artists. More about her work and upcoming events can be seen at julietorres.weebly.com.

Joyce Ann Underwood is a writer whose identity as a Floridian has inspired much of her work. Growing up in Crescent City, Florida, she spent many afternoons listening to the old-timers tell stories about just about everyone they had ever known. Her love for storytelling would grow into a refined passion at the University of West Florida where she received a BA in English and Creative Writing in 2009. Joyce blogs at First Person Narrative and has been published on Offbeat Home, HIV Here&Now, and in the now defunct publication *Kairos*. She lives with her husband and daughter wherever the military takes them, which at the time of this writing is Fayetteville, NC.

Sarah Vallance recently won a Pushcart prize for an essay published in the *Gettysburg Review* in Winter 2014. She also received a Special Mention in *Pushcart XL* and a notable mention in *Best American Essays 2015* for an essay published in *The Pinch*, in Fall 2014. Sarah is a graduate of the City University of Hong Kong MFA program.

Jill Vasileff was born in Detroit, Michigan and currently lives and works in Stockton, California. She holds a BFA from Parsons School for Design, NY, and an MFA from Bard College, Annandale, NY. She has exhibited internationally in New York, California, Detroit, Dallas, Washington DC, Germany, France, and the Netherlands. Artist website: jillvasileff.com.

Jennifer Wheelock's poems have appeared or are forthcoming in many journals and anthologies, including Negative Capability Press, *Stone, River, Sky: An Anthology of Georgia Poems*, *Diagram*, *River Styx*, *Atlanta Review*, *New Millennium Writings*, *The Inflectionist Review*, *Garbanzo*, *North Atlantic Review*, *The Peralta Press*, *Comstock Review*, *The Emily Dickinson Award Anthology*, and the online journal *Blaze*. Her poem "Feeding Francis Bacon" appears in the book *Thirteen Ways of Looking for a Poem: A Guide to Writing Poetry* in the chapter on formal verse. She holds an MFA from Georgia State University and a PhD from Florida State University. She lives in Los Angeles and works at UCLA.

Kim Ablon Whitney's novels have earned special distinction from the American Library Association, Bank Street College of Education, and *Booklist Magazine*. A graduate of Tufts University, Kim has an MFA in creative writing from Emerson College. She lives in Newton, MA with her husband, three children, and dog. She is a member of the PEN New England Children's Book Committee and coordinator of the Susan P. Bloom Discovery Award.

Angela Woodward is the author of the collection *The Human Mind* and the novel *End of the Fire Cult*. Her collection *Origins and Other Stories* won *The Collagist*'s 2014 prose chapbook competition and will be out from Dzanc in 2016. Her novel *Natural Wonders*, also out in 2016, was the winner of the 2015 Fiction Collective Two Catherine Doctorow Innovative Fiction Prize.

Circumstance

Theodore Dawes

Godfrey knew to expect nothing—he'd suffered enough exemplary lessons. Nevertheless, he rode the Manhattan train with hope, as if he carried, in an Igloo cooler secured with transparent tape, a liver he acquired for his own transplant surgery. He wore a windowpane tweed sport coat, new and trimly altered, with lapels as narrow as his knuckle, and he'd soaked his chest, neck, and crotch with an old-fashioned cologne that smelled of pine boughs and hay bales. This Monica, he thought, might get drunk enough to fuck him: the dating app graded their compatibility at eighty-six percent, and in her uploaded photos she appeared sufficiently overweight to be approached without terror. She might even get drunk enough to fuck him without a condom: he could hope. He did hope. A pregnancy would drive her to him, clinging as if to an overturned hull after a wreck on gray, violent seas. He would bear her across the frigid water, to the stony, desolate shore on which she'd be obliged to homestead. Monica's last name was something-or-other freighted with pointless syllables and hawking sounds, the last name of a diner princess, an auto body heiress, the kind of last name that paid inexplicable cash for Audis and tacky mansions in outer boroughs— perhaps her parents squatted on piles of dinars or rupees or Yap wheels that their exotic customs would oblige them to share. Godfrey patted his sparse new mustache, bits of which kept flaring up like twisted bristles on a brush head. Yes, Monica's large-gutted father would lift his splattered apron and distribute handfuls of the flawless rubies he cached amidst his belly's canopy of black hairs. This dowry could carry them to someplace leafy—Westchester or Greenwich, Godfrey figured—where lilacs bloomed in the English-style gardens, where dwarflike Hondurans drove constant lawnmowers, where pitchers of iced tea were cut with whiskey and consumed with dignity before noon. His pretty children were quiet and amusing, his pretty mistress pliant and amusing. He took an interest in wainscoting and similar decorative features, perhaps wrote a pamphlet or small book about it, *Great Moldings of the Hudson Valley*, sold on spinning tree racks by the cash registers at farm stands and antique shops from Nyack to Rhinebeck. He smelled the churned earth, fizzy and organic, after a thunderstorm passed. In autumn he wore hairy sweaters against the ice-flecked wind, against its freight of decay, and feared nothing. Into this mild paradise he had died a little, little by little, for several days.

As his train, an express, passed platforms, Godfrey's fancy mounted. Filigrees corkscrewed into his eyeballs and coarse red bricks scraped streamers of transparent skin from his forearms. They imposed themselves, elbowed him, until he shivered. "God spare me from outrageous nonsense," he said aloud. He pressed his forehead against the greased subway pole. His chest ached. He took a prescription vial from his pocket and chewed a blue pill. It would be fine. It wouldn't be fine. Either way.

Annika, his therapist, had advised against dating. She thought employment a superior distraction, if he wanted one, or charitable volunteering. Godfrey found it difficult to take her seriously. Parodically short-haired and Semitic, she kept on her desk studio portraits of her four Savannah cats, and through all the humid summer still wore a leather coat with a hem at her knees. What wisdom could such a punchline impart? Nevertheless, Godfrey liked her. She maintained her office on a leafy block near Prospect Park, on the first floor of a sandstone row house. She kept ashtrays out, a gesture Godfrey so appreciated that he didn't bother smoking. And she conveyed a convincing impression that their conversations would produce, in time, a useful result. "Don't forget, sex is a trigger, too," she told him. "As much as liquor. More than liquor. Look at the spring."

"Oh, the spring, the spring. How many months must pass before we forget about the spring?"

"It's only August, Godfrey. It's only three months."

"Three. A number. Merely a mere number. Anyway. Is liquor a trigger? Is anything, identifiably?" Godfrey sprawled across a leather loveseat that was as soft and vulgar as an obese aunt's embrace. His brogues stamped the cushions with white dust. When not covering his eyes with his forearm he stared up at a framed poster of a twisting, penile horse by Delacroix. The beast shivered at his attention; it sweated. "I'm civilized, now. I tipple nightly, but only tipple. I feel quite controlled."

"You shouldn't 'tipple' at all," Annika said. "Come on."

"Well, I do, and it's grand—I'm grand, I should say. No problems."

"You're better. But you're only *better*."

He raised himself up on his elbows and, turning his head toward Annika, gathered the muscles of his face into a noble pose: sucked, pinched, pouted. He resembled a Roman bust, and with his delineated, attractive chin he indicated the paths of constellations. "Destiny thrusts itself upon its chosen," he said, "whether or not they wish to assume its obligations."

"Hmm," Annika said. She recorded Godfrey's remark with a soft pencil. Its lead hissed across her legal pad like a broom through a bed of decorative pebbles. Someone somewhere prepared a laurel wreath.

"I shall not disappoint. I won't allow it."

Annika sighed. She rubbed beneath her glasses. "How are we doing with the meds?"

"We're taking them." Some of them. Godfrey had most recently removed clozapine from his rotation, as it left him—he enjoyed repeating this to himself—like a tapped maple, rooted and drooling. Other pills he skipped off and on, as their aesthetics struck him, as they offended him—the capsules of brittle yellow cellulose troubled him most, and tablets with more than four sides. He maintained, he felt, a viscosity of mind that meant his instinctive patterns of medicating worked, or meant that none of the pills he swallowed, the fistfuls of pebbles and lugnuts, had an effect in the first place. Either case qualified as victory—over whom? Oh, it hardly mattered. "They're something."

"Look, do you think this is going to be a productive thing for you?"

"Productive. Productive?" Annika displayed sometimes a dreadful obsession with productivity, an almost Victorian approach, Godfrey thought. "Productive," he whispered. All afflictions mental, moral, and spiritual cured by the unceasing application of vigorous labor. Cured by the turning of great steel wheels to vent steam valves, by feeding one's fingers to tacking machines, all in some vast unventilated workhouse where rats run over your feet and flakes of lead paint drop like pollen into your thermos. Stunted children in burlap tunics drive pigeons from swinging rafters and haul in harnessed teams wheelbarrows full of slag. Their dormitories stink of fish oil burned for heat and light, and their blankets, stitched from the hides of euthanized horses, seem to flicker beneath halos of fleas, mites, and like biting things. Labor's hideous innards are displayed, dissected and pinned: the crime that sustains. Godfrey donned canvas coveralls. He tugged the plastic brim of his paint-splattered cap. He counted his fingers and finished at seven: three stubs remained, scaly and pink, resembling cooked prawns. Mop buckets sloshed and stank, their bleach and mildew eroding his lungs. His tubercles creaked. "My gracious," he sighed.

"Godfrey?"

"Yes," he said. "Yes, I think it's just the thing."

"Is this—have you met this girl—or boy, I don't know—already?"

"No." Godfrey cleared his throat. "Girl, for Christ's sake."

"Sorry. So?"

"I initiated a correspondence online with a few candidates. Perhaps I should have mentioned it last session." He affected, or attempted to affect, a bashful mien: averted eyes, mild smile, coy nibbling of his lower lip. Annika appreciated these little efforts. "I likely could have: your reaction has been milder than I anticipated. The candidate on whom I settled is a fetching creature, or fetching enough. She fetches me, more or less. I have her photo on my phone: care to see?"

"That's not necessary, Godfrey." Annika bit her lip, revealing gray front teeth. "So you're confident this is a right decision? A healthful decision?"

"Yes. It should be. Why not?"

Annika scratched her blotter with the blunt glazed nail of her little finger. "All right. I'm nervous, but I can't tell you what to do."

Godfrey twitched and wished his mustache was so full and luxuriant that he could twist its tips and tug it down over his smile; what an emptied-out life it is when these gestures are unavailable. Poor Annika's obvious attraction—an essential thing, like a bird working the magnetite in its beak—had overwhelmed her training, the jealous darling. Were she fifteen years younger; were she to propose something explicitly. She stood above him, she stood atop her desk, her rayon slacks removed, flung in fact; they dangled from the potted rubber tree that dustily survived beside the window. She made a victory 'V' with her fingers and pried open her lathed, discreet labia. Godfrey got underneath, planted fervent kisses without and within, then, muttering romantic epithets in gutter Italian, donned her like a comic hat. Annika emptied her lungs, a stomped bellows, then laughed a laugh like fingers running on the rims of water glasses. Her legs flapped like unclasped chinstraps. How perfect. Godfrey dashed about the office with her balanced atop him, leaping like a stag, evading the slapsticks of whistle-blowing harlequins, the batons of policemen alerted by nosy upstairs harridans, the butterfly nets of social workers. An upended vase distributed limp daffodils and stinking brown water. Navajo pottery tipped and smashed on the floor, no less artistic in pieces than whole. Their audience laughed, clapped, whistled, hurled roses and lace garters and sacks of gold ducats.

"Godfrey?" Annika snapped her fingers, then rapped on her desktop as if serving a warrant. "Jesus. Godfrey."

"You're so valuable to me," Godfrey said. "But no. No, you can't."

He met Monica at an awful bar a few blocks above Union Square. Electronic music vibrated like flatulence and the expensive beer tasted like thick water. All fell apart before he could grasp at anything—he should have known. Monica sat with her fists balled atop the table and the corners of her lips twisted as if suspended from wires. She'd quickly stopped asking questions and there was something frantic about the way her eyebrows shifted, like rats digging through a tunnel block. He finished his second drink while she still nursed her first. His volubility ascended, hers curdled. Still, Godfrey liked something about the strain he read on her dark and avian face. Her constant blush reminded him of sand used to cover the blood at an accident scene. She might have been chewing her cheek. It all flooded Godfrey's brain, tapped a workingman's sweat on his brow, shook his extremities as if electrodes had been applied.

He blabbed.

"It's just so distant," he told her, almost shouting to achieve a volume audible above the background throb. "It's such a long ride. Not that I minded so much today. It's easy to sit, of course, I always prefer sitting to the alternatives, and at least I looked forward to an amusing destination. Was that an odd way to phrase it? Did it come across as condescending? It's difficult to judge your own tone, you know. I need to take great care, greater care. But daily, the ride, it doesn't thrill me. No. I'm way out there, you know, in the ass-end of Brooklyn. Right in its intestine. Inhabiting my own stinking fissure. It's terrible, but it's also terribly cheap. My liquid assets are presently modest and my circumstance requires caution. But at that it's terrible."

"Terrible," Monica said.

"It *is* terrible. And it's tiny and dark and incubating centipedes and silverfish. And this strange crystalline mold—I guess it's mold—that's appeared in the bathroom. It's consuming the drywall above the tub. A great slime-edged hole. It's ridiculous, like I live in a Jacob Riis photo. I think it's being farmed by my landlord—he lets himself in when I'm not home. I know it. I see stuff knocked around, rifled. He's this old Hasid, looks like a prophet or a forest hermit. *You* know. He always has old food, crusts of stuff, mustards, flakes and oils and whatever, worked into his beard. He resembles those terriers with stained faces. He's trying to trick me into breaking my lease, I'm quite sure. So he can pass my apartment to some Israeli cousin. It's happened before. But I'm prepared: I know how to work it. He won't get me." Godfrey gulped from his vile pint. His throat felt raw and inflated, like a mating frigate bird's.

"Oh," Monica said. "You've come up for air. Amazing."

"What?" Godfrey made a vague gesture with his fingers in the air before his face, warding off evil. He observed for the fifth or ninth time on Monica's left shoulder a mole that any passionate surgeon would have lustful dreams of twisting off, a plump ripe fruit dangling. They should have been lined up with scalpels and lances. "All right. I see your point. You may have one, approximately."

"Are you always just about this much fun?" Her brown lips winked like a cloaca.

"Yes, just about." He sighed and ate an ice cube he took from Monica's empty highball glass. Its cranberry residue felt filthy on his tongue, like he'd licked a penny. Monica stared at his pinched fingers. "I'm not anti-Semitic, by the way," Godfrey said. "If that's what's bothering you. I see how you might misconstrue. I meant only to offer a fun anecdote. It felt fun, didn't it? It was fun. But nothing negative. No. I have a great affinity for those people. I love delicatessens and Joseph Roth, jars of pickles and arid climates. And I'm frightened of Arabs: a dreadful culture, don't you think? Though I enjoy their cuisine. I admit that. A halal street cart is a lovely resource, though I try not to eat from them—I don't trust the sanitation. Where do they piss? Jars, or what? Coffee cans? Do they wash their hands? They don't. They can't. But never mind that."

"Never mind that," Monica echoed.

"Never mind it." He felt a fizzing in his nose, and caught scents of ozone and torched wiring. "Actually, my maternal grandfather may have been born Jewish. It's unclear, of course—war orphan—but it's plausible. He emerged from some Ural hamlet, some rustic Slavic pock on the horrid east. You can imagine them wearing pointed caps and wading through goat shit. I suppose you can see it in my eyes—the blood, that is. I've always thought of them as steppe eyes. Windy, inscrutable. Tartars, I imagine, wandered through, and did the things that Tartars do. My lenses are perhaps too thick to tell—are they?"

"Sure," Monica said. "No."

"Yes. They obscure that east in me, I think. They anonymize my face, for sure. Which I can't say I mind; I hate to draw attention. But look, there *are* documents, but nobody in my family has ever had the leisure to requisition all of them. Or the interest. My grandfather drank a bit and when drinking couldn't control his hands, so—you know. There were those who suffered, and those forced to hear of suffering, over and over. I suppose that's sapped our motivation."

"Well, Godfrey—"

"Well? All right, then, if you like a story; he came over in—" Monica raised up her hands, then slapped them on the table. Godfrey looked at her fingers as if they'd dropped from the sky, shat by a seagull as it passed overhead. "The problem? There's a problem?"

"Oh my god, shut up," Monica sighed. "I'm sorry, but shut up, please."

"Ah," Godfrey said. He pressed his hand to his breast but found that he'd neglected to arrange a handkerchief. He soaked a cocktail napkin with sweat. "Is this what happens now?"

"It sure is." Monica offered a single sharp wave and turned her head as if dismissing a beggar child. She ran a hand through her oiled hair. "I don't want to be cruel, but it's always one of you. Always one like you. And I can't stand it."

"I don't know what you're saying." Clapping his hand to his face, he felt, admiring, the construction of his own bones, their reassuring elegance. "Or rather I do, but it's arrived unexpectedly. Like a killer in one's doorway. Wasn't it all all right? Is it my hair? You object to my hair? It's thin, I admit this, I'm bursting with frank admissions tonight, Monica, but that's a sign of virility, I've read. Really, it looks thinner than it is—it's so pale. You see?"

"It's not your hair."

"Then there could hardly seem to be a problem," Godfrey said. "Unless you've misrepresented, terribly, your store of good sense and good will and good humor."

Monica generated in her throat and expelled from her mouth a vibration like an animal's warning growl. "You want to know? You don't stop talking, and it's nonsense. I can't waste my time," she said.

"Yes? And what have *you* said? I'm verbose, certainly, okay. But what have you said? How else were the gaps—the dreadful gaps—to be filled? And were you to attempt to fill them, how empty, spiritually, would they have remained? Like trying to shovel a hole full with vapor, I should think. Yes, helium vapor, shoveled. Just that efficient."

"What? What are you even saying? Jesus. I won't waste my time. You're—" She shook her head. "Just never mind, never mind. I'm a magnet. And I don't have *time*."

"Okay, then." Godfrey pointed at Monica, wagging his finger as he spoke. "Vapid. Shallow. Fat. Fuck you." He folded his arms. "You go now."

Monica's blush, never gone, darkened and spread, a vat of wine upended, a bus compacted and its organic contents decanted. "Fuck *you*." She took up her purse, its long strap whipping, and, standing, kicked her chair, which listed and clattered. "*Fuck* you," she added. This varied emphasis seemed meant to communicate anger of some particular degree or specialized type: oh well. She attempted to spin on her heel, as one does, but her shoes weren't built for it, no, her torso outpaced her legs and she almost fell, catching herself on the edge of a neighboring table, which rocked, sloshing drinks. The table's occupants—a man wearing a blue shirt with white French cuffs and gold bands on his pinkies, accompanied by a woman whose makeup made it look like he'd punched her—seemed ready to leap up in disgust, in righteous rage, abandoning their tab. Monica walked away with her fridge-wide shoulders hoisted and stiff.

Godfrey watched her merge into the crowd of standees. Her distracting ass resembled a lathed globe secured in a sleeve of taut cotton; how nice a thing, any little thing, with her might have been after all. He felt a stab in his kidney, or so. She'd shown some vim at the end: a shame she'd otherwise been so awful. "Well," he remarked to her vacated chair, "what a bitch."

In late May, after a half-hearted attempt to kill himself with pills, Godfrey spent a fortnight in the country at Wheatfields, a private institution spread across several hilltop acres overlooking the Connecticut River. Though his attendance had been, in the end, compulsory—certain trusts on which he relied were controlled, still, by his father, who *insisted*—the time spent had at first seemed of value; really, a delight. He tramped each day along tamed paths of soft pine needles, watching fawns browse and pressing his fingers into patches of spongy moss. He hurled branches, plastic disks, and rubber dolls across the neon lawns for Miss Piggy, the institution's ever-moist therapeutic Newfoundland, to fetch. He swam in the long, pale-tiled pool until his burning eyes were as red as an albino's and a crust of mosquitos had formed above him. On the fourth day his roommate hanged himself with shoelaces from the radiator in the gent's, and Godfrey thereafter enjoyed private accommodation.

Still. The poetic memoir on which he hoped to get a good start fell apart, or away, or whatever, as his energy dissipated. He couldn't remember upon whom he meant to pour, from the cauldrons stationed atop his tall ramparts, verses of molten blame, let alone arrange them metrically. The volumes of Landor and Ludlum he'd brought along remained unread, still packed; he struggled to get through the copies of *US Weekly* and *Men's Health* that littered the dayroom like crushed Styrofoam on interstate shoulders. While there were women about— most of the day was coeducational—they seemed so frail and useless: unwashed sweatshirts and hair, bruised cheekbones, taped-up wrists, hesitant congested whines. They couldn't bear his pursuit, he couldn't bear the pursuing, and even had he found someone to want, and she possessed the structural integrity to bear the weight of him, his penis had been withered by the pills they served in paper cups on his meal trays—it was a salted slug, a phantom limb, newsprint suspended in water; he held it up to the light, tweezed, and saw a translucent sliver of bad sashimi, quivering and mercury-toxic. Horrors, he thought: horrid. Essential humors had been vacuumed from his ducts and veins. Most aggravatingly, Wheatfields proved unable to provide dry cleaning, and the launderers on hand—the custodial staff, doubling—were not talented: unacceptable creases embedded themselves in his collars, which also began to curl at their points, lint streaked, whites went beige. When Godfrey presented his list of concerns—on personal letterhead, in his excellent calligraphy—he was prescribed a new regime of spansules that pummeled him into helpless sleep for three hours in the afternoons. These impossible people. He felt as if they piled stones atop him to extract a confession of witchcraft.

Genius was the problem: its rootlessness in the world. It was a four-dimensional object adrift in three-dimensional convention. The whole could never be observed; its face always appeared mutilated. A fearful monstrosity, like a hydrocephalic child or a calf with five legs. Only the most practiced—no: the most gifted—could conceive of the whole that existed on the lee side of their perception, and even they shrank when confronted with its non-abstracted fact. They feared it: they could not reconcile it with their blunted experience: so they struck, claws extended, venom sacs pulsing, at the intruder. Hence the bound albums of prescriptions. The ambulance rides in the company of police sergeants. The shivering nurses with their hypodermic poniards. The newsstand clerks who think he's stealing pornography. The waiters who rub their genitals on his silverware. The residents of adjacent apartments who listen to him masturbate. The women who look at him and laugh on the train, at the post office, in the pharmacy. The stray cats who, rolling and lolling on the sidewalk, provoke him into fits of weeping. The idle sewer workers who want to batter him with long wrenches. The livery drivers who think he's a stain on their backseats. The blood relations who refuse his late calls, who refuse his collect calls. Godfrey's peculiar genius—a numinous apprehension of the universe's authentic shape, its tendons and tissues, its knotted veins, its hollow bones—lacked any outlet or consequence that could be appreciated by a general audience, that would beg their pardon. He was a hog famous for biting off the fingers of curious toddlers, the famous mad hog who also arranged, unnoticed, the apple cores and corn cobs from his trough into glyphs that predicted droughts and solar eclipses. If only he could conduct arithmetic by clopping a hoof; if only he could grip a paintbrush in his savage teeth and cover a canvas with spots and blots and streaks that invited interpretation. This was an impossible mode in which to exist, this in-between state, but alas, no one had remembered to provide Godfrey with the glossy brochure that listed his alternatives.

In the end they begged him to stay: for himself, for themselves, but enough was sufficient, as he liked to say, and Wheatfields had, at that moment, no legal hold on him. He informed the administrator on duty— Dr. Peltier, an ovular man who wore an uneven blonde beard against which he should have been sternly advised, and whose soft chest, like that of an uncooked fowl, was a pleasure to poke—that he would involve the police, involve federal agencies, if his duffel and trunk were not shipped with all haste to his Brooklyn address. Godfrey clipped the identification bracelet from his wrist with scissors he plucked from a canister on the front desk while the receptionist pressed herself, gasping, against a wall. Outside, he bolted down the handicapped ramp like a driven foxhound, baying and dripping froth as he pursued his musky quarry. At the front gate he plucked the navy ballcap from the head of an immobile, flange-necked security agent, donning it while making pistol shapes with his free hand. He whistled "Tell Her About It" and then "You May Be Right" as he followed the curling country highway—passing toppled stone walls and farmhouses with missing roofs, stands of birch that should have been lovely and likely were, brooks from which trout arced like gobs of silver mucus hawked—down to the village. On the Greyhound back to New York he felt a clarity and a calm. Above the bus twilight coalesced, forming straight streaks that portioned out the sky like the city's grid. If angels descended, long-haired pretty angels, bright and sluttish angels, strumming on lutes made from mastodon ivory and unicorn gut their favorite anthems of liberation—well, perhaps they did, and it was Godfrey's failure to take in their unambiguous signaling. He sat by the toilet, which emitted a nostalgic odor of camphor, and visited it several times to vomit. He recorded, in the white space of a subscription card shed by a previous passenger's *Redbook*, a few fresh lines:

> "When enemies in silver masks thread wires 'neath your skin—
> Pour noxious tonics down your throat, and shove your Self aside—
> Tear off their demon masks! Punish and purge them of their sin!
> For I in dearest Reason dwell—in living Art abide!"

A beginning: a beginning began. Shifting winds blew sand from buried monoliths. Defoliants burned vines from the walls of Mayan temples. Godfrey tapped his mechanical pencil on the seatback before him. "My estrangement," he muttered. "A passing derangement. No." He ground his teeth happily, scrawling, counting beats. Genius, unearthed, asserted itself. Sunlight bathed it. Shadows bent around it. They had him so wrong: things were going great. ❧

Marly Youmans's CATHERWOOD

Emily Barton

When my college roommate was in graduate school, I took the bus from New York City to Virginia to visit her. She lived on the outskirts of Charlottesville in a spooky, derelict mansion Thomas Jefferson had designed. It had no heat. Dish soap froze on the sink, shampoo in the shower. She was then in the thrall of James Merrill's *The Changing Light at Sandover*, and in its honor we bought a Ouija board. We poured an offering libation of whiskey into an antique teacup and set it on the planchette. After a time, we made contact with . . . something. Neither of us sensed we were controlling the planchette, and yet, when we asked the spirits if they had a message for us, their response came swiftly: PREJUDICE HURT.

One afternoon when my friend had to go to class, she plunked me down in a horsehair armchair and gave me a novel to read: Marly Youmans's *Catherwood*, which tells the story of Catherwood Lyte, a woman who emigrates with her husband from England to the New World in 1676. They help found a settlement in upstate New York—perhaps, who knows?—where I live now. Early chapters describe their lives in fascinating detail: they live "like badgers in holes," their houses nothing more than "cellars" lined "with smallish timbers and bark." When I first read this, I too was writing a novel that took place in a primitive locale, and the economy and vividness of the descriptions enthralled me. I sank into the scratchy armchair and kept turning the pages, fascinated by Youmans's language and Catherwood's thoughts.

But *Catherwood* turns out not to be a novel of settlement life. About a third of the way into the book, the main character loses her way as she heads home from a wintertime visit to neighbors. She is carrying her year-old daughter, Elisabeth, with her.

The story of anyone alone in the woods is frightening, uncanny. But a settler woman, unused to her harsh environment, hopelessly lost and protecting her baby? I couldn't turn away. That first time I read *Catherwood*, I was still a decade away from becoming a mother. Yet despite the uncomfortable chair, I read the book in one long sitting, breathless to find out what happened to Cath and Elisabeth. I later reread the book as the mother of a small child—again all at one go, my heart beating in my throat, this time because I was anxious both to reach and to forestall the inevitable conclusion.

In most stories, lost people return in the end to where they started. That is the arc of the "lost person" plot, which bends toward home, however much that place or concept has changed with absence. Hansel and Gretel eventually make it back. So does Odysseus. But Catherwood's fate is different. It's as if, in telling a story of the New World, Marly Youmans wants to make that world *entirely* new. The whole rest of her novel—all its uncharted territory—lets Cath wander. She wanders page after page, chapter after chapter. She wanders past the point at which the reader thinks she *must* reach human habitation. Only in the most spectral, dreamlike fashion does she manage to rejoin society. In all other respects, the novel ends with its main character still out in the uncharted wilderness. She could lie buried beneath my house, on this ordinary city block.

When I write, and when I teach writing, I focus on plot—not a common predilection for a literary novelist. We are supposed to think about intelligent people's issues such as language, imagery, and theme, whatever that is. Yet plot is what makes a story a story, the sine qua non of storyhood, the thing that keeps the pages turning. And I tend to think that once you are deep in a good plot—either as its writer or as its spectator—it can only lead, always and ever, to one inevitable (yet, in a good fiction, still somehow surprising) conclusion.

When Catherwood Lyte steps off the edge of the known world, she shows me an alternative that hints at the nature of discovery. Marly Youmans, claiming her territory as Henry Hudson once did this river, has no fear of unfamiliar lands. This writer knows she won't lose her reader. The question "Will they keep turning the pages if Catherwood never gets home?" doesn't seem to cross her mind. Instead, Youmans takes a lively interest in all of her vast, lonely world's particulars, even when they're so frightening as to be nearly unthinkable. She helps me, as a writer and teacher, to be more of an adventurer, to have a higher tolerance for risk, for oddity, for the plot that doesn't tie off where you think it will.   ❧

Ode to Trains Departing Billings Railyard

Jeffrey Alfier

You wake the world like a hammer dropped,
like morning's aftertaste of a drink at last call.

Trestle and ballast shoulder you through towns
made of rivers and mines, north country

stops held by grace and dirty snow.
Coalers, grainers, flatcars and tankers

clocked by a shimmer of diesel
heat, move the world on your back.

All forks in the road are settled by the fists
of switchmen. The iron smell of your departures

is the perfect hunger of that one phone call
granted a fugitive trapped on his way out of town.

River Country

Jeffrey Alfier

July, and a man fishes the Yellowstone
from the trestle of a derelict rail bridge.
In the near distance, a young woman
with a new backpack, stares down
Route 89 toward the interstate.

She hangs a thumb in the air
for southbound traffic. The worries
of her parents back home
in White Sulphur Springs are carried
by the soles of her new Sketchers.
Her ears still hold to the Van Morrison
an old man played in his Dodge truck
as he gave her a lift the length
of Meagher County.

A Bozeman busboy hangs from her heart.
There is, in her coat pocket, a gift for him,
a song she wrote to unfold in his voice
as he laces her lines between the strings
of his guitar, his fingertips calloused
with chords she wants the night air to touch.

What they have is not boxed candy
or a Hallmark crush—it is earth
and humid sky, railroad ballast, coarse
stones of the Gallatin River they'll steal
barefoot over, to a palm reader
back in town, on West Main, their music
weaving into their skin, unrinsed
by water, nor the miles between
them, even when she lifts her hand again
on that highway north, her lifeline in the air.

Color Palette Blue #3

Sarah Kennedy

Commuting between Philadelphia and Camden on the PATCO train, I sit on old vinyl seats in a train car that looks like it hasn't changed in fifty years, or has only changed in the ways that the colors have faded or darkened over decades of exposure to skin, cleaning products, and the sunlight that flashes in and out of the windows as the train crosses the Delaware River along the Ben Franklin Bridge. I look at the yellowing walls, the speckled spearmint floor panels, and the durable dark green and tan vinyl, and I know the combination of colors is ugly, but it makes me comfortable. It reminds me of places that make me happy—of other places that haven't changed for decades, like my grandfather's kitchen.

A picture I drew when I was eleven was still scotch-taped to my grandfather's refrigerator when he died fourteen years later. The picture was called "Santa's Workshop." In the background, a single shelf spanning the length of the paper was filled with various toys, including a Jack-in-the-Box, a dollhouse, and some storybooks. A reindeer observed from the sidelines, his head poking in from off the page. My first attempt at drawing the reindeer's head had been vigorously erased but it had apparently been drawn with equal vigor, and the faint outline of its misshapen form was still visible alongside the second, final, version. When I was young, I would draw pictures every time I went to my grandfather's house, and the refrigerator display would change with every visit. "Santa's Workshop," though, was the last drawing. It's rare to be able to pinpoint "the last time" you do something that was, in an earlier phase of life, commonplace. You almost never know, when doing something for the last time, *that* you are doing it for the last time. Surely, when I drew and colored "Santa's Workshop," I did not know it was the last picture I would draw in that house, but by the next year I had moved on to other small adventures, leaving that drawing to remain on the fridge, the colors fading a little each year until Santa's suit was a washed-out pink sometime in the early 2000s.

Grandpa's couch, which he called the *davenport,* had hefty wooden arms and brown and orange woolly plaid upholstery. The television was a piece of furniture in itself—the screen encased in an enormous wooden shell that sat alone on the rug beside the rocking chair. Looking at pictures taken when my mother was in college, I would see a room identical to the one I knew so well, different only in that the pictures had a cast of characters that no longer existed: a living grandmother, a father with long hair, and a mother with short skirts. I understand the desire to update a space, to tear out the old faded trappings of a time that has passed, but it's hard to argue that nothing is lost. Memories imprinted on physical spaces are lost. When I was twenty-seven, I moved from an apartment with a bright modern kitchen with white cabinets and a black-and-white checkered floor into an apartment with rust-colored linoleum, buttery yellow cabinets, mustard countertops, and pale yellow flowered wallpaper. There was little natural light but the whole room felt saturated with an old dark glow. All of my friends loved that kitchen, not because it was a throwback to a decade—the 60s—that was nearing its fifty-year revival in fashion and home decor, but because it felt like all of our grandparents' kitchens, imbued with stagnancy and love.

The entire PATCO fleet is being renovated. The main objective is to update the technology of the cars, but the technological improvements will be accompanied by an interior redesign. Over a thousand PATCO riders participated in a survey to choose the color palette for the new seats, floor, and wall lining. "Color Palette Blue #3" won. The new seat cushions and floor will be an icy periwinkle and the walls and the seat frames will be slate grey. Black armrests and handles for standing riders will provide a flash of contrast to the cool tones that pervade. Looking at the computer-generated graphic posted on the PATCO website to display the winning design, I understand the psychology behind these color choices. The cool muted tones are neutral, calming, and evoke a feeling of spaciousness. They are sterile, and perhaps sterility is a good thing for public transportation. They are unobtrusive, intent on not invading our minds and emotions.

The PATCO cars themselves are not being replaced—they are being completely refurbished, but the exterior shell and major structural components will remain the same. In small batches, the train cars are trucked to a facility in western New York where they will stay for two years, gutted and then slowly rebuilt, remade, reborn. The company that works on them is called Alstom. The town in western New York that serves as home to Alstom's rolling stock manufacturing division is called Hornell. In addition to boasting the largest passenger rail car facility in the United States, Hornell is the town where my mother was born and raised, where my grandmother and grandfather lived until they died, and where my mother's only brother lives to this day. It is the place I've been talking about—where my grandpa's house at 13 Mays Avenue didn't change for decades, where I went to buy ice cream cones in the same ice cream parlor where my mom worked as a teenager. It *is* that place imbued with stagnancy, decades of sameness, and love, and now it is the place that where the train car interiors—the ones that remind me of Hornell, of times and places that are warm and old and familiar—will disappear. It is just a coincidence—nearly all small towns in the United States probably manufacture some small part of the lives of Americans living and commuting in cities—but it's hard for me to think of the PATCO cars arriving on flat-bed trucks in the town where my mother was raised and not feel awestruck by the unexpected places where the past weaves its way into the present and ensures its grip on the future.

When I was young, it was hard to imagine that Hornell existed beyond my knowledge of it. Grandpa lived at 13 Mays Ave and Aunt Eileen lived on East Washington Street. The ice cream shop, the pizza shop, the school and its tennis courts and ball fields were all on Seneca Street, and the pet store was across from the school swimming pool on Adsit Street. The old JCPenney's department store and Friendly's Restaurant were about as far as I ventured, all the way down near the pedestrian mall on Main Street, almost a mile away. There were times when we drove further—to the James Street Park, to Aunt Dorothy and Uncle Gene's house, to the Chinese restaurant that I remember as the only restaurant I ever visited with Grandpa—but these locations felt impossibly distant from my walking world there. Looking now at a map, I see that the James Street Park was just under two miles from 13 Mays Ave., and Aunt Dorothy's place was probably only a mile away, but it was across the four-lane highway that cleaved the town in two when it was constructed in 1972, so they might as well have lived in another city altogether. There were other things in Hornell that I had never seen or even heard about, and one of them was the Alstom Corporation and its rail car manufacturing plant down on Transit Drive.

For the bulk of its history, Hornell was a railroad town. In 1851, pre-railroad years, it was a tiny village with 700 residents. In 1852, after the opening of the Erie Railroad transformed it into a station stop on the first passenger railway from New York City to Lake Erie, the population started to grow. In 1852: 1,800; in 1865, over 5,000; by 1890, over 11,000; and by 1900, 14,000. And Hornell wasn't just any old railroad station town. It became home to the Erie Shops, the largest steam engine repair complex for Erie's rail cars. By 1891, visitors to Hornell would find a town with three hotels, four banks, five silk mills, a fairground with a horse racing park, a shoe factory, and a world-class opera house visited by the Russian Symphony Orchestra, John Philip Sousa's Marching Band, and the magician Harry Houdini.

In 1930, Hornell's population was over 16,000, but like for so many railroad towns, what followed was not pretty. The beginning of the end came in the year my mother was born, 1948, when Erie switched from steam to diesel locomotives that required less service. Hundreds of workers in Hornell were laid off. In 1960, Erie merged with the Delaware, Lackawanna, and Western Railroad and the Hornell accounting office was closed. In 1970, Erie discontinued passenger service. In 1972, the year after my parents got married at St. Ann's Church with a reception at the Ponce De Leon Restaurant, the Erie-Lackawanna Railroad went bankrupt and the Hornell repair shops closed completely. In 1990, when I drew "Santa's Workshop," the population of Hornell was 9,500 and dropping. After the Erie Shops closed, the facilities were leased for a time to General Electric and then to Morris-Knudsen, and then in 1995, Alstom began leasing the site. In the last twenty years there have been periods of hope and periods of despair as Alstom competes for contracts to renovate the nations's aging subway and rail cars. After years of uncertainty and layoffs, it won the PATCO contract in 2010, and while this allowed the company to start hiring again, it is a trickle compared to Hornell's old railroad days.

I knew none of this when I was young. It's difficult to overstate how much I loved Hornell and how little I knew of its deep, permanent depression. I played with the girls across the street whose father was, and continues to be, the mayor (in office for twenty-eight years so far, he is the longest serving in New York State). I sat at St. Ann's Church for Sunday mass where the priest's arms shook with Parkinson's and they read from thick song books instead of the photocopied song-sheets to which I was accustomed. I spent hours in the must-smelling cellar helping Uncle Bobby with his carpentry projects, occasionally rummaging through the stacks of old board games from when my mother was a kid. I followed Grandpa through the supermarket, smiling as he tipped his hat at the people we passed. He seemed to know everyone, and everyone knew him. Emmett Clancy: lifelong Hornell resident, baseball star, World War Two vet, grocery store owner, snow plow driver, Erie Railroad switch operator. He flirted with the cashiers, much as he flirted with me: "Now don't hit me when I say this," he would tell me, "but you're a good looking girl."

When it was time to leave at the end of a trip, I would hide between coats in the walk-in closet while Mom and Grandpa shouted back and forth about how it was ok, she'd leave without me and I could stay and go to Hornell Elementary School for a year or two. "It's just up the street," Grandpa would say. "You just walk up to the corner and you're there." As I got older I knew it was a joke but I still wished that maybe, someday, I could stay. Maybe for a summer? A summer in Hornell meant trips up to my third cousins' farm and to the old wooded homestead at Hartsville Hill where the small stone foundation of Grandpa's childhood home lay hidden in the woods. It meant playing in the next-door neighbors' above-ground swimming pool. It meant rising early with Uncle Bobby and hiking down Mays Ave to the Canisteo River with fishing poles and lunchboxes ensuring we'd be gone until at least noon. It meant playing tiddly-winks on the green outdoor carpeting in the screened-in front porch as the Hornell Evening Tribune was tossed on the front steps by the paperboy in the late afternoon.

And then there was the food, an unchanging bounty of items that

I never ate elsewhere: powdered doughnuts from a box, salted Planters peanuts, bologna, whole milk, yellow slices of cheese, soft sticks of real butter that were never refrigerated, soft sandwich bread with no crunchy grains inside. I didn't know it was a kitchen stuck in 1965, but I knew that it was food I would never see at my own house and would never bother even asking for. I can still taste the Oscar Mayer bologna on soft bread with butter and yellow mustard, served on a white plate at the round table with the faded plastic table cloth and round cloth placemats.

An old bronze grocery store scale sat on the counter next to the fridge, a relic of the days when Grandpa owned a store. After his time as a grocer ended, he never lost his knack for guessing an item's weight—I could hand him an orange or a coffee mug or a carton of ice cream and he would stand in the middle of the kitchen, skinny legs spread with knees slightly bent, and he'd bob the item up and down in his open palm, testing its heft and density. "Ehhhh—fourteen ounces," he'd declare, and I'd scurry to put it on the scale. He was always right, even in the years when he couldn't remember how old I was or where I went to college, in the years when he paced all day between the living room and the kitchen, anxiously tapping his fingers on the kitchen counter and watching through the window for any disturbances in the neighborhood, constantly moving from one room to the next, forgetting as soon as he was in one place what was happening in the place he had left just a moment before.

"I'm losing control," he told me the last time I visited. "Where's Bobby?"

"He and mom went out. They'll be back at nine."

"That's right. Thank you."

"Grandpa, can I get anything for you?"

"No . . . I'm just looking for a can of beer but I can't find one."

"I don't know where to find one either."

"Well, I'm just going to look in here one more time."

The carpet in the dining room along his path between the living room and kitchen was worn thin from his constant shuffling back and forth. There was a stack of old fedoras and fishing hats on top of the refrigerator. He never left home without a hat, but he didn't leave home much anymore. The air in the house felt caged and desperate. Grandpa would wake from his frequent naps and hurry up from his armchair to investigate what was happening in the other rooms, as if life was transpiring in the places he could not see. But no, it was quiet everywhere. There was nothing new to see.

After Grandpa died in 2005, Uncle Bobby continued to live in the house, and upon my mother's insistent prodding, he renovated the kitchen. The space is barely recognizable—the water-stained drop-ceiling panels are gone and the ceiling is two feet higher. The grease-stained peeling wallpaper has been replaced with new drywall painted bright salmon orange. A peninsula counter with tall stools bisects the room, lit by sleek hanging pendant lamps. There are large windows, stainless steel fixtures, maple cabinets, and the old buckling linoleum has been replaced by tiles. It is, by every standard, more attractive and more functional.

I miss the old kitchen, choosing to imagine a time before the anxious sadness began. It is easy to wax nostalgic for old, beaten-down places when you were present for neither their heyday nor the worst of their decline, when you don't remember the time when their colors were vivid and new, when you have no memories of what used to be. That kitchen was old and faded by the time I was born, and so was my grandpa, and so was Hornell. I just didn't know it. My mother told me about an argument she had with her father sometime during college or shortly after. They were bickering about something—anything—when unexpectedly my grandfather erupted with a defeated proclamation: "Whatever I've done, remember that I never asked you to come back to this town." It was the greatest gift—permission to leave, permission to invent herself anew. Permission to extract herself from the constant weight of memory and to have a daughter who can yearn naively for a place that no longer exists. A place, perhaps, that never did.

Several years ago, I was helping a friend and her boyfriend look for a house to rent. Every time we drove by a little bungalow with peeling paint and a teetering porch, she would joyfully exclaim, "It could be so cute! It's a fixer-upper!" The boyfriend and I would correct her: "No, it's just shitty." I think about her while sitting on the PATCO train one morning and I look around at the dingy jaundiced walls and the saturated dullness of the seat's thick vinyl. I think about the elisions that make nostalgia possible. I think about whether it is places or people whose memory elicits the greatest longing. I think about how to love the past without grasping to keep it alive. I wonder if Hornell can be remade like these train cars or if the shell is too big and too broken to be occupied anew.

The Shape of Things: Various Artists

Jason Rohlf, *Tar Beach*, 2015, Acrylic on shop rag, 15" x 15"

Loren Britton, *Lay on My Chest*, 2015, Mixed media, 17" x 28"

Bonny Leibowitz, *Teater*, 2014, Wood, acrylic and oil paint, 5" x 1" x 2"

Suzan Shutan, *Tic*, 2014, Paint, wood, and Color-aid, 12" x 10.75" x 1.75"

Stephen B. MacInnis, *Nifty Fifty #29*, 2015, Mixed media on paper, 7" x 9"

Meg Lipke, *Surplus*, 2015, Muslin, fabric dye, string and yarn, 12" x 24" x 6"

Julie Torres, *Free Falling*, 2015, Acrylic on panel, 14" x 8" x 8"

Lauri Lynnxe Murphy, *Spill*, 2010, Cast resin, oil paints, piano wire,
and sculpting epoxy, dimensions variable
(110 variably sized units, 2" - 4" in diameter, mounted on piano wire)

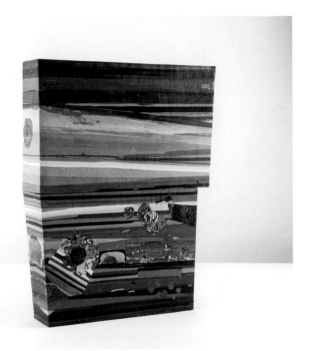

Laura Moriarty, *Hangover*, 2015, Pigmented beeswax, 16" x 9.5" x 3"

Jill Vasileff, *Pink Hum*, 2011-2013, Acrylic on branches, 16" x 16" (dimensions variable)

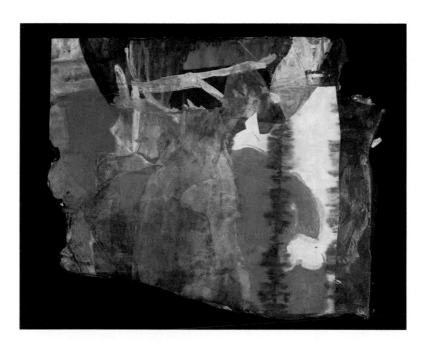

Stacy Leeman, *Book of Esther C5*, 2015, Sumi watercolor and collaged paper, 16" x 19",
Photo credit: Robert Colgan, Courtesy of Sharon Weiss Gallery

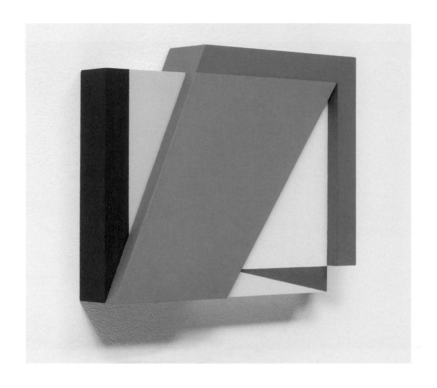

Connie Goldman, *Shift VI*, 2015, Oil on Panel, 9" x 11" x 2",
Photo credit: Kim Harrington Photography, Courtesy of the Artist

Ricardo Paniagua, *Intersections in Dimensions*, 2015,
Polychrome cast fiberglass/urethane resin, 16" x 12" x 5"

Noé Jimenez, *Corolla*, 2015, Acrylic paint and 35mm print, 7" x 5",
Photo credit: Abigail Clark Lupoff

Susan Still Scott, *Fish Head*, 2012, Acrylic and oil on canvas, plywood, staples, glue, polyester fiber, 9" x 13" x 18.5"

Susan Carr, *My House with Toothy Cloud*, 2015, Wood, oil paint, wisdom tooth, 8" x 12"

"A Town of Accreted Myth": Lauren Groff's THE MONSTERS OF TEMPLETON

W.B. Belcher

Last summer, for the hell of it, I created a list of twenty debut novels that I'd recommend to friends. There was no method to this madness, except that I wanted to list novels that captured my imagination and stuck to my ribs. Old standbys like F. Scott Fitzgerald's *This Side of Paradise*, James Baldwin's *Go Tell It on the Mountain*, and Marilynne Robinson's *Housekeeping* were no-brainers, but a more recent book that I come back to again and again, and one that I recommend to many friends, is Lauren Groff's *The Monsters of Templeton*.

As Groff explains in the "Author's Note," *The Monsters of Templeton* is set in a "slantwise version" of Cooperstown, New York. To be fair, I should point out that I worked at Glimmerglass Opera in Cooperstown for three summers during the late '90s, so I share an affinity for the lake and the village that she depicts, but my recommendation has less to do with my own personal experience than Groff's confident prose, colorful characters, and imaginative storytelling.

Willie Upton, a flawed, sarcastic, loveable, and often infuriating narrator, reluctantly returns to her hometown after a string of poor decisions, including a crack up of an affair with her archeology professor. On the day she arrives home in Templeton, a leviathan washes up on the shores of Lake Glimmerglass. Soon after, her mother confesses a secret concerning the true identity of Willie's father, and Willie sets out to piece together her parentage by unearthing the town's secrets. All the while, Glimmey, the dead lake monster, rests in the background.

Mythmaking, storytelling, and reinvention are themes that many debut novelists explore, but Groff dives in with flair and originality. Beginning with the discovery of the lake monster, the fantastic weaves its way through history and family secrets, through ghosts and gossips, and through relationships buried and unburied. All of these discoveries speak to Willie, her personal history, her crisis of identity, and her ability to come to terms with her family, her past, and her own mistakes. Willie is a researcher and an archeologist—digging up the past is her work. She chips and brushes away at clues until she finds the truth behind years of "accreted myth." The reader is on a similar journey, chipping and brushing away at the narrative to discover how the town's history or the lake monster's tale, for example, reinforce Willie's self-discovery.

Beyond Groff's affection for the setting and her cast of characters, I'm also drawn back to this novel because of its genre-blending, which is completely original and endlessly interesting. She melds the fantastical (ghosts and lake monsters) with the history novel, a coming-of-age story, a genealogy narrative, and the small town tale; each angle strengthens the other, and they all serve Willie's character and her journey to find the truth.

Lauren Groff has gone on to become one of our best novelists. Her *Fates and Furies* hit the shelves in the fall of 2015 to much anticipation and acclaim. For those of you who loved *Fates and Furies* or Groff's second novel, *Arcadia*, I hope you'll go back and check out *The Monsters of Templeton*, which was an ambitious and endearing debut, and one that is never far from my desk, cracked binding and all. ❧

The Room Where Elizabeth Bishop Slept

Paola Peroni

Flavia Banti had just returned from her father's funeral in Rome, and to her surprise she missed him less now that he was dead than when he was alive.

She was fifty-seven, and on a rare good day she could shed eight years from her age. She held a chair in Comparative Literature at Columbia University, wrote literary criticism, and translated Italian classics into English. She was respected; some said she was brilliant. She was miserable.

One week after the funeral, a cab drove her through the big iron gate of the famed artists' retreat, and a gothic mansion surrounded by smaller buildings came into view. The place had once been the estate of a millionaire, but it reminded Flavia of the landscape in a Grimm's fairytale. In the office, the secretary gave her a key and introduced her to a man who was going to show her to her room.

"Welcome," he said. "I'm Diego."

His hair was cropped short, and he wore army pants and a loose shirt with sleeves rolled over bulging biceps covered with tattoos. To Flavia this was the sloppy uniform of middle-aged adolescents with artistic pretensions that she disliked even among her students. The smile on Diego's face was too obstinate, and she refused his insistent joviality.

"Ready when you are," she said, before grabbing her suitcase and following him out the door.

"You're a translator," said Diego. "What are you working on?"

"Giacomo Leopardi's *Thoughts*."

"I'm afraid I don't know him."

"I'm afraid few do," she said. "He was born in the wrong country, and in the wrong century."

On the way to the room Diego went over rules and regulations. The house resembled that in Hansel and Gretel, but made with stale confectionery and cake. Diego motioned for Flavia to be quiet as they climbed the creaky stairs.

"The room where Elizabeth Bishop slept," Diego said, after closing the door. She could tell he had expected her to erupt with joy.

The room was a shabby affair, dark, with a stained blue carpet, a small desk, and an iron bed. Flavia opened the three doors against one wall and discovered they were all closets.

She said, "Where is Elizabeth Bishop's bathroom?"

"Down the hallway," he said. "You'll share it with the two other residents of the house. Adam and Jack, a screenwriter and a novelist. Great guys."

She was past the age for sharing bathrooms, let alone sharing one with two men she did not know. In the office the secretary told her there was no other room available. Flavia was ready to leave, but the next train was not until morning, and her brother and his girlfriend were arriving in New York that night from Rome. She had offered them her small apartment for the month she was going to be gone. She had done it to please her father and placate his worry for his reckless son.

Now she was trapped.

She was furious with the colleague from the Creative Writing department who had convinced her to apply for a residency. She was furious with the committee that had admitted her. She was furious with her penniless brother always in need of a place to stay. She was furious with her father for dying. She was furious with Mark because she could not let go of him. And she was furious with herself because this was her life, and she knew she could not blame anybody else.

Dinner was served in the main house. The carved wood furnishing of the dining room was gloomy, all pretensions gone astray. There were about twenty people, their age ranging from twenty to sixty-five. The spark in their eyes was a mix of ambition, envy, and expectation. She dismissed the cordiality that greeted her. She was introduced to Adam and Jack, the two other guests residing in her house. Adam was a small and wiry man in his early forties, but Jack was a hulk of over six feet, close to her in age, with a huge stomach overflowing his ragged pants. He was so large and unpolished that she dreaded having to share the bathroom with him.

For all the friendliness, the pecking order was strictly observed. The most prominent writer—a fat woman with the confidence to match her weight—presided at the head of the table, with Diego in attendance to refill her plate. The guests deemed more deserving sat adjacent to her, and the rest were dispersed randomly at the far end.

Flavia glanced at the buffet. Some effort had gone into its presentation, but not quite enough. It was cafeteria food with an attitude. There was vegetable lasagna, lamb and roasted potatoes. Salad seemed the safest choice, and she helped herself to some.

The appeal of the place was clear to her: the known came for adulation, the-up-and-coming for prestige and connections, and the young and hopefuls for free meals and affirmation. She sat between a painter from Germany obsessed with giving orange the place it deserved in the history of art, and a playwright working on a drama about Seneca's life.

"Twelve hours is pretty long for a play," said Flavia, turning from her meager salad to the playwright. "I guess the audience is not one of your concerns."

"The play dictates the length, not the audience," said the woman.

"So you're just a scribe," Flavia said.

"In a way," said the woman, giving the thought serious consideration.

Jack was sitting across from them. He kept to himself. His head was bent over his plate. Flavia could not finish her salad.

The German painter turned to her and said, "What brings you here?"

"I needed a place to stay so that my brother could have my apartment to himself," she said.

"That's ridiculous," said the painter with a thunderous laugh.

"I agree," she said, but of all the reasons for being there it seemed the least preposterous.

After dinner, it took her a long time to wash. The bathroom seemed clean, but she could not be sure, and so she performed acrobatics to prevent her skin from touching any surface. When she returned to the room, she flopped down on the bed. It was too early to sleep, and she could not focus enough to read, so she leafed through some literature about the history of the colony that she found on the nightstand. She heard Jack hauling himself up the stairs, and then a door slam. He moved around in the adjacent room; then he started talking. She could not make out his words, and she lay in the dark listening to the modulations of his voice. After silence returned, she slipped out and went quietly down the stairs.

The light was on in the small kitchen on the ground floor.

"Hello," said Adam, peeking out.

"I need something to eat. Any suggestions?"

He motioned for her to follow him into the kitchen, and she was relieved to find bread and cheese. They sat at the small table, and he poured her a glass of red wine.

"Food is not one of the draws of this place," he said.

"It's best not to dwell on the draws of this place."

"I came here to get away from my work, but all I have been doing is discussing the movie business," Adam said. "Everybody wants advice on writing a screenplay or getting a novel adapted for the screen. It's worse than being in Hollywood." He paused, worried. "I hope you don't want to be a screenwriter too?"

"I don't want to be a screenwriter. I don't want to be Elizabeth Bishop. I don't want to be here. I don't want to be who I am. And I don't even want to be somebody else," she said, biting into a piece of cheese with the force required for a steak.

Her ferocity startled him. "Right. You just wanted something to eat," he said.

"What's wrong with the guy upstairs?"

"Nothing. He's just quiet and reserved."

"I heard him talk out loud in his room," she said.

"He calls his son at night to read him a story before bedtime," he said, and left without saying goodnight.

When she returned to her room, she was restless and did the one thing she had promised herself not to do: she phoned Mark. He did not answer. He was probably busy with his wife. Mark taught philosophy at the same university. He was ten years younger than Flavia, and they had been involved before he had decided he wanted a child and had married a pretty girl almost half his age. His changed circumstances did not seem to him to be an impediment to their continued involvement, but their ideas differed as to what this involvement entailed. Flavia demanded emotional engagement, but Mark stayed willfully disengaged.

Sleep did not come until dawn, and it was too late to bring relief. She woke up at noon. The silence was eerie, and the grounds were deserted. In the main house she found a lunchbox with her name on it. The moist bread of the tuna sandwich seemed to be sweating, and the two chocolate chip cookies crumbled at the touch. She left the contents of the lunchbox in the refrigerator in case Adam and Jack wanted them, keeping only an apple.

It was a mild and sunny May day, and she walked down the road leading into town. A horse track was a short distance away, and she paused to observe a few kids jumping. She had been a fine rider herself but—unlike her father—the demands of work had made it impossible for her to continue. Her stepmother had burst into laughter when, two years earlier, she had announced her intention of using all her savings to replace her father's horse with a more agile animal.

"Giving your eighty-four year-old father a more agile horse would be like sending him on a vacation with a twenty-year-old escort," her stepmother had said, only strengthening Flavia's resolve to go ahead with the plan.

On one of her visits to Rome she had consulted with a trainer, made the necessary arrangements, and finally presented her father with an exuberant mare. Her father was not demonstrative, but Flavia knew he was pleased from the renewed enthusiasm he took in his daily riding routine, which he kept until the last day of his life when—before jumping an obstacle in the ring—the horse shook him off its back, killing him instantly.

The town was small, and Flavia took fifteen minutes to walk along the main street that ran across it. The usual shops sold the usual brands. Among the pervasive sameness she was able to find a bakery that served decent coffee. She ordered a sandwich with melted cheese and vegetables. It was oversized and—though not unpalatable—the taste was lost in the abundance of ingredients. There was always too much of everything, she thought. Too much paper wrapped around gifts, too many bags to carry groceries, too much air conditioning or heat, too much rush, too much ambition, too much hope and joviality. And for all this abundance food was no less bland, homes were no more comfortable, life was no more meaningful, and despair and loneliness were no less palpable.

She waved at the waitress. "Can you turn the air conditioning down?"

"I'll see what I can do," the waitress said.

"You're making the second mistake I made. You go away in search of something and all you discover is what you've left behind," her mother had told her thirty years before, to dissuade her from moving to the United States. Her mother had done the reverse. She had married Flavia's father and moved to Italy from Boston.

"What was the first mistake?" Flavia asked.

"Thinking nobody equals your father," her mother said.

Her parents had divorced when she was five years old, and her mother—unlike her father—had never remarried.

As a young girl Flavia had made up stories about her father for her friends: fabulous trips they had been on together, and wonderful gifts he had given her. She did not do it to impress them. She did it for herself. Her father was handsome, elegant and brilliant, and what he lacked in warmth, care, and devotion she filled in with her imagination. But whenever her mother got wind of these tales, she confronted her.

"Don't make him into something he is not. Don't lie to yourself," her mother said, as Flavia covered her ears and flew into a rage.

To the end of her father's life Flavia had blamed his inattention on the demands of others, whether it be her stepmother or her brother. She could not accept that despite her efforts he showed little interest in her.

"I am proud of you. I wish it mattered. I wish it was enough," her mother always said to her.

But her mother knew better than anyone that no love can make up for the one we're lacking.

Years later, after her mother had been diagnosed with cancer, she had said, "It won't be as bad as when your father left." She had said it without bitterness or anger, and not without humor. It amused her to repeat it, especially after having undergone some debilitating treatment. "It's not as bad as when my husband left," she would say, and nobody knew what to say in response. And at the end, she grabbed the doctor's arm to ask, "Why don't you speak to me in English?" The doctor did not speak English, Flavia explained. They were in Rome, and people spoke Italian here.

Dinner was the only meal at the colony where attendance was mandatory. The man sitting to Flavia's right was a poet working on a collection of sonnets all beginning and ending with the same line.

"How do you choose which work to translate?" the poet asked her.

"The author must have been dead for at least fifty years," Flavia said, shifting the overcooked vegetables on her plate with her fork.

"A measure to ensure the lasting value of the work, I suppose."

"And a precaution against running into the author and not being able to enjoy the work any longer."

"Oh," said the poet.

A young woman returned after refilling her plate, and took the one empty seat next to Flavia. She announced with great fanfare that the prominent writer at the head of the table had agreed to read her novel, and might give it a blurb.

"A burp?" Flavia said.

"A blurb," said the novelist, resolute in her enthusiasm.

"It's one and the same, really," said Flavia.

The novelist was affronted. "Why are you so bitter?"

"In America you are supposed to be Mary Poppins," said Flavia, holding up a depleted carrot. "Mary Poppins is positive. Mary Poppins finds an element of fun in every job. Mary Poppins gets along and loves everyone. But I am not Mary Poppins."

"Mary Poppins doesn't scream into the phone that she wants to speak to a fucking human being and not a recording," said Adam. He had overheard her screaming on her cell phone that morning.

"Nobody is holding you here. You're free to leave if you don't like it," said the novelist.

"But I am also free to stay and criticize it," said Flavia.

Jack, sitting across the table, was observing her. She waved her fingers at him, but his grave expression was unyielding.

It was exhilarating to be disliked. It took no effort. All you had to do was call things by their real name. She was free of the deception and lies required by the desire to please. Mark believed that her compulsion for confrontation was as demanding a master as the need to be agreeable. For all his brilliance, Mark—like everybody else—was uneasy with dissent.

"I worked too hard for a B," a student once told her.

"I don't grade the effort, but the quality of the work," she had said, ending the conversation.

She refused to be corrupted. She was generous with her time, but not with grades.

The Dean had recently summoned her to his office.

"There is a widespread feeling among students that you are too demanding," he said.

"I am a professor. I get paid to be demanding."

"You have strong opinions and you're outspoken. Some perceive you as negative. You need to be more cautious."

Flavia's eyes widened. "My only obligation is to do my job in a professional manner, not to garner consensus," she said.

"Do me a favor, think this over," said the Dean, as he showed her to the door.

"The land of the free," she said with a smirk, and walked out.

But after thinking it over she had to admit that something had eroded in her. There was a new edge to her dissent. Defiance was tinged with discontent. She had exhausted her personal fund of compassion. Her students now seemed to her demanding and pampered customers she had little interest in indulging.

"You antagonize everyone," Mark had said after she reported her conversation with the Dean.

"I refuse to lie."

"Nobody is asking you to lie, just to be a little more accommodating."

"I should give students a grade they don't deserve? Praise work that I believe is worthless? Exchange pleasantries. Agree with whatever is being said. Keep my opinions to myself. And exude cheerfulness with everyone."

"That's not what I'm saying."

"Then what are you saying? Please tell me since you have all the answers."

"I don't have all the answers. But you don't like the answers I have."

It was dark outside when she came back to her room. Leopardi's *Pensieri* was open on the desk next to a laptop. She read the first paragraph, but she was unable to carry the meaning of one language into another.

The cell phone rang. "You called last night," Mark said. He was in a good mood.

"You're just an idea, Mark," she said as if he had interrupted her thoughts. "And I hold on to it so that when I pass a man's clothing store I have someone to buy for."

She hung up knowing he would not call back. He could take her or leave her, and she could do neither.

Dazed, she lay on the bed with her eyes closed. Jack's voice reached her from across the wall, its variations in speed and tone a soothing melody beyond words.

When all was silent again, she got up, flicked the light on, and sat at the desk. She leafed through the book, skimming it, until she came to a passage that read, "Nothing is more rare in the world than a person who is habitually bearable." Language had returned to her, and the immersion in the work of a great mind stirred her with unspoiled joy. The feeble glow of dawn seeping through the window, and a bird chirping outside reminded her of the arrival of day. She massaged her eyes, slipped into bed, and fell asleep.

Her interaction with the other guests was limited to dinner. She often ran into Adam in the kitchen of their house where they both went for a snack at night. But after their first encounter, they had both refrained from speaking. Then one night, she was boiling water for tea and he turned to her.

"Why Leopardi's *Thoughts*? What is its appeal?" he asked.

She sat at the table dipping a tea bag into a cup of water.

"It's an implacable investigation into the nature of human relationships and their universal governing principle: selfishness," she said.

"It will not make Mary Poppins' reading list," he said.

"It will not make most reading lists," she said.

"All the more worthwhile that you're translating it," he said.

She raised her teacup in his direction. "Thank you," she said.

On her way to the room she passed Jack in the hallway, and they nodded. There was something inaccessible about him that seemed worthy of respect. She did not mind that he kept his distance. All she wanted from him was to hear his voice at bedtime.

Slowly she settled into a routine, working through the night and sleeping until noon. To her surprise, time went by no slower and no faster than it always did. She took daily walks into town for coffee and lunch, and on the way back she stopped at the horse track to watch the riders. Sometimes she ventured into the stables to hear the horses' neighs and smell the hay. She pictured her father, leaning forward on the horse, getting it ready to jump until the animal gave a sudden jerk, pushed its front legs into the ground, and shook him off. He must have had a last few fleeting thoughts. Did he think of her? Did he remember the horse had been her gift? She summoned all the imagination she had left. She needed it to believe that her father had been thinking about her before his death.

Alone in her room in the evening, she waited for Jack to call his son. As soon as she heard his voice, she lay on the bed and closed her eyes. It was the best part of the day.

The topic at dinner was the Pulitzer Prize, which the prominent writer referred to as the Pewlitzer Prize to everyone's delight.

"It's meaningless. They never come up with a creative choice," said the prominent writer, cutting a piece of meat.

"They might as well give it to Philip Roth every year, even when he doesn't have a book out," said the young novelist, eager to concur.

Flavia settled her fork down. "They should change the rules and give it to Hermann Broch. He deserves it and he's dead. Nobody will be upset," she said, loud enough to be heard by everyone. "I read he was a guest here which adds to his credentials."

"Never heard of him," said the prominent writer, washing her food down with a glass of wine.

"Broch was an Austrian writer," said Adam, hesitating. "He immigrated to the United States at the outbreak of the Second World War. He's considered one of the giants of Modernism."

Nobody was interested. Jack alone was attentive, but as usual he did not say anything.

"You think of yourselves as poets and writers and not only have you never read Hermann Broch, but you don't even know who he is and have no interest in finding out," said Flavia, indignant.

"We've had enough of your European snobbery," said the prominent writer.

"Ignorance, not European snobbery, should elicit your contempt. Literature would be better served by it," said Flavia.

"Do you enjoy provoking people or is it only a way of calling attention to yourself?" the poet asked.

"A mix of both," Flavia said.

The conversation swiftly drifted to more familiar ground, and the prominent writer resumed her monologue before the admiring crowd.

Flavia turned to the woman next to her, who had just arrived that morning.

"What are you working on?" she said. Her proficiency at small talk amazed her.

"A memoir about surviving cancer," said the woman.

"Surviving it wasn't enough?" said Flavia. She thought of her mother who, before undergoing a mastectomy, had said she did not care since her breasts were no longer of any use to her.

"I hope people can learn from my experience," said the woman, defensively.

"That's very optimistic."

"I want to make the most out of my life," she added. "I want to help others."

Flavia nodded. "Good luck with that."

Later that evening, when she walked into the kitchen she found Adam eating a sandwich.

"Do you think people have sex here?" she said.

He laughed. "You mean casual sex? Among the guests?"

"Yes, random, animal, shallow intercourse?"

"I wouldn't know," he said, cleaning his glasses with the edge of his shirt.

"Forget about nurturing the creative process in a supportive environment. How about nurturing healthy frolic in a bucolic setting? It might provide a welcome distraction, and dissuade some from writing another novel or a memoir."

"You should bring it up at dinner," Adam said, amused.

"I bet it was after he returned from his residency here that Broch declared literature was the domain of vanity and mendacity."

"I'm afraid your efforts on his behalf did not succeed."

"Failure is my business. I caused my father's death in an attempt to please him," she said, and dropped on a chair. "But maybe I wanted him dead."

Adam was quiet and then he said, "We all want our parents dead at some point."

"Do you have children?"

"A boy and a girl."

"You should be home with them."

"You may be right. I wanted to get away from everything. I don't know what I was hoping to find."

"What you left behind," she said, knowing that what she had left did not amount to much.

In the morning a loud sound awoke her—somebody was knocking at the door. She slipped on a shirt and a pair of pants.

"One moment," she shouted, and rushed to the door.

Jack was standing in the hallway next to a suitcase. "I wanted to say goodbye. I'm leaving."

"I didn't know," she said. She had only two days left, and had expected to leave before he did.

"I'll check out the Austrian writer you mentioned," he said, and held out his hand.

She leaned against the doorpost as his empty hand hung in midair. Something was giving way inside her. She felt herself shrinking—a barren sack of grief and rage. And before she could stop herself she started to cry.

"I'm sorry," she said, wiping the tears from her face. "I don't know what's wrong with me."

He placed his hand on her shoulder. "It's okay."

"We should all have somebody who reads to us before we go to bed," she said.

In the stillness of the afternoon, she lingered in the garden of the estate trying to name the different varieties of plants. She named them in English and in Italian. She needed both languages. She lived suspended between the two, and more and more it seemed to her that translating somebody else's words was the only way she had to reach another soul. ❧

THE BOYS OF MY YOUTH by Jo Ann Beard

Suzanne Cope

I picked up my copy of Jo Ann Beard's *The Boys of My Youth* in an as unexpected place as possible: from the English book exchange shelf at a bakery in Baja, Mexico during my honeymoon. Stuck between Agatha Christie and Robert Ludlum was the decade-old advanced reading copy, the kind sent to reviewers and booksellers to garner excitement and reviews before publication. A young Jo Ann's face was on the back with lists of tour cities and marketing efforts. I knew from my first post-college job at a publishing house that this package was presenting the potential of a book—and I remember years ago having heard about it as one does the most anticipated books of the season. It had come amidst the late-1990s memoir boom, and was billed as a memoir-in-essays with the signature piece having been published in *The New Yorker*. But I left with it because I felt some echo in the back copy of my own writing, which had stalled in the past year due to an overflowing adjunct teaching load and wedding plans.

That morning I rescued it from among the mass market paperbacks, aware of the strange path it must have taken to arrive in my hands, and devoured it from under my umbrella poolside. I had earned my MFA in creative nonfiction over a year before and was teaching composition and the occasional creative writing class at a handful of local colleges. In another month I would be starting a new full time teaching job. These ten days in the sun were meant to be a last chance to read magazines and drink margaritas at lunch, to relax after a busy summer and before an intense new instructorship. Yet my marriage was just beginning, and I hoped my new position would allow me time for my creative work—challenges I would figure out in due time, I reasoned. Yet by the time I finished Beard's book I knew I was done resting and ready to get on with the rest of my life. Her prose not only connected me to my past—a girl full of potential, a young woman with so many stories left to live—but she also reminded me why I was a writer. *The Boys of My Youth* did what few books do: it left me wanting to read more—not just to learn more about Beard's story, but more so to learn more about *how* she told her story.

The first lines of the opening piece, what we would now call a "flash" essay transported me back to my youth: "The family vacation. Heat, flies, sand and dirt. My mother sweeps and complains, my father forever baits hooks and untangles lines . . . I am ten. The only thing to do is sit on the dock and read, drink watered–down Pepsi and squint." I had been like our narrator: few friends except for those in my books, sitting, reading, waiting for life to go on. The tension of the brief essay soon heightens as it tells of a near-death experience for three local teenagers, witnessed by Beard and her family and juxtaposed with the insecurities of young Jo Ann at ten. A girl on cusp of puberty. Our adult narrator chooses the details young Beard notices to show the severity of the almost-drowning: skin like "Silly Putty," legs "shaking like crazy." But what we end on is the self-consciousness of the pre-teen, hiding her own flat chest, concerned about her outfit. Jo Ann was a girl like so many of us had been—like I had been. Her youthful self-centeredness butts up against human mortality, and the reader recognizes what our young protagonist will soon learn. *How did she do that?* I wondered as I read through the short piece a second time. And then I asked myself, *How can I?*

Yet it was the essay "Cousins" that took my breath away. We start in utero: "Here is a scene. Two sisters are fishing together in a flat-bottomed boat . . . They both have a touch of morning sickness but neither are admitting it . . . My cousin and I are floating in separate, saline oceans." In creative nonfiction we are often exploring the boundaries of our genre—can we write a scene if we aren't there? How can we know what's true if memory fails? Here Beard gives us a poetic answer: of course she couldn't know what her mother and aunt were wearing, or hear their argument about "worms versus minnows." But we also don't doubt her. These are the people she knows most intimately and I believed her "emotional truth," as we learned to call it in graduate school. I yearned to revisit pages from my manuscript at home, wanting to infuse them with my new understanding of the potential of the words I might use to represent my own experience.

The essay continues with non-chronological scenes from the lives of these cousins who are as close as sisters, ending with one of the last times they were together with their mothers. In each, our lens is both focusing on our narrator and also beyond her, the "I" and the author's eye effortlessly intertwined. In the second scene of the essay a deer nearly collides with their speeding car, the sky "black and glittering with pin holes," and besides the adrenaline-fueled relief of the narrator and her cousin, we also see a car wrapped around a tree just off-scene, underscoring how fraught their sense of both innocence and invincibility is.

"Could have wrecked my whole front end," her cousin said before going back to singing along to the radio. Our author knows about the car in the tree, as the reader now does, but do our characters? In the end it doesn't matter. And suddenly I could see my experience from a similar vantage point: I finally understood my role as writer was to be in the metaphorical car with my characters, but to also see beyond them in both time and space. And I needed my own time and space—and inspirational prose—to learn this.

I returned from Mexico to the waiting arms of my internet search engine, ready to find everything else Jo Ann Beard had written. Yet she had only published a single novel since her nonfiction collection and a handful of essays. The author, like her memoir, had left me wanting more. But more so she, and the work she has given us, reminds me of potential—that which will someday be realized and that which may dissipate down the muddy river or up into the glittering pin hole sky. And in either case, it can make a damn good story. ぇ

Blessed Holy Fuck

Alan Hanson

simple like saturdays
before it's mowing lawns in tennis shoes
and a quick snack then hinge-fixing before noon:

in a fever dream
i thought odd things
like surfing alligators
up the moat to your home.

and every sign on the freeway,
every letter on every building,
had been replaced by my own thoughts.
i saw a billboard in bunker hill
that read "i want to eat fourth-meal with you."

i sit in the arts district
whispering 'petaluma' 'petaluma'—
trying to find words that sing
as the sparks do in your name.

the gliding, hungry fashion chix
walk by in a cloud of camel blues
and one with a murmuring radio
does what's what and turns it up:

but the disc jockey is me
and for once my voice sounds clean
as i say "all my favorite songs are about you"
and then i
spin the hits—

the fog it lifts,
i'm doing the twist!
and you're smiling at me,
or about to.

Children Left to be Raised by Wolves

Carrie Messenger

The children in the photographs in the old woman's album had no style. Or maybe, it would be more accurate to say they had a style, but one that was alien to me, both ancient and inappropriate. Scraggly, wild hair. You couldn't tell the boys and girls apart, like they were all one kind of creature, and wild, furtive eyes, ready to bolt, the way they had when the police came calling. The jeans were clean, but bulging at the cuffs, as if the jeans wanted to grow out, too. They had sandals barely covering their slender feet. They had flowers in their hair. I thought the taller one was the man. There was so much hair flopping in their faces that I couldn't tell whether there were beards, sideburns, something that would guide me other than height, but the old woman corrected me, pointing to the tall one, saying, that's your mother, that's my daughter. See, she's pregnant in this picture, see how her blouse catches a curve? She traced it with her bony, spotted finger. Here. See?

I didn't see it.

She grabbed my hand, pulled my finger to the curling snapshot, and made me trace it with her. That's you, she said. Until now, it was my only picture of you. It's my last picture of her. She was taken before you were born. She was at seven months when they took her. He'd just finished building the crib. We kept it right there by the bookshelf. I kept it until you turned four. I figured, if I found you then, you'd climb out anyway. And look at you now.

She was crazy, crazy as her daughter in her own way. My knuckles hurt where she had squeezed. She stared at me, hard, as if I would look like either the baby in the belly or the tall girl in the peasant blouse with the hair in her face. Any of my friends would have left then, but me, I'm polite. I have the courtesy of my mother, the one in pearls, the one smelling of gardenias, the one who I know is a woman because she has every feminine grace. And maybe I have the curiosity of these other people, these wild animals. Maybe I was already marked one of them since before I was born, and my parents as well as this woman have always been waiting for wildness to out.

How could I come from them? The wild children in the photographs, playing guitars and sticking flowers in their hair? How was that a way to run a revolution? They must have never gotten anything done, unless they only took pictures of their most innocuous activities. If you listen to my parents, the children of the left were dangerous radicals with bombs, who got what they deserved. If I listened to this woman in this room, the only bombs that went off blew up the radicals themselves.

How could I come from my own parents? My father in his pressed uniform, my mother in her pearls, coming in to kiss me goodnight before they went to one of their parties, promising to kiss me again when they came back home. I'd wait for them for hours, building my blankets into a tent with the bedposts, until I finally fell asleep, blankets tangled around me, and who knew if they kept their promise. I would pretend that when they would come home, it wouldn't be them, but wolves wearing their faces as masks. When I told my mother one morning at breakfast, she took away *Little Red Riding Hood*. She must have known, then, that it was her face that was the mask. If they are wolves, the children of this woman here in this room where I couldn't breathe were sheep, and I was a lamb that shouldn't be. I should have been killed in my mother's womb along with my mother when they killed my father. They waited to kill her until I was born, and then they pushed her out of an airplane into the sea. That's what the old woman is waiting to tell me, the old woman, my grandmother.

We all should have died together, the three of us. Everything would have been simpler, cleaner. My grandmother would have had no hope, but she could have spent the last thirty years taking up a hobby instead of standing around the square holding pictures, waiting for a baby, a girl, a woman who never came. But if they killed my mother before I was born, my own children wouldn't be, my boys, wrestling each other on the kitchen floor, picking me wildflowers when we walked in the park, tugging at my hand with their sticky fingers, demanding it was their turn now.

How could I come from this crazy old woman, who let her daughter dabble in revolution when she should have been studying? This woman was not the grandmother I would have chosen. I wouldn't have wanted to spend my childhood visiting this stuffy, small apartment in this outskirt neighborhood, one I've never had reason to venture to before in my entire life. There wasn't a garden, just a balcony facing traffic, draped with laundry. I couldn't bring my own children here. There would be no place for them to play among the piles of books and papers.

She didn't offer me pastries, just hard candies melted down into the chipped porcelain bowl. The tea she brewed for me was so weak I couldn't tell whether she didn't have money for more, or that was how she liked it. The cup was thin with a pearly sheen, nothing but a checkered, black and gold Art Deco design on the rims. Her family must have had money, once, either before they came to this country or before they joined the left and didn't believe in pretty things any more.

She must not have believed I would come this time or she would have surely supplied pastries. I'd turned down the other invitations, and I'd only accepted this one because my mother took me aside to whisper, it might go better with your father's case if you made a visit. Just one, just once. Until the DNA results are established, darling.

The old woman wanted to keep looking at the photo album. It was the old kind, cream corners glued to black thick paper to hold the snapshots in place. Some popped out as the pages turned, and she wouldn't move on until everything was back in place. Most of the photos were black and white, and in the ones in color, the colors were off, garish like a Technicolor movie, as if that decade never happened except in documentaries.

She paused at a picture of radicals seated around a campsite. The green of the forest made me see spots after I stared too long. She said, He would play the guitar for you and she would sing. Before you were born. From the day she found out about you to the day they took her. Do you sing? She was an alto. What are you?

Soprano.

And you're so short. But you could have gotten that from him. He was short, but feisty. Real tough, like he had something to prove. But he was the kindest of all of them, his group of friends. He took care of everyone. They didn't have enough money for their own place because so much of his paycheck went to making sure his students had enough to eat. I knew him since he was a boy. Oh, if only your other grandmother had lived to see this day. She came to the demonstrations until she got sick, and when she couldn't come any more, I would hold up his picture, too. This one.

He was in an old man's suit for first communion. It was too big for him. Maybe it belonged to a cousin first, but if so, why hadn't somebody altered it for him? Maybe there were more cousins coming down the line. He clutched his *Book of Saints* to his chest. His hair was cut short and it stood up in spikes. You could see his big, luminous eyes. It was easier for me to think of this boy as my father than the hairy short man in the first picture she showed me, even though it was impossible for this boy to be a father. It seemed like a strange choice of the other grandmother to bring this picture to the demonstration. They hadn't killed this boy on the day of his first communion. They killed a radical, a wild, shaggy man, a dangerous man. The other grandmother must have been hoping they would see the boy within the man. The fact that this very boy became the man, for somebody like my father in the uniform and my mother in the pearls, was all the more reason to kill him. In their eyes, he turned out to be a wolf in sheep's clothing.

It was the photo of my mother on the first day of school when I knew without doubts. I knew, but I didn't say anything to her yet, this little old woman, my grandmother who wanted so much more from me than I would ever be capable of giving. Not just because of what had happened to me, but because of what was in me. Maybe I changed in those last two months in my mother's womb, when she was being tortured in detention. Or maybe I was the kind of baby who couldn't protect their parents, who couldn't make them choose safer, easier ways. My boys were that kind of baby. I wouldn't risk anything for myself, but everything for them.

I knew because the nervous grin of my mother holding her mother's hand at the school door was the one my youngest son flashed at me when he wanted to tell me he was worried, but would be all right. That I could go, as long as I came back. Now when I would watch him, it would be like seeing a ghost, exactly the ghost this old woman was so hungry for. I didn't say anything, though, until we'd worked backwards through the album, to baby pictures that looked like me except the surroundings were wrong, the decade twenty years earlier than mine, as if I'd been photoshopped into somebody else's movie set.

Now you see, she said to me, closing the cover gingerly. Now you know what the DNA results will show you. I didn't want science to show us why we are family. I wanted history, the history that was stolen from you the way that you were stolen from us. But she couldn't help herself, and the phrases she'd been practicing since the first grandmothers found their grandchildren through DNA were not enough for her. She had to add, The history that was stolen from you when those people murdered your parents.

You are telling me, I asked her, my voice starting out cordial but wavering as I went, that my parents murdered my real parents? Which am I meant to be most distraught over? That my parents aren't my real parents? Or that they are murderers? One alone might be enough for today. I was polite and my mother's daughter. Only the teacup trembling in my hand gave me away.

She wasn't polite, this crazy woman, her dark eyes feverish, bony hands waving wildly as she talked. Your parents are murderers and you are not who you think you are. I've spent the last thirty years looking for you. Every child who came to look in the library where I worked at the circulation desk, I'd stare into their eyes. When you were at the university, I'd walk through the halls on all my lunch breaks. I thought, maybe you'd like music, too. She grabbed a folder and spilled out the ticket stubs of decades' worth of musical events. Why did you deny what you love? she said. Why weren't you where I looked for you? Why did I have to look so hard?

I wasn't allowed to go to the library when I was small. My father, with his deep and abiding love of private ownership, always said, any book worth reading is a book worth owning. I didn't finish the university. I started with my class and attended the lectures, but I was too nervous to sit for the exams. I didn't go to concerts often, because they made me cry. I sat at home and played records. My ex-husband called me agoraphobic, first as a joke when we started dating and I wanted to stay at my home or his but not go out, and then for real when he said my problems were scaring the boys and pretty soon nobody would go outside anywhere.

I have a lovely apartment with a garden. I don't get out much now, except to the market and to take the boys to the park. The alimony is good, and even if it wasn't, my parents would help. The wolves, I mean, the uniform and pearls, not the parents dropped from the plane into the sea. My ex-husband is a successful dentist putting braces on the city's upper middle class children. The kind of child I was, once. Dentists aren't often found on the left. They rip out people's teeth. What they do would be considered torture if you didn't have to pay them so much. My ex-husband has asked me, no matter what I find out, yes or no, not to share it with the boys. Or with him, either. He says he doesn't care. He already knows me, and he's already found me wanting.

I don't have grandmothers any more, I told her. They both died years ago, when I was little. So you can be my grandmother if you'd like. I thought I was making a grand gesture, more polite than my mother in the pearls, as kind as my brand new father clutching his children's *Book of Saints*.

I *am* your grandmother, she wailed. I don't need your permission to be what I am.

But I've been waiting my whole life for permission to be who I am. Lambs have to ask the wolves. Wolves don't ask to be lambs. They just put on the masks.

I didn't take a taxi to the house on the hill. I rode the metro, packed with people, packed with DNA and history. I imagined swabbing the insides of people's cheeks, pulling at stray hair on the collars of coats. So many ways to find out you weren't who you thought you were. You could go around asking about political parties now and those of thirty years ago, but most of the older people on the metro car would lie and the young wouldn't care. DNA doesn't lie. I've watched enough soap operas, though, in my years as a housewife, to know that results can be contaminated by human error, or human desire if there's enough money involved. I didn't care any more what the results would be. I knew from my child's nervous grin on the face of my mother as a girl. I'd known my whole life that something was wrong with me, and now I knew there was something wrong with everybody else.

My mother held her pearls at her throat and said, What a lovely surprise. She had the kettle on and there were éclairs that the maid had picked up that morning, so they weren't fresh, she could send the maid out again, but I told her I didn't care. My mother was worried to see me out of the house and wanted to know first where the boys were. When I said, with the neighbors, she didn't like the answer. She never liked the neighbors. She wanted me to bring them up the hill, where she could watch them, which meant the maid would watch them. There had been many maids since the one I'd loved when I was a girl, the one who'd read me *Little Red Riding Hood*, who sang the songs that my mother must have sung to me. Not this one in pearls, the androgynous one in sandals, the tall one who towers over her man. I can't figure out how to say "real." They both are unreal, the wolf, the wild one. Maybe mothers are always unreal.

She fingered her pearls with her blood-red fingernails and waited for me to speak.

You knew what the DNA results would be all along, didn't you?

You have the results?

I don't need the results now.

So now you think you know something. You know nothing. You don't know what it's like to want a child. Yours came so easily. I held my breath for you, and you didn't even know how lucky you were, both times.

She was jealous of me and my fertility, jealous of my hairy flower mother and hers. Which was worse, the murder or the kidnapping? The kidnapping. Because if you hate people so much you want them to die, you shouldn't want their children. She must have been so confident that she could turn me into her. A book worth reading is a book worth owning. A child worth raising is a child worth owning. I didn't say anything. The cream oozed out of the éclair as I pressed it with my thumb.

There were five miscarriages before you, darling. Five. You didn't have one. You can't know. So many dead babies, so much blood. I couldn't try again. The doctors said it would kill me. But your father needed a son. And I needed something to love.

But I wasn't a boy.

Your father saw you and he fell in love. He didn't care whether or not you were a boy once he saw you, so little you fit in his two hands, like a puppy or a kitten, so tiny! How nervous we were as we waited for you to grow. And I, of course, never cared as long as you were ours.

The words binding me to her again. Ours. If you wish it, it must be so. If you wish it, your adopted daughter will dutifully forge a relationship with the crazy old grandmother so that when your husband stands trial, the court will see that his attitude toward radicals and their families has relaxed. He's a kind man, a gentle man, a father, not a murderer and kidnapper any more.

Why didn't you try what you said you did, when you told me I was adopted? Go and see the nuns?

You fell into our lives, don't you see? We didn't have to try anything. You were there. You needed so much care. You were so little. We gave you everything. It wasn't something I thought about. It happened. Wasn't it a good life, darling? You remember when the boys were little, how much there is to be done, how you never sleep, but you don't care because there is a baby in your arms?

The idea of my mother, sleepless, a baby in her arms. It must have been maids who were sleepless, the maids she ran through as if the job description stated it was only to be temporary. I don't mean that she didn't love me, didn't take care of me. But her vision of herself never matched the reality. She couldn't see her mask, although she could see that I couldn't manage keeping mine from slipping.

They'd admitted I was adopted when I was first contacted by the old woman, when her letter stayed in my pocketbook for days before I could bring myself to finish it. Yes, I was adopted, she was right about that, but not the rest, that was crazy. I was adopted, but they hadn't wanted to tell me to make me feel I was anything less than theirs because I was, I was their everything. I was from an orphanage, nuns handled the paperwork, but from what they understood, my parents died in a bus crash that I survived, and the distant relatives still in the countryside, although heartbroken, were too poor to take me in. No loose ends. Everything virtuous. Poor but noble. The perfect orphan story, straight from a soap opera. Rags to riches because I was such an adorable baby. I earned my fate through my cooing.

They had to tell me I was adopted because they knew the first court-ordered DNA tests would reveal that the DNA was an impossible match for us, and the next step would be to match my DNA with one of the grandmothers, the whole group of them who stood in the square, and although they weren't sure there would be a match, they knew I would know I was adopted. My parents were doling out truth and building new lies for scaffolding. When the DNA showed my grandmother was my grandmother, were they planning to claim the nuns had tricked them into taking a baby without knowing the origins? Without knowing that the baby's parents had been killed by my father? Bad origins twice: the murdered and the murderers. Bad by nature, worse by nurture.

What child doesn't think, maybe I'm adopted? Waiting for the wolves who wear the masks of parent faces to fool the careless child. My father, on the stairs of the house on the hill, sneering down at me, when he'd found out that I hadn't failed my university exams, but hadn't taken them in the first place: you're no child of mine. He was right.

I put the teacup down. The pattern that had once seemed so delicate resolved into a military crest. The pearls themselves were a uniform.

Your father will be home soon. Can't you wait to talk to him? You can help him. You're the only one who can. I'm losing you, maybe my grandchildren, too.

I didn't respond.

Don't let me lose him. He's all I'll have left.

I can't keep him from prison.

But you can decide how long he goes. Darling, he isn't young. All I ask is that you remember how much he loves you. She folded her hands around her teacup and crossed her ankles together. The interview was over. She wouldn't say another word because she wanted to end on this sentimental note. All I ask is everything of you, darling.

I stood in the garden waiting for my father. The cushions were out for the chaise lounge, and I could have walked to the gazebo, but to sit in comfort would reveal me as part of the world of the pearls. I'd wait to sit in my own home, on chairs paid for by skillful dentistry. The rosebushes were pruned so tightly they looked skeletal, and the lawn as regular as Astroturf and as lush as a painting. A green so bright I thought of the Technicolor photographs at my grandmother's.

I knew my father wouldn't approach me in the garden. He didn't meet people, not even halfway. People came in to talk to him, either once he was ensconced beyond the massive oak desk in the study or propped up in his club chair in the den, cigar in hand. He didn't enter rooms or exit them. He was already there, the space already claimed and shaped by him. I tiptoed around him when I was little. I only came to him when I was called. Which is not to say I didn't love him, or that I feared him. When I was little, he would pull me up into his lap and listen patiently while I narrated inventions. He would hide candy and small treats he thought I would like in his pockets: change from other countries, stamps with birds and flowers, pencils with cartoon characters. He wanted to see me every day, no matter how late he returned from his office. He called it the viewing, and sometimes I would turn it into a performance, ballet steps, warbling I called opera, poems about rabbits in the garden. As I grew older, sitting in his lap seemed ridiculous, and I became self-conscious about the viewing. I didn't want to perform, and what teenager wants to be looked at? I stopped seeking him out, and he didn't meet people halfway.

He was done with me when I dropped out of the university. I wasn't a boy, which would have meant an army career. What my mother had hoped for me was at least a few years at the university and marriage. When it was a few months at the university instead, she found me my dentist, the son of a childhood friend of hers. I'd known him all my life. When he came to my house or I went to his, he expected a viewing. He liked to examine my teeth. He found mouths erotic, and it was an efficient step to kissing and things that can be done with mouths that would horrify my mother. When I married my dentist, my father warmed up to me again, although I never remember speaking to him alone, always my mother and my husband in the room instead, as if we were trapped in some play on a country estate where all principals must be on stage at once. When I had the boys, he was transformed, bringing out tin soldiers to scatter on the rugs, the patterns terrain. When I was divorced, it didn't matter to him because I'd produced the boys. His heirs were here, an heir and a spare. They could run two branches of the armed forces between them. I could be dumped from the plane now.

My mother called me back inside. Darling, he's in the study. You can take his tea in to him, she said, handing me the tray. As if I needed a reason to talk to him, when he was the one desperate to talk to me.

I didn't take the tray. She had to put it back on the sideboard. Behind the desk in the study, he looked shrunken, not that much younger than the old lady who was my grandmother, and his uniform didn't fit so well any more, as if he was shrinking too fast for adjustments. The medals gleamed; epaulets framed his shoulders. He waited for me to say something, as if I were the supplicant. But I waited for him to speak first.

Your mother says the situation has changed, he said.

Yes, I said.

What do you want me to do? he asked. I was the supplicant. He couldn't ask me to save him. It wasn't in him, wasn't within the uniform.

Can you kill her, Daddy? I don't want to go back there. You should have seen her apartment. And it's so sad, her story.

He scowled. It isn't funny, he said. We didn't raise you to be flippant.

What do you want me to do, Daddy?

His eyes flickered. He knew what my mother wanted him to ask, but he couldn't do it. Either he didn't want to debase himself and ask a favor of me, or there was something in him, maybe the part that put those old knees down on the rug for my boys, that wanted to be punished.

Nothing, he said. There is nothing for you to do. What do you want from me?

I do want to know if you were the one who killed them. I know you must have killed radicals. Killed their friends. But did you kill them. Did you kill my mother and father?

Your mother is in the garden. I'm your father, sitting here before you.

But we both know that's not true. At least, not wholly true. I have many parents.

What would you believe? That I killed them? That I didn't kill them? If you know the truth before the DNA results have come, you must know this truth, too.

I did. I knew. He was a man who liked to delegate, but wouldn't shirk from something hard. He prided himself on being a hard man. There would have been bargains between brothers. He would have tortured and killed other mothers for fellow officers who needed babies, too. He'd be complicit in the crime, but able to look at his child and not see a copy of his victims' eyes. If the wolf had killed my parents, I would have felt most bound to him, I think. He would have been the parent who mattered most. But he lacked the courage of his convictions. He was a murderer, just not my murderer.

You didn't kill them, Daddy.

Thank you. Tell your mother I'd like my tea now, darling, will you? He didn't look up from his newspaper as I left. I didn't stop to talk to my mother. I walked all the way home, down the hill, the whole city spread out before me.

I didn't testify for leniency for my father, the murderer, and my mother, the kidnapper. I didn't testify for my grandmother, either. I stayed here, insulated by the money of my dentist, bringing up my own wolfpack. We're alone, set adrift in the island of childhood, those years before school when a parent is everything to a child, but we're surrounded by family. My father snug in the prison, my mother high in the mansion on the hill, my grandmother out in her tiny apartment, my parents falling from the plane into the sea, if you drew a circle, there I would be in the center, with my boys, neither left nor right. Nothing will be the same. Everything will be the same. I'm the one who's right. I'm what's left. ã

Joe Klein's WOODY GUTHRIE: A LIFE

Holly George-Warren

Thirty-five years ago, the first biography of folksinger Woody Guthrie became a kind of bible for me, a wannabe music writer who'd just moved to New York from North Carolina. In *Woody Guthrie: A Life*, Joe Klein, primarily a political journalist, had crafted an in-depth history of the author of "This Land Is Your Land," a self-mythologizing populist hobo riding the rails and toting a guitar emblazoned with the words, "This machine kills fascists." Guthrie's story reads like a combination adventure novel, history of American folk music, and study of Dust Bowl-era populism.

When the book was published in 1980, Guthrie was thirteen years dead, and by then, his legacy had been nearly swept aside by the tides of popular music. Klein won the cooperation of Guthrie's three wives, various family members, and associates like Pete Seeger and Alan Lomax. He set out on his own journey, digging deep into the life of the complicated troubadour, raconteur, and wordsmith. Traveling to Guthrie's native Oklahoma and spending months in a room in New York with the prolific songwriter's copious writing, including manuscripts, correspondence, and lyrics, Klein excavated mountains of material to digest and analyze. In between were stints at Florida's Beluthahatchee Swamp (where Guthrie and his third wife lived in a tent) and the Brooklyn State Hospital, where Guthrie suffered the long, torturous decline caused by Huntington's disease, the hereditary scourge that killed his mother.

In Klein's telling, Woody Guthrie comes alive as a very flawed but brilliant human being, an artist whose timeless work has inspired generations of songwriters, from Bob Dylan and Bruce Springsteen to Billy Bragg and Wilco. He tells Guthrie's story with all its color and complexity—the ugly and the beautiful—but without sensationalizing scabrous events or turning biography into hagiography. It's clear that Klein had no agenda other than seeking to understand the man and the artist without making moral judgments or offering armchair psychology. Yet, Klein is perceptive in helping decipher his many contradictions: in describing Guthrie's failed attempts at writing a follow-up to the well-received memoir, *Bound for Glory*: "Although Woody paid lip service to the ideal of simplicity, he was burdened by the constant pressure to produce greatness." Klein, seemingly, took this lesson to heart, by letting Guthrie's story unfold in a natural, organic way—making it an engaging read. Klein's eye for detail and his judicious selection of examples from the perhaps millions of words Guthrie wrote bring Woody to life.

In the book's introduction, Klein spells out his M.O., which exemplifies his choice of simple eloquence trumping overblown dissection:

"Woody Guthrie was a man who was born on the frontier and died in the city. At times, I've been tempted to view his progress from Okemah, Oklahoma, to the Creedmoor State Hospital in Queens, New York, as a perverse metaphor for America's progress through the twentieth century—but it really isn't. It is only one life, sad and triumphant and utterly unique, and I have tried to present it as accurately as possible."

That was the lesson I learned from Klein's book as I embarked on my career as a writer, a journey that started at a railroad apartment on St. Mark's Place. Interviewing dozens of musicians and telling their stories in magazine profiles, I was mostly drawn to complicated artists, usually of the indie-rock variety, whose emotional baggage made its way into their songcraft, as well as C&W icons like Johnny Cash, George Jones, and Merle Haggard. Eventually, I began a lengthy biography of the ultimate "good guy," Gene Autry, the singing cowboy idol of the 1930s and '40s. My travels took me to Oklahoma, Texas, and California—Woody's old stomping grounds. When I learned that Autry had a hidden dark side, I grappled with how best to present this difficult material. Without making leaps—comparing Autry's downward spiral (which fortunately righted itself) to the country's plummet in mood following WWII—I discussed his foibles in context with the whole story of his long (sometimes tragic), event-filled life. I knew acknowledging his demons would not be welcomed by many of the biography's readers—longtime admirers who believed in the myth of the Man in the White Hat. In fact, at a Los Angeles book signing, one such fan—a man from Ohio in his 70s—told me that at first he'd been dismayed to discover Autry's more human side in my book. But he gradually realized that as he accepted Autry as a flawed hero, he could forgive his own father who'd abandoned the family when he was a baby—he'd always wished for a dad like Gene Autry (who never had children).

Like Klein, I endeavored to include the unpleasant facts in an evenhanded way without sensationalizing them or roasting Autry over the coals for his errant behavior. The same approach came in handy when I tackled my next biographical subject—the very complicated, mercurial artist Alex Chilton, cofounder of the ill-fated band Big Star. Based on the feedback I've gotten, I think I pulled it off. As I begin writing the biography of Janis Joplin, I'm sure I'll be thanking Joe Klein yet again for guiding the way. ೋ

Heart Attack

Sarah Vallance

Lying in bed one night in our tiny apartment in Somerville, I am seized by a tremendous pain in my chest. It feels like someone has taken a tomahawk to me and is beating away at my ribcage with all their might. I roll over onto my side and try to catch my breath but the pain is excruciating.

I decide to wake my girlfriend, Laura. "I think I might be dying," I whisper, knowing that Laura is someone who does not like having her sleep disturbed. I tell her about the crushing pain in my chest, the likes of which I have never experienced, and I manage to alarm her sufficiently for her to forget to be angry at being woken. She rings her mother back home in Australia to ask for advice. Her mother runs a bed and breakfast and is a person with no medical experience or expertise, but she tells us over speakerphone that I am having a heart attack. I am thirty-four, healthy, slim, a non-smoking vegetarian, and I do not believe I am having a heart attack. I tell Laura I think we need a second opinion. She calls a doctor friend who lives in Cambridge. It is five o'clock in the morning when she makes the call. Take a couple of aspirin, our friend suggests. I do, but the pain doesn't stop.

The year is 1997 and Laura and I have left our home and our dog in sleepy Sydney to spend twelve months in America. I am at Harvard studying the access of very poor elderly African Americans to healthcare. Laura is taking a couple of subjects for her Masters degree in marketing and using her spare time for sight-seeing. My scholarship has provided us both with excellent health insurance, as Laura reminds me, before picking up the phone and calling Blue Cross.

"Don't!" I shout. "It will pass! No!" but pain prevents me from leaning over and wrenching the telephone from her hand.

Laura passes me the phone and a woman who introduces herself as "Cindy," asks me to rate my pain on a scale of one to ten. This seems to be an odd barometer, but I tell her it's probably an eight. She asks me to describe the pain. I say that a couple of hours ago it felt like someone had stabbed me with a tomahawk, but that now the pain is more generalized and it feels like a pallet of bricks has been dropped on my chest from a great height. "You need an ambulance ma'am. I am sending one now," she says.

"No, please!" I say. "I do not need an ambulance! Don't I get any say in this?"

I barely have time to heave myself out of bed before eight people appear inside our living room. Two firemen, a policeman, three emergency medical team people, and two ambulance officers. Back home it would take a bomb blast to get such a turnout.

"What's going on?" I ask.

No one speaks.

"Can I please get dressed?" Laura helps me into some jeans and a t-shirt and grabs a jacket from the wardrobe. I am told to keep quiet, strapped to a stretcher, and carried down the front steps of our apartment.

Double-parked in the street outside are an ambulance, a police car, an emergency services station wagon, and a fire truck. The neighbors peer out from their porches to see what's happening. "She shot me!" I want to say, clutching my chest and pointing at Laura, because we are in America after all. Instead I close my eyes and pretend I am dead. There is a certain indignity in being carted out of one's home on a stretcher.

I am lifted into the ambulance and a woman hooks me up to a portable ECG machine. Probably because I am in shock at the sight of all these people, and in an ambulance for the first time in my life, my heartbeat is irregular, or so the woman administering the test tells me. We are about to pull away from the curb when one of the ambulance officers asks about my insurance. Laura leaps out of the ambulance, races back inside the apartment and reappears moments later waving my Blue Cross card. The siren wails and we screech around the corner to Cambridge Hospital, to make up for the time we lost trying to determine whether my insurance would cover the ambulance ride.

I am wheeled inside the emergency room. It's noisy and it reeks of disinfectant. I happen to hate hospitals. I don't care much for the medical profession either. My last experience with a doctor, four years earlier, had been an unhappy one. A bolting horse had hurled me out of its saddle, and I had landed on a rock, the back of my head taking the full force of impact. The neurologist I saw in hospital told me I had suffered a Traumatic Brain Injury. After seeing the results of my psychometric tests, he told me my brain would never recover. I would not work again, nor finish the PhD I was a third of the way through researching. For the better part of a year, I lay slumped on my sofa at home, drawing a disability pension, thinking my life was over. Only my brain *did* recover, most of it anyway, and here I was, four years later, on a scholarship at Harvard. Doctors, I learned, make grave mistakes.

We wait for a stall to become available, and Laura kisses me on the cheek and looks at me with concern.

"I'm fine!" I say, mindful of how pathetic I look on this tiny white bed, and squeeze her hand.

The emergency room is packed full of people who have overdosed or poisoned themselves with alcohol. I happen to have a vomit phobia, and an emergency room for the sufferer of emetophobia is a bit like standing outside the guardrail on the roof of a skyscraper for a person with a fear of heights. In the bed to my left, a woman wails. "She's coming down after a bad night," the nurse shouts over the woman's howls. I am someone who finds the sound of an adult howling unsettling. It's fine if they have just lost an eye, or been attacked by a crocodile, or found out someone close to them has died, but at any other time is it really necessary?

To my right, protected from me by nothing but a flimsy green piece of polyester, is a white man in his fifties who can't stop vomiting. I know he is white and in his fifties because he keeps opening my curtain to talk to the nurse who is trying to attend to my heart attack. "Well, this should teach you not to drink two bottles of vodka a day," the nurse says, snapping the curtain closed. "Please nurse," he begs her. "The yellow pills, the ones that stop . . ." and he's off again. Between hurls into his bucket he keeps opening my curtain. I want to tell him to get the fuck out of my cubicle but I worry what he might do with his bucket full of vomit.

A different nurse performs another ECG on me. This time the results are normal. That would seem to be a good sign and I propose I leave. The nurse informs me that a bad reading followed by a good reading is bad. Could it not be the machine, I ask? The machine inside the ambulance and the machine here in the emergency ward are different. No, that isn't it, she says, walking out of my cubicle and leaving the curtain open. The man beside me shrieks "I'm vomiting blood!" but no one seems to hear him but me. He has changed positions and is now sitting on the side of his bed inches away from me. His bucket is poking through the curtain. "Nurse! I've filled this one up," he shouts, "I need another . . ." I close my eyes. I am in hell.

They wheel me out of emergency into a private room in intensive care, Laura trailing behind. "Just give me some painkillers and send me home," I beg.
No one listens.
A needle is stuck inside one arm so my cardiac enzymes can be tested every two hours, and a blood pressure bag attached to the other, so my blood pressure can be measured every fifteen minutes. At five o'clock in the afternoon, I tell Laura to go home, and I spend a long and uncomfortable night in a very cold room, visited every so often by

an officious nurse with a crew cut, who demands I pee into a plastic receptacle. She becomes even snappier when I tell her I do not need to pee. I lie on my side, clutching my chest, pretending I'm lying on a beach somewhere, watching the waves lap the sand, waiting for someone to fan me with a palm frond or bring me a daiquiri.

A young doctor with a face like Danny Bonaduce, swings by in the morning and tells me my problems are suspiciously similar to those of a person who has snorted too much cocaine. I look at her for a moment and tell her I have never used cocaine in my life.

"Well, we believe you have," she says.

"Well you're fucking crazy," I tell her. "I don't use *any* illegal drugs. I've *never* used *any* illegal drugs."

That happens to be true. I would very much have *liked* to use illegal drugs, but I always hung around with the wrong crowd. And then I had my accident. Drugs can do a lot of harm to a person with a damaged brain. So can alcohol, of course, but I chose to ignore that fact. And it is legal. I also happen to have a highly addictive personality. One snort of cocaine for me would mean the start of a slippery slope which would leave me in a gutter somewhere, my mouth wrapped around a crack pipe. I tell the doctor none of this. She sticks another needle in my arm, like she might a garden hoe into a dry bit of soil. Once the pain passes, I speak.

"You can't march in here accusing someone of using drugs," I say. "It's completely unethical. Why don't you do a drug test? And then you can apologize."

She doesn't do a drug test, nor does she apologize, but when the cardiologist appears, some moments later, she tells him she suspects I have a history of drug abuse. Like many people with brain damage, I struggle with impulse control, and I do not deal well with being accused of something I haven't done.

"What the fuck is the matter with you?" I shout. "I just told you I've never taken any illegal drugs!" And then I say it: "I'm studying at Harvard!" and the words make me cringe as soon as they leave my mouth.

"That just confirms it," she says under her breath and turns to leave the room.

"What a *bitch!*" I say to the doctor as he scribbles something in the folder at the foot of my bed, which is probably "psychotic," "aggressive" or "patient displays challenging behaviours."

I am still fuming when Laura arrives with chocolate, licorice, and some nice red grapes. She sits down on my bed, takes my hand and listens patiently while I tell her I am still traumatized by the vomiting man.

"Poor you," she says, giggling at my misfortune. Laura, herself an easy and frequent vomiter, derives much mirth from my emetophobia.

We are interrupted by the nurse with the commando haircut, who keeps snarling at me because I refuse to urinate in her plastic dish.

"She's a lesbian, isn't she?" I ask Laura quietly when the nurse leaves the room. Laura is my compass on such things, and I look to her for social cues.

"Yes, darling, I don't think there's any doubt about that."

"Why is she so rude?" I ask.

Laura shrugs. "She is what's known as a *grumpy* lesbian."

"What about the sisterhood? Shouldn't she be nice to us?"

"Maybe she doesn't like Australians," Laura suggests with a half smile. "Or perhaps we are not butch enough for her."

I mull this over and nod.

Laura looks like a taller, slightly heavier version of Kate Winslet, and I've always thought that I have the wholesome looks of a Sunday school teacher. People are almost always surprised to learn we are gay.

"But she's a nurse," I say. "Aren't they meant to put aside their prejudices and be pleasant?" I ask.

"It's America, darling. No one puts aside their prejudices when it comes to healthcare," Laura says, and as we giggle the woman reappears and shouts "No eating!" picking up Laura's shopping and dumping it in the drawer beside my bed.

"We weren't eating," I say, but she has gone.

Personally, I have no plans to eat until I've made it home and had a long hot shower to scrub away whatever airborne microbes from the vomiting man may have penetrated the space between us.

But I am not leaving yet. First I am to be given thallium to test my heart through a CT scan, both before and after I exercise on a treadmill. Then comes a three-way chest X-ray, an ultra-sound of my heart, a lung CT scan, and a breast ultra-sound. Laura looks worried. "I'm fine," I tell her, and she bends down to kiss me goodbye before I get wheeled off into another room for more tests. "I'd be dead by now if it was a heart attack," I say to reassure her. "Most likely," I add, as she waves to me from the door.

"Why do I need a breast ultra-sound?" I ask, but no one answers.

In the middle of the ultra-sound, my breasts glistening with KY jelly while a nurse in a short skirt rubs a white dildo across my chest, the curtain yanks open and the Professor from the School of Social Medicine at Harvard who is supervising my research appears at the foot of my bed.

"My God, Sarah, are you alright?" she says. "What on earth happened?"

I pull the sheet up over me and tell her the whole story.

"Would you like me to talk to the doctor?"

I assume she means the doctor that thinks I'm a cokehead, but I'm not sure.

"No, I'll be fine. They say I can go home now."

Another nurse appears on the other side of the bed. "You can go home once you've had your TB test."

"My what?"

"Your TB test. We scratch your skin, it only takes five minutes."

"TB?" I look at my supervisor and she shrugs as if there must be a mistake. "*Tuberculosis?*"

"Yes," a nurse says. "The doctor thinks you have TB."

"Which doctor?" I ask.

"The lung doctor," the nurse says.

"She doesn't have TB," my supervisor says, before shooting me a look that says, "Do you?"

She offers to stick around to find out why they think I have TB, but I urge her to go. It's been humiliating enough. I thank her for visiting and tell her I'll call her in the morning to let her know what happens. At seven o'clock that evening I am allowed to go home, with strict instructions to attend a clinic the following Wednesday.

Cambridge Hospital has its own TB clinic, or it did in 1997. Tucked away to one side of the main entrance, you find it by walking to the end of a very long corridor. They would prefer patients to use the side entrance, so as not to share their airborne droplets with anyone else, but I do not have TB so I use the main entrance. The waiting room is packed with Hispanic men wearing cowboy boots and sombreros. I give my name to the woman at reception and am told to sit. The wait will be one hour. Laura surveys the room quickly and realizes that sitting for an hour in a room packed with TB patients isn't going to be a whole lot of fun, so she decides to go for a walk. I take the only spare seat, wedged underneath the brims of two enormous hats. As soon as I'm seated, the men on either side of me start coughing. One of them spits thick globs of green and red phlegm into a large see-through plastic shopping bag. I put my hand over my mouth before deciding to step outside for some fresh air. When I return I stand near the exit, and take short, shallow breaths through my nose.

Finally my name is called, and the doctor, a man who tells me he is a Professor of Respiratory Medicine at Harvard, examines my lung scans.

"It's TB," he says.

"It can't be," I answer.

"It is. I'm 98% sure of it," he says, squeezing his eyes together.

"Impossible," I say, shaking my head.

"You tested borderline positive to the skin test," he says.

"But borderline positive does not mean positive," I say.

He points with a biro to a CT scan of my lung lit up on a backlit box. "See those white spots? That's calcification. At some point, you've been exposed to TB."

"No," I say. "I had pneumonia once. I've had those spots since then."

"That's not pneumonia," he says. "Have you ever travelled through the developing world?"

"Yes."

"Where exactly?"

"Philippines, Thailand, Fiji, Palestine, Egypt . . ."

"How long were you there?"

"About four months in the Philippines and the same in Thailand and Fiji. A few days in the others."

"My money is on the Philippines," he says, tapping his biro on the desk.

"I was never sick in the Philippines," I say.

"That doesn't mean you didn't come into contact with the bacteria that causes TB," he says, cocking his head. "You have inactive TB."

He goes on to tell me that there is a law in Massachusetts, which stipulates that any person found to have active or inactive TB, must be treated.

"But I'm not sick!" I say.

"You're not sick *now*," he says. "But you have had a TB exposure which means there's a good enough chance you'll get it back. One in ten, in fact. And it won't be in the lungs next time. There's a good chance it will kill you."

"Can't we wait 'til then?"

"No," he says, and exhales.

"Can I ask you something?"

"Sure," he says, cocking his head again.

"Being coughed all over by a waiting room full of TB patients can't be great for those of us who don't have it. What's the risk of transmission like?"

"Did you see the ultraviolet lights out there?" he says, using what I imagine must be his teaching voice. "Those lights kill the bacteria. No one sitting out there is going to catch TB."

I didn't believe it at the time, but it's true: ultraviolet germicidal irradiation kills the droplets that cause TB.

Outside, I find Laura sitting on a bench reading the *Boston Globe*.

"I don't have TB," I say.

"Of course you don't!" she says and hugs me.

"But the doctor thinks I do."

"What?"

"I don't!" And I look at Laura who I can tell is worrying about the risks of transmission, and whether *she* might have tuberculosis. We have been together five years, sharing the same bed and the same toothbrush on occasions, when she gets home late and drunk.

"It's very hard to catch, Laura," I say.

"But you caught it! And you don't even know where or how."

It's a good point. "Look, I don't have TB, okay? Please believe me," and we leave it at that.

The following week I visit a clinic in Porter Square. It's kind of like a methadone clinic, except the drugs meted out are for people with TB. A nurse who looks to be in her fifties comes out to greet me. She tells me her name is Frances. I shake her hand and she smiles and asks how I am. She is the only medical practitioner I have met in America who has smiled at me, or asked how I am. I tell her so. She is from Haiti, she says, giving me an even bigger smile. The Haitians look like they could teach white Americans a bit about bedside manner, I say. She laughs, and tells me I am her only white patient. White people suck, I want to say, although I am sure by this point in her life she has reached that conclusion herself.

We chat a little about Haiti and Australia and she leaves the room and returns with an armful of pill bottles.

"Now you're going to need to take six of these tablets every day for a year."

"What is it?" I ask.

"Isoniazid. It's the best treatment we have for TB. You'll need to come back to the clinic every fortnight for more drugs and to have your blood tested."

I look at her and nod.

"There is a slight chance you will develop chemically-induced hepatitis from the treatment," Frances says. "That's very rare, though," she adds, nudging my arm. "In the meantime, you can't drink alcohol."

"No alcohol for a year?" I cannot hide my shock.

"That's right," she says.

I would rather die than spend a year without alcohol, but I keep that thought to myself.

Four weeks after I start taking the drugs, I feel terrible. It's like a very bad flu. My glands are swollen and I ache all over. I shuffle from my bed to the bathroom to the kitchen and back to bed and feel like I have run a marathon. I haven't had so much as a sniff of alcohol. Unable to drag myself to the clinic, I postpone my blood test appointment for another fortnight and keep taking the drugs. I start to lose weight and my eyes look like they are retreating inside my head. Alarmed by my appearance, Laura calls a taxi and takes me to the clinic.

We follow Frances into a small room and I tell her I have spent the past month in bed. I describe the symptoms.

"That doesn't sound good at all," she says, giving me a worried look.

Later that day, once the blood test results are ready, she calls me at home.

"Sarah! You've got hepatitis!" and she sounds as alarmed at the news as I am. "Stop taking the drugs immediately! They can be very dangerous to a person with liver damage. Rest up," she says, "and drink plenty of fluids. And take good care!" She calls me every day for the next week to check on me, and tells me that in her seven years at the clinic, only one other patient has developed hepatitis, and he had HIV. Later I learn that only 0.5% of patients under the age of 35 develop hepatitis from Isoniazid.

I toy with the idea of calling the TB doctor and telling him that while I *may* have had inactive TB, I *definitely* now have hepatitis. In the end I don't bother. I summon up all my energy to buy a large bunch of flowers for my favourite nurse. I surprise her at the clinic between patients. She throws her arms around me and hugs me, and I thank her for being so kind. "I'm so sorry!" she says.

The final months of my scholarship passed with me in bed, for the most part, nursing my poisoned liver. We moved back to Sydney to our home and our dog, and I saw another specialist who said he could virtually guarantee I did not have TB in any shape or form. He was 98% certain of it. The white spots on my lungs were scars from an old case of pneumonia. My mother remembered me being vaccinated against TB when we lived in England when I was seven. I asked the doctor if the vaccination could have caused a borderline skin test result. "Absolutely!" he said.

No one ever told me what caused my chest pains. But Blue Cross picked up the $10,000 hospital bill. That seemed like a lot for the privilege of spending a couple of hours only inches away from a man vomiting up his own poisoned liver, being accused of taking cocaine by a resident doctor, being snapped at by a rude nurse in intensive care, and prescribed a course of treatment for a condition I never had that happened to lead to something that made me sick. Really sick. Next time I think I'm dying, I plan to lie perfectly still, not wake a soul, and wait for death to seize me.   ࢷ

Kent Haruf's PLAINSONG

David Huddle

I've recently placed Kent Haruf's *Plainsong* on my mental shelf of books that I recommend to readers who will appreciate them—and occasionally to readers I judge to be in need of a specific book. Its companions on that shelf are James Galvin's *The Meadow*, Marie Howe's *What the Living Do*, Dorianne Laux's *Smoke* and *Awake* and Andre Dubus's *Selected Stories*. I realize that I sometimes recommend these books as a doctor prescribes a medicine.

The people in *Plainsong* feel no self-pity and probably don't realize how deeply they are suffering. If they know how dire their circumstances are, they don't dwell on the hardship and don't talk about it. They navigate as best they can—and often do so out of intuition that seems more animal than human. They rely on their resourcefulness, their willingness to work hard, and their ability to face down their fears. They're small-town and rural folks. Self-reliant to a fault, they nevertheless need at least one or two people to care about them, but they *feel* that need more than they understand it, and they know that caring people are hard to come by anyway.

Plainsong is a humble book, one that overtly risks sentimentality. Its language is so plain that a reader is continually astonished by simple words generating so much empathy and emotion. The power of the novel comes from the strength with which readers connect with its characters. I came to feel that Victoria Roubideaux, Ike and Bobby Guthrie and their father, and the McPheron brothers were my relatives. I lived their struggles with them almost as deeply as I would those of my brothers, my parents, my children, my aunts and uncles.

I teared up reading scenes where the *Plainsong* characters suffered hardship. Here's a passage from the first of those scenes, the one where newly-pregnant, seventeen-year-old Victoria Roubideaux comes home from a day of school and working the evening shift as a washer of pots and pans at a restaurant to find that her mother has locked her out of their house:

Mama. Let me in now. Do you hear me?

She clutched at the doorknob, pulling and twisting it, and she knocked on the window, rattling the hard little pane, but the door stayed locked. Then inside the house the dim hall light went out.

Mama. Don't. Please.

I also teared up when the characters I'd come to care about had some good luck. And these were often instances of one person's need somehow matching up with a different need in another person. Victoria, for example, is taken in by elderly bachelor brother farmers—she needs a safe place to live, and the McPherons need the enlivening presence of a young woman and her baby. The end of the scene where she moves in to their farmhouse ends with such countrified decorum that I can hardly bear it:

> She looked at him, then at his brother. Thank you, she said. Thank you for letting me stay here with you.
>
> Well, you're welcome, Raymond said. You sure are.
>
> They stood awkwardly inspecting the floor.

I would admire the writing in *Plainsong* and the beauty of its composition if it had nothing else to offer. But I love the book for the author's vision of how humans can sometimes manage to fix each other. Were he alive, Kent Haruf would probably be quick to point out that such healing is a rare occurrence. But the simple possibility of it is a ray of light to those of us who spend a lot of time groping around in the dark. ⮞

The Woman in the Barn

Jaclyn Gilbert

Joseph and I are soon to be hitched in my sister's house with white sideboards and purple geraniums sprawling from black pots.

Joseph didn't give me any kind of engagement ring. He gave me a wooden clock. I told him, Joseph, let's be more like the English and go for carats, our value in carats, with a thirteen grand baseline.

But he said: Lydia, our people bequeath clocks and china and tools, family tokens and borrowed things, useful things.

There's a woman outside—she's still locked up in Joseph's family barn like a cow.

I've only seen her once, caught a glimpse through a crack while I waited for Joseph to finish his plowing. It was April, just before our fourth courting walk. The woman's hair was flying wild from her mull cap as if someone went and took all her bobby pins, and she was screaming something about *Martyrs Mirror*:

I am but dust and ash approach thee, she said.

Usually, in church, we see it as our sacred privilege to recite, O my savior and redeemer, those defenseless lambs, who were sacrificed by water fire sword and wild beasts.

The woman kept asking for chalk, a board, something to write on.

Listen, my hands are dry as flint. I had to tell her.

Later during our walk, I asked Joseph:

Is she a wild beast? The kind of woman who'd scrape out her own eyes, knock out her own teeth? Like a rabid dog I once saw my father shoot when it stole chicken eggs from the coop because there was no mercy, God had no tolerance for that!

But Joseph answered me, Lydia, she can't be any of those things. The devil Himself has possessed her. She's not fit to marry or bear any kind of child. We can't trust her hands for needlework.

Our winter seasons for sewing have always been long like a slumber while the men dry tobacco the little boys speared. They work the cows too hard in the barn milking up the light of day. Dusk at four and dinner at five. We go to bed early. We pray before we sleep.

Dark blue, they tell us to wear on our wedding day. O be humble before God. Like a bruise. And dark colors to absorb the light. We will have to keep the lights dim for the ceremony.

There was something like dust in the woman. The way her dry lips cracked. Screeching out words like chalk scraped over hard dark black. That chalk she kept asking me for, to write out symbols and things about God's consuming flames.

She said to me: Here's rue for you, some for me . . . I would give you some violets!

Violet, whose violet? Violet the color of my eye when Joseph hits. He started when I wondered, pressed him, whether the barn woman truly deserved this. Sometime not long after, he asked for my hand, and I gave it.

Next to the Bible, *Martyrs Mirror* is our most sacred book. I've begun pressing fresh lilac between some of the pages.

Luke said, Blessed are ye that weep now, for ye shall laugh. I am waiting for the flowers to dry.

I've seen a picture of an English wedding. In the house of a family I clean for every week. On Thursdays I scrub for twenty an hour this English house, but don't I dare touch a current of spark. No vacuum or washer and dryer either. No electric iron.

In the picture, the bride, she's let her hair down: lilac-strewn. I'd like that too. Some flowers in my hair to scatter after all's been said and done.

I am seventeen and Joseph is twenty. We don't go by legal age, more by what our family thinks is a good fit and these weeks of courting we took. Long walks barefoot by the far creek holding hands and hiccupping words like chimes. The soft sound bells make I used to mistake for laughter.

The woman in the barn did smile at me, said she too had wanted more than china, more than a clock. Perhaps she asked for chalk so she could write out a different story.

Mankind: the essential thing, the useful thing, she said. But it isn't always! she howled.

Joseph noticed me during volleyball practice one Sunday after Church, after choir. I have never liked running much. He used to watch me slap my hands wildly. I would giggle, but during our first walk in the woods Joseph told me to stop that. He told me I wasn't very intelligent.

My mother has asked about my eye. I said wedding china fell down from the hutch when I was getting the new house ready.

She told me to be more careful. This is your sacred life beginning, Lydia, she said. Your house with Joseph will be under God.

At first bruises are purple, like broken moonlight. I've started counting the nighttime stars. Someone's missing teeth, I think. More sweet lilacs pressed next to the words of Timothy:

If we suffer, we shall also reign with Him.

The creek where Joseph and I took our first courting walks glittered with shadows from the spring tree leaves. Against the water there was a sallow color like ripening corn, white to greenish gray and yellow. Joseph once kissed me there. I tasted sunlight and the fields and plough wheels turning around the soft dead dirt.

I've practiced twisting lipstick tops when cleaning the English family's bathroom. Stole the matron's rouge into my apron pocket and caught myself doing it in the mirror.

I had stared at the barn woman's face that day and wondered about violets and lilies and hundreds of colors bleeding into flowers and how different each petal looks depending on which way you turn it under the sun.

Eye bruises, they must take a long time to heal. We aren't allowed to watch our reflections in this community.

I started coating the tender rings round my eye with flour dust. I tell my sisters and brothers it is leftover from so much pie baking these final days before the wedding.

In school they taught us to write out *Sorry* in chalk. Our Father Our Creator we had to write. I'm Sorry we wrote it one hundred times over on the blackboard: I will not talk when someone else is talking.

The barn woman approached me when I told her. Then she licked my wrist.

Devil's tongue, it gets us into trouble! she screamed, We are full of sin! She lay down in the hay then, laughing.

I am pressing more lilac next to Samuel who said:

Consider and hear me, O Lord my God: lighten mine eyes.

The English have lace underwear. I found some in that matron's vanity drawer while cleaning. The word is lingerie, but I would never say it out loud:

Joseph, would you love me in lingerie?

The woman in the barn was small like early daisies. She wrapped herself around rafters with arms like frail stems, skin like pollen dust. Sunlight leaked through the sideboard cracks, got caught in her eye: a fire like the sharp dots English tools make. Electric saws splitting wood. She stared into me.

What if I go blind, the bruises leak to my eye, my brain? I want to go back and ask the barn woman. I would tell her I clean houses to pay for prescriptions, fancy ointments and stark white swathes.

It's been weeks since Joseph last hit me by the far creek. My bruises faded shadow blue, like pearls. Joseph says he's giving me this short time to heal before the wedding.

Stray straw fell out into the barn as the woman howled among the rafters. She touched her face like it hurt, like it was mine.

Maybe I'll bring her more than chalk if I go back. I'll bring her dry corn fodder and tobacco leaves, cow grease, swine oil, saddles, harnesses, ropes, discs, and wheels. I'll bring her eyehooks and nails and twine. Some truss board too. I'll bring her water from the river.

I want to believe the sun is enough to tell the time, that Joseph and I won't need a clock beside our bed after we marry.

The creek water drips into a river that winds long away from the community. It gurgles under the highway, grows murky from black underthings and inky spiders. It laps and eddies around sediment making clay. We could build things, I cried to Joseph when he last struck me, we could, if we let our hair go and wandered past the perimeter.

But Joseph's hand continued down, and he said he had no urge. To follow the flickering silver tail of the river out of our farm. The water tastes like metal, or has the blood finally dried into my mouth like black clay ebony?

I want to believe cold sunlight in the morning and fire at night for warmth are of the same piece. That the quake of lightning shooting sparks along the English lines chattering during storms are needful, natural wants.

Joseph doesn't believe in fear. He doesn't believe lightning can kill. The second time he hit me in the woods he told me to thank the rain. To kneel before it.

I wonder if the woman in the barn ever touched an electric hand-mixer, power drill, reciprocating saw, immersion blender, dishwasher, fuel rotary hammer, pressure cooker, or automatic rifle. Joseph says it's violence. Technology, electricity, all of it Godless and violent.

Daniel was cast into a den of lions, to be torn by them, but God protected him. The dried lilacs crackle beside his name where I'm moving them, the dust of purple faint by black words the woman in the barn would like scratched into chalk white light.

The woman in the barn said there were more than four seasons. Hundreds more than that. Millions, because light is all tiny particles exploding at different speeds and pulses. She said she wanted to read Physics and History and Biology. Evil subjects of war and vanity, she wants to know more than God, but how can we know that?

The last time Joseph hit me he said that fear and love were not the same, especially false love, idol love, which is wanting things, and I am not supposed to want any more than exactly what I have.

Black sparrows and ravens have a sheen of violet satin in their feathers, as if they'd been hiding them all along. The light brings it out in them: lavender silver and gold as natural things more than any useful thing that flutters my pulse, a batting of my eye and quiver in my mouth, like that first kiss I blew for Joseph during volleyball.

He would hit me with a pitchfork in the hayloft if I said lin-ger-ie, puncturing each syllable, and hearing the song of it with my sweet lavender voice.

Did she sit at a wedding table, alone, the woman in the barn? Did she shield her face with her hand as we do against the sunlight? Her eyes crossed and dizzied by the closeness of a corner, where she sat and stared and waited?

She was watching me as she ate chaff in the barn, her mouth frothing white from it: this leftover dust we feed to the cows. I wish I had recited out words like lilac lingerie and black lace spiders and daisy lips and cordless drill through the barn door wall.

Joseph took back my stolen lipstick. He hit me and said I'd burn in hell.

I'll burn for it, this sin, he told me—until I am nothing but dry spark and dust and ash. A feeble flame hobbling from his hands rubbing together and clapping me out.

Tomorrow they'll prop us up blue-dressed and mull-cap-pinned like dolls.
    Joseph, with his heavy clock, black hat, and long dark beard will be waiting for me.

I found the lipstick buried in with Joseph's wool cutting shears. I placed it back in my apron with blackberry jam from the cellar, and carried a leather harness with swine oil and my *Martyrs Mirror* to the woman in the barn. I let her choose the words she wanted. She asked for those of Samuel. Lighten mine eyes, she said.

Together we crushed and let loose the pale dust of dried lilac. ❧

The Bakery Off Flatbush

Steve Monroe

In the Dark:
The sounds of slow moving traffic, breaks braking, tires rolling, maybe a
horn blowing.

The lights rise to reveal the front of a bakery, nondescript, with a couple
of windows and a door.

There are two benches facing each other. It is after the morning rush,
about 10:30 AM. No one is there except A WOMAN, twenties, dressed for
the office, sitting on one of the benches. She speaks into her cell phone.

WOMAN: She has the bigger room! That was the agreement, that she
would keep the beast in her room with her.

That is why I let her have the bigger room. *(Listens.)* I've never called
it that. I've never called it the beast in front of her. I'm calling it a beast
now, to you, because I thought you were my friend and I thought
you were on my side. *(Listens.)* Well it doesn't sound like it. It sounds
like you're on her side. *(Listens.)* I have pet it. I've pet it enough for
ninety-nine lifetimes. *(Listens.)* I do hate it. *(Listens.)* BECAUSE IT
IS DEMENTED! *(Listens.)* Oh! It's nice to you when you're there.
How sweet. You're there for twenty fucking minutes. You don't know
anything! *(Listens.)* So I should keep my door closed? I should isolate
myself? I should not feel the benefits of the air conditioning? *(Listens.)*
Its face was right next to mine. I opened my eyes and it was right there.
(Listens.) I didn't scare it! The fucking thing smiled and raised its left
paw like a guillotine! I've got a six-inch gash above my right breast.
(Listens.) So you have talked to her. *(Listens.)* I didn't say I was going to
poison it.

The door to the bakery opens with the dinging of a bell. A YOUNG
MOTHER clumsily pushes out a bulky stroller while holding a white
paper bag in one hand and a cup of coffee in the other.

MOTHER: *(speaks to the unseen baby in the stroller.)* Mommy got us a
croissant. Yes, Mommy did.

WOMAN: *(turns on the bench and whispers.)* I said I would poison it if it ever scratched me again.

MOTHER: A big fat flaky croissant. Can you say croissant?

WOMAN: *(still whispering)* It's not the same thing.

MOTHER: Say it. Croissant ... croissant.

WOMAN: It's not.

The Mother settles on the bench directly across from The Woman.

MOTHER: Croissant. Say it. Can you say it? Croissant. *(Her face lights up!)* Very good! Very good!

WOMAN: Hold on. Hold on. *(She lowers the phone into her lap.)*

MOTHER: Daddy's going to be so proud. So proud.

She pulls a croissant out of the bag, breaks off a piece and feeds it to the still and never-to-be-seen baby.

WOMAN: *(lifts phone again and turns away.)* Yeah. Hello? No. Nothing.

MOTHER: Croissant's a hard word. Yes, it is.

WOMAN: It's ...

MOTHER: Croissant's a very hard word.

WOMAN: Hold on. Just ...

The Woman again lowers the phone to her lap.

MOTHER: And you said it. Yes, you did. You said it.

The Mother breaks off another piece of croissant and feeds the baby while The Woman looks at her.

The Mother notices the Woman looking.

MOTHER *(cont'd)*: Can I help you?

WOMAN: Are you going to be long?

MOTHER: Excuse me?

WOMAN: Are you going to be sitting here long?

MOTHER: I was going to sit here and drink my cup of coffee and eat my croissant. Why?

WOMAN: I'm having a conversation. (*The Woman holds her phone as proof.*)

MOTHER: Forgive me for invading your phone booth.

The Mother turns her attention to the baby as if she just put an end to the conversation.

MOTHER *(cont'd)*: Is it good? Is it good?

WOMAN: *(back into phone.)* Hold on. I know you have to go. Just . . . hold on. *(To the Mother.)* I was here first.

MOTHER: What?

WOMAN: You clearly saw that I was talking—

MOTHER: Are you even a customer?

WOMAN: And yet you plop yourself right across—

MOTHER: Did you buy anything?

WOMAN: This is the only spot I get reception between here and the subway.

MOTHER: Then get a better phone.

They stare at each other. A stand-off. Even though they're both still sitting.

Finally the Woman raises her phone to her ear, still keeping her eyes locked with the Mother's.

WOMAN: Jean, I'm going to have to—Jean? Jean?

She stands and holds the phone to the sky searching for bars.

WOMAN *(cont'd)*: Hello? Hello?

Skyward again.

WOMAN *(cont'd)*: Jean? Jean?

Jean is clearly gone. She disconnects and tries re-dialing. Nothing. No service.

WOMAN *(cont'd)*: Shit.

She stuffs the phone in her purse.

The Mother meanwhile has returned to feeding the baby.

MOTHER: Isn't that good? So good. So good.

WOMAN: Thanks a lot. Thank you very much.

MOTHER: Oh, you're welcome.

The Woman starts off.

WOMAN: *(slightly mumbles.)* I hope your baby chokes on the croissant.

MOTHER: *(STANDS QUICKLY!)* What did you say?!

WOMAN: *(turns to the Mother)* You and your fucking strollers, you're ruining the neighborhood!

The Woman exits.

MOTHER: *(calls after her)* Then move, sweetheart, cause we're not going anywhere!

She continues to stand looking after the Woman.

MOTHER *(cont'd)*: *(screams)* Asshole!

She sits, clearly shaken.

MOTHER *(cont'd)*: *(half to herself, half to the baby)* Do you believe that?!

She takes deep breaths trying to calm herself.

MOTHER *(cont'd):* I just want to sit here and have a nice cup of coffee.

Her cell phone rings. It startles her. She takes it out of her purse. She looks at it warily, as if it might somehow be the Woman calling.

MOTHER *(cont'd):* Hello . . . ? Hello . . . ? Oh, yes, yes. Sure. Two o'clock tomorrow? Great. And that's with Cherry? Yes. No. Cut and color. Cut and color. Yes. Thank you. See you then. Uh-huh. Bye.

She disconnects and puts the phone in her purse. She takes another deep breath. She is clearly still upset.

MOTHER *(cont'd):* What an asshole.

She turns and looks into the stroller.

MOTHER *(cont'd):* (small laugh) Asshole, yes. *(Another laugh)* You shouldn't say that but this time I'll make an exception. Asshole. Right.

The Mother doesn't see the Woman reenter.

MOTHER *(cont'd):* She was a total asshole.

WOMAN: Excuse me.

Startled, the Mother stands and places herself between the stroller and The Woman.

WOMAN *(cont'd):* (holding up her hands indicating she means no harm) I just want to say I'm sorry. You had every right to be here and I . . . should have never said that about your baby and I just wanted to say that I'm sorry.

The Mother puts her hand to her chest.

MOTHER: Thank you.

The encounter has clearly left both of them emotional.

WOMAN: Well . . . you have a nice day.

MOTHER: You too.

Again, the Woman exits.

The Mother sits. She pulls the stroller to the previous position. She tries to gather her emotions, maybe even wipes a tear.

She turns and looks to the stroller.

MOTHER *(cont'd):* No, she was not an asshole. It turns out she was not an asshole at all and you have to stop saying it.

Pause as she continues to look into the stroller.

MOTHER *(cont'd):* I know mommy said it but mommy was wrong.

Pause.

MOTHER *(cont'd):* Don't say it.

She holds up her finger to caution.

MOTHER *(cont'd):* I said to stop saying it.

Pause.

MOTHER *(cont'd):* One more time and we're going home.

Pause.

MOTHER *(cont'd):* One more time.

Longer pause as the Mother stares.

MOTHER *(cont'd):* That's it! Let's go!

The Mother stands.

BLACK OUT

THE END ❧

NEW DARK AGES by Donald Revell

Josh Kalscheur

Shortly after I finished writing my first book, *Tidal*, I started to feel anxiety. The momentum and rhythm of drafting, revising and ordering the manuscript was over. The image systems and the concrete nouns in which I had lived and moved were no longer available to me. The landscapes of rebar, pandanus and potholes were gone. I felt an aimlessness. I would sit down, write, and hours later, end up with retreads of old poems. I worried, in some nonsensical way, that by writing a book I had forgotten how to write.

Around this same time, in 2011, I began reading the work of Donald Revell, whose collection *New Dark Ages* was recommended to me. It is a book of sentences. It is a book that is aware of God, of a faith in God. It is a book that contains beautiful music but does not privilege sonics above meaning-making. It is a book whose stark images are not domineering. Its principal concern is not story-telling or to create a dramatic series of images, but to distill thoughts and reach for universal truths while also bending and reimagining images and narrative through syntax, enjambment, and repetition.

This approach is apparent in the book's first poem, "Survey," which after a seven-line first sentence, departs from its descriptive opening:

> When a man talks reason, he postpones something.
> He gets in the way of a machine that knows him
> for the sad vengeance that he is, somewhere close
> to the bald name of his city ...

The break from the second to third line adheres to Revell's idea that a line break should enact the intensity and pressure of a religious conversion. The syntactically straightforward second line is subverted by the prepositional phrase in the third, "for the sad vengeance that he is." This is a representative move of *New Dark Ages,* and one which invites the reader to think critically, to meditate on a particular universal truth that does not stand still and goes beyond the simple reenactment of a human condition.

I am compelled, when I read *New Dark Ages*, to grapple with how my life has the potential to negate the lives of others. The poems never fully release the reader into comfort, which makes the book so deeply human. Take, for example, the sonnet-length sixth stanza of "Against Pluralism":

Feeling comes from nowhere and goes nowhere.
It is not a train. It is not one instance
of lovemaking or a lifetime spent together
running the dogs, dying finally face down
in the yard bed of herbs. We are all the same.
Or, rather, we should believe we are the same
in order to be happy with the same things
and not to be stealing from each other.
We put each other in camps. I crush my lover with a kiss
and then it is impossible to love her.
What must die if we are to live without barbed wire
and bad sex is the very idea of otherness.
And to kill the idea, we have merely to find
one victim in ourselves who will die for nothing.

The poem declares a stasis, as feeling "is not a train. It is not one instance / of lovemaking." Eventually, though, this declarative tone is interrupted by the repetition of the phrase "the same" in lines five and six. The hesitance in the repetition, the fact that it recants an original thought (from "We are all the same" to "…we should believe we are the same…") is a departure from earlier lines in this stanza. This hesitant moment turns again, though, as the speaker declares that "bad sex is the very idea of otherness." Is this true? Is this partially true? Not at all? I am not sure but I have thought hard on it, just as I have wondered if "happiness divides us, sometimes / in God's name, sometimes in the name of History." I have wondered if "happiness vends a kind of generosity / that keeps its distance and wants nothing…" I have wondered if "Exhaustion is a last line of defense / where time either stops dead or kills you." I consider the responses. I am not anxious. I work through the thoughts and then I find myself writing, just as Revell might have done when he wrote *New Dark Ages*. Here is a thought and now another and there is the thought again. There is no escaping it. ❧

Lift Off

Lania Knight

The first time I run away with Rob to Fort Worth, I'm sixteen. My father drives 550 miles from Kansas to find me. It's not that difficult. He and a Fort Worth Police Officer pull up the driveway to Rob's dad's house while Rob is away at work. It's the summer of 1985. They sit me in the back of the unmarked police car and drive me to the station downtown to show me the concrete cell I'll live in if I try it again.

The next time, my whole family converges on Fort Worth with the youth minister and a friend from church. They don't want me in a jail this time—they want to rescue me. After tense negotiations—Rob twirls a black, brushed metal throwing star in his fingers while he stands, sur-rounded, in the middle of our bedroom—I ride home three hours with my mother to Conroe, Texas. She promises she'll treat me like an adult.

But when we're home and I'm talking to Rob on the phone, my mother will yell from the bottom of the back stairway that it's time to hang up.

I'll whisper a minute longer, asking about his wallet, anything to keep talking. It's camo-colored. It's got Velcro. I made fun of it the first time I met him. I've seen pictures of the cousin who gave it to him—tall and wiry. He swings the nunchucks. They both do.

Rob speaks quiet and low on the phone.

Mom says he has the voice of the Devil.

"I got it right here," he'll say. There'll be a tearing noise—the Velcro—and then he'll say something like, "I'm looking at a picture of you. Know what I'm thinking?"

"What?"

"You got a nice ass. That's what."

My mom will holler again. "What did I say?"

I'll hold my hand over the receiver and yell back at her.

"You've got to get out of there," Rob's voice will soothe in my ear. "She's never going to treat you right. Come to Florida with me. We'll make it work this time. They won't find us. We'll go far away," he says. "Merritt Island."

"I don't know." I'll slump into the unpainted drywall in the hallway. I'll pick at the hammer dents in the plywood on the floor near a flattened nail-head. My dad left the summer I got my period, the summer he banged a hole in the drywall over the stairway and kept saying, "Fuck, fuck," until he stomped down the stairs and out the back door.

"I gotta go."

In the car with my mom, I'll stare out the window the whole five miles to town.

We'll have this conversation, again: "He's a bad influence."

"He's fine," I'll say. "You promised everyone that I could talk on the phone."

"Maybe you'll meet a nice boy at church."

"Nice boys are dull."

"Keep your mouth shut," she'll say. "You're giving me a headache." She'll light a cigarette and crack open the window exactly one-half of an inch.

I'll turn to my own window. I'll stare at the fields. I'll keep my mouth shut.

For the next two weeks, my mother drops me off each morning on the highway in front of Conroe High School. I wait until the cars pass, and then I walk across to school. That perfect GPA, the extra math class I took as a freshman, the memberships in Mu Alpha Theta and the National Honor Society, those are all behind me now. Rob has a plan for me. I don't care if I lose my spot as valedictorian. My friend Kim has moved back to Kentucky. My other friend Janet has graduated. There is nothing and no one to keep me in Texas. I don't like the new kids in the youth group at church, and I can't bring myself to talk to Danny, the youth minister, about what's happening to me. He was there in Fort Worth when she made the promises, but he was on her side because he believes in the literal version of the Bible. Even if she is mean, I'm supposed to honor my mother.

And according to her, the voice of the Devil is inside me, so I must be up to no good.

"What are these?" she asked me once. She was examining padded round discs she'd found on my dresser. "What are you doing with these?" She held them up and shook them at me like they were sinful.

"I put them in my roller skates," I said. I was trembling, even though I was telling the truth. They were pads I'd bought with my own money at the Roadrunner Roller Rink because the skates she bought me didn't fit. She thought I was stuffing my bra, like I wanted to be sexy.

Here's another conversation: "You need to apologize to your brother next time we talk to him on the phone." Maybe we are almost at the drop off point near my high school where she pulls over to the shoulder on HWY 105, directly across from the high school. My brother has gone away to college. On days when no one else is home, I stare into his room.

"Tell him you're sorry for that time you bit his you-know-what."

"I was only a baby."

"You hurt him. You need to say sorry." Another cigarette will be clutched in her fingers, hands gripped tight on the steering wheel.

The day at school will be long and slow, and I'll feel lost in the hallways, like everyone is a stranger even though I've known most of them since first grade. Later, on the phone, I'll ask Rob what he thinks about my brother and if I should say sorry.

"She's keeping you down," Rob will whisper through the receiver. "She wants complete control of you."

He's right, and I know it, too. It's time to leave again. "You're right," I'll say.

I bring an extra piece of clothing to school each day and hide it in my locker. Panties. A bra. The T-shirt I bought in Kansas when I lived with my dad that says, "Auntie Em: Hate you, hate Kansas. Taking the dog. Love, Dorothy." A pair of jeans and a pair of shorts. We have a plan. On Friday, after I've asked my mom for money to buy tickets to the football game, after I've shoved all of the smuggled clothes into a little duffel bag and left all of my textbooks in my locker, I'll walk out onto HWY 105 and wait for Rob.

He's eighteen and has brown hair and sky blue eyes. He's a California state Tae Kwon Do champion. His shoulders are broad and his muscles ripple beneath his white t-shirt as he helps me strap on my helmet. He doesn't look like the Devil. He starts up the Honda 350Four—it's a small bike—and I swing my leg over the seat behind him and wrap my arms around his waist. He flips out the metal footrests for me, and I lean into him. Conroe High School melts into the distance behind us with the August heat.

We stop at a yard sale near the town of Cut and Shoot and buy a little arm cushion that I wedge between my legs. We pass the Coushatta Indian Village I visited as a child with my grandmother, where I bought handmade turquoise jewelry and watched Indian boys my age dance with beads strung across their bodies. On the second afternoon of our long ride, we nap on a concrete picnic table at a rest area in the Florida panhandle. We drive on, shifting positions when his leg cramps or my arms go numb from holding tight to his waist.

Our tiny cinder block apartment is across the street from Merritt Island High. The first morning, I call to see if I can enroll myself, and they say no, I need a guardian's signature.

Rob goes to his uncle's jobsite to beg for work, and I stay in the little apartment by myself as long as I can. Rob is very clear that I am not to interact with any guys while he's gone. At night, he tells me stories about his day. The men in his family do drywall, snowmen when they're sanding, white speckled hands, arms, and faces when they're taping. Evenings spent at the bar. One of them lives here in Florida. The rest are in California. Rob grew up playing with his cousin beneath bar tables with beer bottles and pull-tabs. I hang on his every story about the jobsite, about his childhood and his cousin, about his long days at work with his uncle, ready to shed my own life.

I go to the Merritt Island Public Library down the street and take magazines from the free stack. I cut out coupons for groceries we can't afford, taking my time to separate the paper carefully on the dashed lines. Rob comes home tired, speckled with white mud and dust. I start going to work with him because he says I have to when a guy in a nearby apartment takes an interest in me. I walk around the jobsite, a high-rise near the beach, and stare into the ocean. I am careful not to talk to any of the men.

Rob starts telling me fantasies to turn me on. I feel dead inside. I don't want to have sex with him. He whispers things like this: "Imagine we're on the beach and a man walks up to us. He's handsome. He wants you, and we go back to his apartment."

"The three of us?" I say.

"Yes. I watch him put his fingers in you, but you only come when I'm inside."

My breathing gets faster, and I close my eyes.

The first time Rob and I went all the way was at a Motel 6. This was before I ran away that first time. I skipped school, my friend Kim, who eventually moved to Kentucky, covering for me that night with a lie about a sleepover. When Rob was finished, he rolled away.

"Well, we've done it all," I'd said.

"Not everything." He proceeded to turn me over and show me where else you could have sex. I thought things would get better. I'm not sure why.

In Florida, I sleep a lot. We don't have much food. It's been weeks, and Rob hasn't been paid. He's working under the table. His uncle has gone to California. His uncle's son, the cousin who gave Rob the camo wallet, is coming for a visit soon. He's bringing money. In the meantime, I hang my panties to dry on the shower rack, and I drip-dry my body on the bathroom tiles after each shower. We steal pink hand soap and thin toilet paper from the gas station at the corner. We buy a loaf of white bread and a tub of margarine and a shaker of garlic salt at the convenience store. The white bread reminds me of my great aunt who liked to eat onion sandwiches. She died just a few months after the first time I ran away. I spoke with her on the phone days before she passed, feeling light-years away from her little clapboard house on Robert Street in New Orleans, her laughter and orange hair and costume jewelry. "Are you okay?" I'd asked her when she was in the hospital.

"No," she'd said. "I'm in pain." She sounded angry. I thought she was angry at me. I thought I'd done something wrong. After the funeral, Rob came to see me, and we had sex all day in a dark room. Something died inside me, but I couldn't say no. I'd already told Rob once that I wanted to break up, and he'd tried to kill himself. In the spring, weeks after I'd met Rob, his cousin called me. He found my phone number in the camo-colored wallet—Rob was visiting him in California. He said Rob had nearly overdosed on pain meds when I told him, during a phone call, I wanted to break up. I'd imagined Rob sitting in an old brown reclining chair, clutching his chest.

"I don't know what to do," the cousin said. "I've never seen him like this."

In Florida, I wake up hungry, and each day it gets harder to fill up on bread and margarine. We can't get food stamps until next week, so we go to a soup kitchen. We're staying here until I turn seventeen in November, and then we'll go back to Texas to live with Rob's dad. I'll be an emancipated minor. I'll go back to high school. We'll sell the motorcycle to get money for the plane tickets.

At night, the evenings are cooler, and Rob's sex fantasies now include the cousin. He tells me stories about him, about the three of us, and I try to form images in my mind and hold onto them long enough to feel something inside.

It's October. I see a health worker at a county clinic and get birth control and feminine hygiene products and other toiletries. Rob waits outside in the parking lot. The young woman asks my age, and I tell her eighteen. Her long brown hair falls forward across her face as she writes my information on a form. She's so pretty, and I want to tell her something more about myself, something true, but I don't want to go home. She hands me a paper bag with a three-month-supply, and she says please come back if I need anything else. "I will," I say.

The cousin arrives in time to see the space shuttle *Atlantis* take its maiden voyage. He's tall and thin and has the same eyes and cheekbones as Rob. I shake his hand and welcome him to Florida. We drive up HWY 1 to Titusville to watch the launch in the morning. The ground shakes under our feet, and my chest vibrates with the deep rocket engines firing. The white light from the base of the shuttle cuts through the hazy morning sunshine like overly bright distress flares, shooting downward. Lift off occurs and I'm shouting and clapping and crying with everyone else parked for miles and miles of roadside viewing.

A few days later, I call my mother on her birthday.

Our conversation goes something like this: "I wondered if I might hear from you today."

"I'm safe."

"Where are you?"

"I'm safe." It's all I'll tell her. Her years of suspecting me of being a bad girl have come true. "How is work?"

"Fine."

"Oh."

"You're making my heart hurt," she says.

My chest squeezes tight. If she dies from a heart attack, right here on the phone, it'll be my fault. "I'm sorry," I say. I hang up. My head feels like it's in an astronaut helmet. The rest of the world has been suffering while I have been on my little adventure down here in Florida. I sit by the payphone as the coins clink inside the metal chamber, looking at the tall weeds growing at the edge of the concrete beside the convenience store. I feel like I'm being squeezed inside a tube of metal made for something or someone much smaller than me.

Rob's cousin has brought money, easier days, and California sunshine, which I didn't know before was different than Florida sunshine. He and Rob skip rocks along the beach, bouncing them over the waves. We go to a casino. I'm too young, but they sneak me in. The cousin goes to the bathroom, and Rob and I wait in the lobby. He sees me watching. He knows my head is full of the fantasies about his cousin he's been whispering to me when we grind against each other on the mattress in the back bedroom. "I guess I have to let you fuck him," Rob says.

"Okay," I say. I don't notice that he hesitates. I don't catch it until I rewind the scene later.

We ride home. I sit in the middle of the seat. I put my hand on the cousin's leg and tell him what we want to do with him.

"Seriously?" he says.

"Yeah," Rob says. "Serious."

We go to the apartment, and the cousin sits on our brown recliner, the one we salvaged from the side of the road. "I'm surprised," he says.

I don't say anything. I'm buzzing, supercharged for the first time in a very long time with the thought of having sex.

Rob has it all planned out. We put a blanket on the living room floor. He turns on the TV and the radio. Reggae music. I don't want the TV, but there's a flash in Rob's eyes, and I give in. We all slowly undress. The cousin lies down on the blanket, and I lie on top of him. We kiss. He's big, and he goes all the way inside me. Rob straddles me from behind. It's hard to coordinate all three of our bodies. They don't quite fit. But somehow we make it work.

When Rob finishes, he pulls away and gets up and walks toward the kitchen, slow and creaky like he doesn't want to leave his cousin and me alone.

The cousin whispers to me that I'm beautiful. He brushes my hair to the side, looking up into my eyes. I shake my head. I say no. One of my tears falls onto his face, and I wipe it away quickly. Light from the TV illuminates his brow, his nose. I'm alone with him. I haven't wanted to be alone with anyone in so long. It feels good, and it feels bad.

Rob walks in the room and says he's going to bed. He says my name. What he means is that I'm going to bed, too. So I do.

The next morning, when the cousin has gone out for a walk, Rob wakes me, his hands wrapped around my neck. "How could you do it?" he says. "You're killing me."

I drop off the bed and fall onto the floor, unable to breathe or answer him before the room goes dark. I wake, tangled in the sheets with him crying beside me, wiping my hair from my face.

"At least you didn't come," he says. His voice is quiet. Calm.

Here's the conversation I wish we would have: "I did come."

Pause. "Do you love him?"

"I don't know. But I do know I don't love you. I'm leaving."

But we don't have that conversation. I can't see my way out. In addition to threatening to kill himself when I tried to break up, Rob often proves to me how strong he is, holding me down after a session of tickling, pressing his hand or foot into different parts of my body, explaining how he can take me out. I'm afraid of him, but he's been my ticket out, my release.

So I wait. The cousin leaves. Rob and I return to Texas. I talk to my parents occasionally, but seldom see them. Rob and I stay together. He tells me if I ever cheat on him, he'll kill me, no questions asked. I get pregnant with him, and I get pregnant again. I have two boys, and I never find the courage to leave him. He finds another woman and leaves me instead. I let him go, holding my breath in case he changes his mind. He berates me in public and on the phone — in that quiet voice, his jaw clenched — and he tries to negotiate with me for sex. I'm destitute, but I don't want him back.

One day, I meet a woman at the library where I've started working part-time. She's a counselor. I have no health insurance, but she says she'll let me come in once a month for $35.00. She'll give me books to read and homework assignments, if I want them.

It takes me a long time to say Rob's name in our sessions. We talk about other things, a new guy I'm dating, the kids, my job. Anything else. After a year of therapy, I finally tell her a little about him. She teaches me to visualize locking him in a deep freeze when I feel like I can't breathe, when the room starts getting dark. We practice what I can say if I decide I want to hang up the phone on him. After months of this and other therapeutic activities like beating a cushion with a foam stick, I finally do something.

Rob and I are standing on the sidelines of our older son's soccer game.

Here's the conversation: Rob starts saying something about a mistake he thinks I've made. His voice starts getting loud.

"Please stop yelling at me," I say.

He continues.

"If you don't stop, I'll walk away."

He continues, his face red, his hands gesticulating his rage. Like how my dad used to get when he was pissed, just before he slid off his belt to beat my older brother or me. Or like how my mom used to get, just before she'd grab a frying pan from a hook on the wall or a wooden spoon from the countertop and commence to chase after me.

At the soccer field, I turn and walk away. A deep part of me doesn't believe Rob won't run up behind me and choke me. But he doesn't. I keep walking until I've launched myself to the other side of the field, and I stand there, far away from Rob, far away from everyone. No one is choking me. No one is chasing me. I can't hear his voice anymore. I can only hear the cheering, the shouting and excitement for the soccer game unfolding on the field, and maybe my voice joins in, cheering for my kid out on the field and for something it'll take me years to understand. Maybe I'm just cheering for myself, and maybe I don't have to understand it at all. ᔕ

Les Abandonnées

Kirby Gann

That stretch of the Boulevard de Clichy where she stopped to remove her shoes was framed by great waves of graffiti, spiky stalactite designs rushing wild across the stone walls and rusted roll-gates, crowding the wide and otherwise empty street. The air stank of garbage. A heat flushed through her body and the stench closed in like swaddling cloth, salt mixing in her mouth with the evening's wine, a static sheen of perspiration about her eye sockets. It was that time of year when the generous vacations of the French closed half the city, transforming the Paris she knew into an empty and strangely quiet museum. No cars had passed by despite it being Saturday night and the boulevard a main thoroughfare not far from Pigalle's perpetual raunch; the Métro had shut down until morning; she was a young woman, slender, fit, pretty, with a long walk ahead. Whether bad luck or the result of bad decisions—it didn't matter which—she was on her own.

The wall she leaned into for balance greeted her bare shoulder with the previous day's warmth (she was a hygienic person, compulsive in keeping her hands free from public surfaces; she kept a sanitizing gel in her purse). A patch of its heat lingered on her skin as she came away and started off again, each hand clasping one shoe like some outdated and clumsy telephone. On her feet their effect was strikingly different: these were sleek, tight, six-inch Italian heels and her legs looked fantastic in them. Yet after hours of standing in a hot and cramped apartment her feet not only hurt but felt mauled, like maybe some real damage had been done. Once freed, they ached expansively, and she tested her weight on them with a few experimental steps.

Striding barefoot through Paris might be the height of ridiculousness, but there was no one before whom she needed to keep up appearances now. The graffiti alongside her seemed elusive and strained toward language without quite achieving it, the shapes almost forming into letters she could identify—words you can't find on your tongue when you need them. She glanced over every few steps to see if she could snatch something from the corner of her eye in case a person was meant to read it in that way, on the run, but none of it conformed to any alphabet she recognized. The source of the stench ran street-side to her, where a row of overstuffed blue bins aligned against the curb looked like open-market stalls presenting wares of rot: discarded food in undone takeout cartons, half-bagged dog droppings sacked atop withered flowers, bottles with a final swig for the fruit flies. She began to move as quickly as her blighted feet would allow and breathed through her mouth, the stink heavy enough that it should have been visible.

Her first August in Paris. It felt alien, off, and it appeared she had the place to herself. At the office some of her colleagues had warned her, playfully, of the weird change the city underwent this time of year. They called themselves *les abandonées*, a title for those low enough in the hierarchy (of which she was certainly one) to be left behind. She had laughed then, and yet—as in so many peculiar instances with the French language—it summed up the experience perfectly: the emptiness was unsettling and she felt abandoned. Perhaps the sensation was stressed in her by her lack of success at the party (she had expected to go home with a boy from Cameroon she'd been flirting with for weeks), or the unexpectedly oppressive heat at that late hour; or maybe it was just that what awaited her was an empty room with an unmade bed, clothes strewn about the floor that she would have to gather and wash tomorrow, passing her Sunday in a plastic chair alone with a magazine as Portuguese maids chatted over the hum of the laundry machines. Regardless of why, the wandering quality of her walk started to gain the weight of an expulsion, a sentence of exile.

Her hip grazed the enchained tables and chairs of a shuttered café as she turned into a lean pedestrian street; a pharmacist's neon sign hovered blue in the air ahead, not quite a beacon. Her strides slowed as she recognized a feeling she did not want, one she believed she had dismissed a long time before: the queasy hollow of homesickness, her first pang of it since she had arrived in January.

She was the kind of person who kept tight control of her emotions; the longing need of the homesick did not apply to her. She was the kind of person comfortable far from her origins, at ease among voices clamoring in unfamiliar languages, calm at work in cities and tribal areas where she knew hardly a soul or how things got done; she had once even denied food and water to refugees who could see stacks of aid awaiting them in trucks (an order from above, not her fault). A strong woman, disconcerted to learn how a long, unwanted, solitary walk through empty streets could bring out the lonesome in her. Perhaps what enhanced this sense of abandonment was that she had last been in this quartier weeks before when it had been overrun by jubilant crowds, absolute strangers dancing and embracing one another in the all-night celebration of France winning its first World Cup title. But there she was, twenty-four years old, an American who liked to describe herself as *just a Kentucky girl*, a woman who brought a small dose of good to the balance of the world even as she'd managed to secure a position and residence in one of its great cities. An especially impressive achievement in light of the bald sticks where she had grown up.

It was a path she had not so much set out on as found herself thrown in to. She had not grown up with specific career goals, but in her sopho-more year of high school she managed to raise enough sponsor money to take part in her church's mission to the Dominican Republic. In a village there they had installed a water filtration system and taught Christ, and she had returned home with a sense of fulfillment the depth of which had been new, unimagined, thrilling to her. Two years later she did it again, to Haiti this time. That trip differed from the first in every way, and ended in failure—either from missionary ineptitude or the design of the materi-als, she never learned exactly. She had been bereft at abandoning people she'd come to consider friends by then to a poverty inconceivable to her before, and without having improved their lives in the slightest. It had been crushing to her teenage self. When she confessed her sense of fu-tility to her pastor as they sat sweating in the airport, awaiting what felt like a narrow escape, his counsel had shocked her: she had her priorities mixed up, he said. The ultimate purpose of the missionary was to teach these people that Jesus loved them. This mission had had its drawbacks and frustrations, he admitted, but to his mind it had been a great success in the end. By the time their flight touched down on American tarmac she had lost her faith, found her life—that was the line she used when summing up her story over drinks, in the rare instance anybody asked.

Eight months in the city and she knew the layout of Paris better than many natives. She'd taken care to memorize Métro routes, took quiet pride in knowing which required the fewest connections to reach a des-tination without having to drag out the small blue *Paris par arrondisse-ment* guide everyone owned and tried not to consult in public. Irrelevant knowledge now, on the street, though she did still possess a basic satel-lite view of the nautilus of arrondissements in her head. If she remained on the Haussmann boulevards it would be daylight before she made it to bed. Possible cut-throughs offered themselves, and she squinted at the blue-and-green plaques screwed to the sides of buildings, uncertain if she recognized the street names or not. It seemed much of her life now consisted of just such episodes, her eyes narrowing as she tried to discern a way forward, to identify whether or not she was lost, trying to recall her exact location in relation to a larger plan. Still, she walked.

For the three boys kneeling at work with spray cans and china markers, the woman's arrival signaled their moment to flee. Thirty minutes from the party and she had entered a dark lampless stretch, swinging her arms with each step even as she was having trouble estimating distances; she smacked the hand carrying both heels into a garbage container near the invisible curb and cried out as the shoes clattered away.

The boys sprang to their feet, shoving their tools deep into the pockets of counterfeit tracksuits, rip-offs of what the players wore for Paris St. Germain. They moved with exaggerated nonchalance while retreating without a glance back toward the noise that had disturbed them. The two youngest, barely in their teens, quickly got to hissing at one another, each convinced the other had failed in executing the agreed-upon escape route. They had been instructed to split up if discovered; instead, all three were angling toward the same long allée that gave out on the Place Napoleon and the Gare du Nord. To anyone observing from some distance the boys looked to be suffering muscular fits, each grunting, growling at the deaf ear of the other, twitching his head to where he thought his accomplice should take off.

Already the night had been tense. The boys barely knew one another beyond a nod around the neighborhood. They both wanted to impress their nominal leader, a seventeen-year-old recently arrived from Clichy-sous-Bois. To come from that beleaguered banlieue marked him as *un bagarreur* without question in their eyes, although unknown to them he had left the place to placate his mother. She had sent him to stay with his aunt (a woman who, she liked to say, had *a real home*) in the vain hope of protecting her son from the tuberculosis outbreak in their housing project. They lived on the ninth floor of a *cité* with no working elevator, climbed nine flights over needles and clochards. At first he had been relieved to get away from the nightsticks the police let fly on kids his age and color, relieved from having to cough up identification papers and detail reasons for occupying a park bench longer than some *flic* deemed necessary, or else risk a cracked skull. But cops were cops everywhere, he learned; it didn't matter if you were in or out of the ghetto-wall the périphérique highway had become.

So he spent his days on the move. *Mytobacterium tuberculosis* was thriving in his blood even if he did not yet know the fact of it. He had suffered from low fever for so long that his body would seem unfamiliar at normal temperature. He slept late, awoke coughing on his aunt's floor wrapped in a sheet gone damp with sweat, and blamed the raw spot beneath his ribcage on too many smokes the night before, too much of something or other. Bowed beneath a headache he would promise himself to lay off a bit today, give his lungs a break. But what to do when the Guadeloupean who ran the tables behind the station had no work to offer? He wasn't the type to push garment racks across rue St. Denis. He hopped turnstiles and rode aimless hours, eyes pegged for an unattended purse or the sagging suit-coat pocket. His hours glazed past as on a video screen flashing the world of goods refused to his kind, another life there glassed off in boutiques he would be asked to leave should he ever dare enter. He bummed smokes, chain-smoked slumped on slatted benches among the stench of the Métro stations, stretching his long legs into the paths of passengers who paced the siding—a game for him, a chance to prove who was boss. It was important that *they* were the ones to move, that *they* made way for *him*, while he himself did not move. All while casting frank appraisal at any female who wandered nearby. Old crone or hot *meuf* lost within her headphones, it didn't matter—if she lingered long enough he would start with the stare and sometimes even kissing solicitations; if she held her ground he would take up the challenge, increase the stakes, whisper the suffering she caused him, describe scenarios to offend a whore.

Rush hour crowds allowed him the pleasure of a little *frottement*. He could press himself into a *gourgandine's* firm haunch—softly at first, the merest graze that could be expected in the confines of the train car—and then he might push more insistently, rock in rhythm with the sway on the rails. Sometimes the woman moved off, switched places with another passenger. But not always. His favorites were the ones who panicked, stricken, stilled in disbelief at what was happening. *Those* he would grind into, thrusting until she had no choice but to exclaim *Laisses-moi!*, leave me alone. Those were best. How satisfying to work them up, to sense their distress like some hormonal secretion sounding the alarm! He would sift his nose up to just behind her ear and inhale deeply, seeing what she could tolerate before she could not accept a moment more, not one more touch. *Laisses-moi!*

Her complaint shook loose his laughter then, his rummy Akar-sour breath a cascade over the pretty white face cosmetically prepared just so. It was crucial that she understand how none of it—his sex hard against her thigh, her stunned outrage—meant the slightest to him. Every day needs whatever thrill that can be drilled from it. In his laughter he wanted her to not only hear but *feel* the utter *mépris*, the contempt in him; she had to understand that this boy knew the score and everyone was in play and he was atop his game, for who knew but one day it could be entirely different, one day they might be alone, and with him disinclined toward such generosity, such *n'importe quoi*. At half the chance he could eat their very hearts.

He made a lasting impression. It pleased him to think that these brief moments of contact—that instant she shouted *Laisses-moi!* and his laughter tumbled forth and the other passengers turned to look as the train screeched along the rails—he liked to think from that moment on he was in her life forever. A presence forever imprinted: his arms, thin as cuticles yet with hard muscle deeply defined, lazing overhead by the balance-rod above, arms ready to crush her *and yet choosing not to crush her*—a woman never forgets a moment like that. She would never know his name but his scent would be there, his heat and *mépris absolu*, returning to her the rest of her life and without warning, some quiet moment as she sought sleep or washed her face before a mirror, or when her mind was not quite with her mate as they made love. Thing was, a woman valued herself too highly. Every woman except his mother, who valued herself not at all.

With a grand sweep of his arm he corralled his young accomplices as their bickering attained an unacceptable level. *Ta gueic*, he said, silencing them both. He told them they could go. Neither moved. He refused to repeat himself. Let them watch—every boy must learn how things got done; it had been the same for him. As he neared the bright graffiti they'd abandoned he slowed enough to make cursory inspection over the baroque designs in red and gold, an elaborate mask over what he'd drawn for the Guadeloupean, a penciled map that led to a fourth-floor apartment whose owner was away in the sun of the very country his mother had fled years before.

At first he took the woman hunched among the trash bins as a drunken *pute* gliding down from her night's work and not worth his attention. He almost decided to leave her alone. She had yet to notice him. She was either speaking to herself or singing a little song, one that carried in that narrow street walled in stone, and in her voice a charm sounded, a sweetness ground out of any whore he knew. When the search for her shoes placed her in a dim wash of streetlight, he sighted the brief dress clutching her fine figure, the step-class legs, the luster in the blonde hair she held from her face as she bent forward, peering about the gutter. She seemed impossible, unreal, something conjured.

His companions slipped in behind him, stubbing sneakered toes on uneven stones, hardly aware of moving of their own will but ready yet, prepared for all that might happen. They cast careful quick scans in every direction for signs of some cruel setup, and found none. Their dulled bodies enlivened, a jittering surge quickened their limbs, astonished to find the night's tedium broken so unexpectedly by such an offering, one they were obligated to accept. Even later, after it was all over and their days returned to routine, after they swore oaths to never speak of this night again, they would waste no time seeking a cause behind what they had discovered each was capable of doing—they accepted what happened as natural; there had been no other options. What else could she or anyone have expected, appearing at that hour and looking like that?

From her own perspective, the boys appeared with the silence of apparitions just as she reclaimed her shoes, three spirits loosed into the world from the garbage bins she had shoved aside. By the time she realized their presence, she was cornered already. *Salut petite*, she heard one say, the tallest and in the center, and with an accent she found unfamiliar. *T'est perdu, non? T'as besoin du service?* The voice exuded an extraordinary politesse she did not interpret as mocking until the others either side of him burst into hatchet-chop guffaws.

At full height she nearly managed to reach the shoulder of the one who had spoken. A peculiar tremor started to push in her veins, a sudden racing she made an effort, instinctively, to hide. She took in each face before her, each pair of unblinking eyes stilled beneath a dull red film, and saw no emotion, not kindness not threat nor even amusement; they were marbled stares that may as well have been awaiting an empty screen to proffer the next pointless show on the schedule. She was not yet ready to believe she'd entered into trouble. She started to speak—it seemed they were waiting for her to say something—but her throat was dry and her voice caught and she had to clear it before trying again, speaking into the vicinity of a collarbone and soul-patched chin. She told them she wanted to be left alone. It had come out in English. Her shoes were in her hands but she could hardly feel them. She pressed them against her chest, sharp heels turned out.

The boys did not move. When she spoke again she had found her French, stepping forward at the same time, and to her surprise they let her through. She felt the concentrated heat off their bodies as she passed through them. Then she was in the street and she did not care where she was headed so long as it was away. For several slow steps she even felt relief, a small hope that fear had been unwarranted, it had been only the surprise of the boys appearing at a time when she had believed she was alone. Paris was after all a safe city, its crimes essentially inconveniences, it wasn't like she was in Monrovia or East L.A. These boys were Parisians, and like every Parisian she'd met, they were not concerned with her one way or another.

A murmuring sounded behind her and she did not look back. A volley of laughter rose and then dropped and it sounded like they had not moved—fine, a few jokes at her expense cost her nothing. She did not look once over her shoulder, not even as she reached the allée, the nearest corner that would take her from sight. And then she did; she looked back. It was like the boys had been waiting for her to do so, like they had been awaiting a kind of signal she didn't even know she was sending. The boys whooped and cackled and smacked hands and by the time she went to run the one that had spoken was standing before her again, it seemed impossible that he covered the distance with such speed but in reality she had not moved very far, her legs were the legs in a dream when you know you must run but discover you cannot. The solid fact of him surprised her, one ropey arm barring her way as he leaned into it, casual, his bronze skin agleam as if oiled, giving off an odor of sugary alcohol and sweat.

Little light drew into the passageway there. Before she was aware of the others she felt hands on her ass, and she twisted half into the wall and half into the arm before her, and she felt hot breaths on her bare shoulders and her neck as she shouted, *Stop.* It made no difference. Someone held her at the waist and she shouted *Laisses moi* and laughter erupted around her, a great party breaking out in the empty alleyway, *laisses moi* suddenly the only French she knew and she heard it sung back to her in falsetto voices. Her arm scraped a stubbled cheek and her skin there stung sharply, and she lost one shoe batting away a hand as it pulled her dress above her hip, her thong snapped back against her and she twisted again and the stone wall pressed her cheeks, that was how she knew her dress was up. Hands scurried everywhere, all over her body and so many of them, rough and pinching and sweaty, her sweat or theirs, she didn't know, it didn't matter. She fought as best she could. She swung the one sharp heel left to her and struck into the meat of a face that ducked from sight with a pained cry that might have been her own. With that strike there fell a kind of pause, one in which the very atmosphere relayed an extra charge as each boy in the alleyway hesitated—not to think it over, no, thinking had fled the scene—but as though to acknowledge her one good strike, a natural rhythm arising to what the moment had reached.

Wait, she said. She wielded the one shoe before her with both hands.

The blows fell then all at once, from every direction. The mocking falsettos and tittering giggles plunged to grunts and gasps. Her feet left the ground and she felt herself floating, aloft in a harness of muscle that pinned her arms to her sides. The tallest boy bounced on the balls of his feet as he directed a series of punches to one part of her face with methodical focus, like it was the only idea he had and there was no way to defend herself against it, where were her arms, the hurt in her face surprised her with each blow, a new hurt each time. Her cheekbone gave way. She may have lost consciousness, she wasn't sure, there was a moment when his fist met her face again and she was startled to find the blows still coming, she had missed part of it. A tooth broke loose and slipped far back on her tongue and panic for air sent her writhing and the boys thought she was fighting back again. Inadvertently one of them saved her by staving his knee into her belly, bringing out the tooth along with the long evening's wine and couscous in a great wide projection. Then she was no longer floating but flying and only for an instant before she smacked against the wall and all wind escaped her, left her retching, unable to even sob.

The boys allowed another pause to gather breath. One had his hands on his knees and he coughed and hacked until he dislodged something from his throat that he left on her dress. Their bodies were not used to this kind of concentrated effort. They watched her push aside a garbage bag to make room within an overturned bin, digging out a small useless shelter, a task that appeared to require a good deal of deliberation. The act inscribed an image into the youngest boy there, one he would remember the length of his brief life—this image precisely, of her shapely bottom in the air with the thong halving its sumptuous valentine and the slow, childlike movement of her crawling into the bin, and the image would confuse him, being both erotic and pathetic, and he would come to wonder what he had wrong with him for it to fascinate him so. When they pulled her back out by the hips their hands had calmed, almost a grace to the whole thing now, they had worked hard and deserved to take their time. They turned her onto her back, they separated her knees, and she didn't want any of this but they had her. What little she would remember of the next twelve minutes of her life was the contortions of her tongue, how it worked to form various iterations of a single word—God—though she would never feel certain of the specific phrases she found, or where they had come from, or who she might have believed was listening.

The next few hours passed with her both in the world and out if it, the sliver of moon above sailing silently along its path in direct measure against the length of the alleyway, its light too meager to reach her, blocked by the city lights suffusing Paris in its roman candle glow, until the earth's rotation took the moon from sight behind the Gare du Nord before the sun had even weakened the night. Her mind waded through a drab crepuscular place where bits of conversation and parts of songs looped and faded in snatches and samples, a braid that kept unthreading in her hands. Her body felt apart from her, distanced by natural opiates flooding her bloodstream as rapidly as her body could create them, capillaries dilating to welcome white cells and fluid to her injuries and inflating one side of her face into the shape and color of a plum ready to be plucked. Pain fluttered in like irritable music heard down an otherwise complacent street, save for brief bursts when her body returned and the music surged to excruciating pain screaming down her nerves and sending her out once more. She did not know that the youngest boy finished last and alone, the others having fled as soon as they were done, and she did not feel his touch once he came back after several minutes spent squatting against the opposite wall staring at her unconscious form and glancing at that white gash of moon, where he believed sometimes he could see its darkest part if he looked long enough. She did not feel his swollen hands fix her outfit to cover her again but his hands were there, tugging the dress back over her thighs, lifting the stretchy fabric over her cool breast. It wasn't that the boy was gentle by nature or felt sorry for what he had done so much as he did not know what he felt, aside from it being different than what he was used to, a shaky, agitated fatigue contorted by emotions that refused to settle, wheeling one into another: contempt and release and pity and fear—even gratitude for the relief of his virginity, for resolving finally the great mystery of a woman's body; disgust, too, for much the same reason, and that she should have allowed such a thing to happen to her.

The way things go, it's like the world unfolds as if it has been all written down already; an uncle had given him that. He gnawed a sore on his lip and shook his head as the notion rattled about his mind. He walked up the alleyway with an eye on the moon that hovered like a scythe about to fall and made half an effort to understand how he felt. He wished he could ask someone about it (perhaps that same, if only he knew how to contact the man, but he had disappeared from his *bidonville*—the plywood and tin encampment where his people lived alongside the A1—years ago), even as he knew the soul he might discuss it with did not exist. It was like a whirlwind had taken possession of him and then dissipated once his companions had fled and his lust had been served. As though he had been a simple vessel used by something greater than himself.

Street cleaners discovered her the next morning, their loud arrival scattering the fat pigeons that had congregated to pick through the strewn trash. At first sight of her bare foot the man who found her assumed she had merely dropped there, too drunk to make it home (he was used to chancing upon such despond on his route). It wasn't until he righted an overturned bin that he understood, when at his touch the girl stirred, and a strange paralysis overtook him as she began to moan, to shake, and to weep. His crew was yelling at him by then, unable to see why he had left his post, angry that the debris they swept down the narrow stream of hydrant water was piling against his rolled mat and spilling back into the street, it meant more work for everyone, they were on a strict schedule and easily fell behind. But the street cleaner, almost thirty and with his wife expecting their first child, could not respond. He only palmed the skin of his shaven head, lips pared back and white teeth shining in the sharp morning gleam, the day's heat already slicking his scalp. Soon the others grew so angry that they too left their posts, eager to scold him to his face—he was the team dreamer, the foolish one—only to stop as well at the sight of the girl shuddering curled against the spattered wall (that was how they saw her; not as a young woman, but a girl). Perhaps because for some time his wife had been teasing him that she could feel she was carrying a girl (she claimed mothers-to-be knew what grew in their bellies, and he never crossed her once a certain framing set to her eyes), he had been contemplating what sort of father might he make for a daughter, it would be different for a son, what sort of world could he bring to a daughter and bring a daughter into ... or maybe because he was the sort of man who acted on impulse, trusting his body to know what to do before he over-thought the task ... or perhaps for no other reason than that he was a human being confronted with the suffering of another human being and already he had witnessed much suffering without acting against it—for whatever reason (later he would find no words to express reason to the police, his boss, his wife, for they seemed self-evident, the reasons), once his crew arrived and fell into that same shocked paralysis, he rediscovered his limbs and moved. He pushed his way through and bent to one knee and ignored the high keening sound she made and whispered supplications in his best, most gentle voice—what could he do, *mad'selle*, where did she hurt most?—and when she answered with nothing other than that sound like a rusty pulley working in her throat, he scooped her into his arms.

He was a tall thin man his comrades had thought frail. They stepped back, surprised, and then burst into exclamations and admonishments at the sight of him swaying with her, this victim of some terrible crime, even they knew not to get involved in that, call the police, an ambulance, what did he think he was doing, have you gone crazy, man? He said something to them, he wouldn't remember what but he knew he said something without looking any in the eye, no, he was looking somewhere over their heads, and in his voice they must have heard his seriousness for they all fell silent. He started with tentative steps, staggering at first before he got the hang of it, and no one spoke another word as he carried her up the allée and past the train station to the Hôpital Lariboisière another block away.

He had done only what humanity demanded—that was how he explained himself to the officers who detained him at the prefecture and during subsequent interviews; how he explained himself to the journalist who visited, and to the crew's manager once he was allowed to inquire whether his job still existed (his position had been filled by an alternate that same day; the entire crew was suspended until the investigation got sorted out). He met with his boss in the company of the American missionary from the Foyer in Aubervilliers, a sensible man who acted as something like a sponsor in whom the street cleaner placed deep trust— the man had helped him gain the work visa after years of undeclared toil, and the small apartment once legal status permitted him to move into a real home with his wife. The missionary insisted that he keep faith. The street cleaner agreed that yes, but in what? The process? It frightened and amazed him to realize the mess he'd made by carrying the girl to a hospital instead of waiting for an ambulance. In fact it was difficult to even believe. But there were procedures to follow in such an event, his friend explained, and the French take procedure very seriously (a characteristic he'd grown familiar with already). Once police informed them that his DNA had been found beneath the girl's fingernails, his uniform soiled with her blood, and once he came to understand how investigators might prefer to connect his immigrant's face to the damage done to hers, the faith he clung to narrowed to what little he found in himself.

The missionary girded him with reminders of the many proofs of God's presence in his life: how else to explain the good fortune that had allowed him to even make it to this moment and suffer this very crisis? Look at how he had fled Togo; he must have been carried in the Lord's hands just as he had carried that young woman. In Lomé he had lain hidden within a stand of trees as he watched his father, a faith healer, hacked to death for supposedly casting spells to protect those who opposed the rule of Eyadema. Later he lost two older brothers, nothing left of them now but the photographs he had kept in an envelope taped to his breast throughout his journey, when he had managed to enter Ghana without papers, tuck himself into a ship in the port of Accra, and be somehow delivered to Marseille, a two-week odyssey without harm or arrest. How else to explain meeting a woman as excellent as his wife, a woman unafraid of work and keeping house even as she prepared to deliver their first child?

The weeks passed. Eventually he was dropped, or set aside, as a suspect—he didn't know if he had been officially cleared or if it was a matter of the incident fading behind more recent crimes with better leads. He returned to work renewed and recommitted to his tasks. The mood of the crew had changed, though he tried to ignore it. They treated him differently than before. They weren't rude or abusive per se, but they left him to himself, they didn't speak to him beyond what the job required. Still he dispatched his duties quickly in order to ease the load on the others. This went unremarked upon but accepted, even as to seem expected; he had to make up somehow the misfortune he had brought upon them, the weeks they went without pay. He considered this a fair deal. Because in truth the street cleaner was a decent man who had passed through many desperate times and who allowed himself few illusions. He took his work seriously. He envisioned himself as a small but necessary cog in a great machine that produced hygiene, order, a home for some twelve million people from every corner of the globe. It was honorable work even if many did not see it that way.

He had much in his mind that he preferred not to pursue. For thirty-eight hours each week he created some small solace by focusing entirely on the activity of his hands. Still there was empty time to pass on the Métro, and on the bus that took him to and from the two small rooms he shared with his wife and new son in Aubervilliers; its single window overlooked the old cemetery behind the United Church of Christ, where he used to rest on a wire cot alongside other men desperate to create a new life and home. His wife forced books on him to read during his commute, either novels she'd enjoyed or else yet another guide to raising children. Rarely did he scan more than a few pages, if he opened them at all.

He didn't wish to think or dwell upon her, but some mornings his mind returned to the girl. Her weight in his arms, the frantic clutch of her hands behind his neck, often set upon him without his wishing it so. The strain within the deep muscles of his back, that wheeling sound in her throat—these blotted out the lines he was trying to follow in some book; they combined and continued within him and in time transformed into a general longing, a kind of sadness about the violence in the world from which there was no perfect escape. When his thoughts strayed too long to such matters he caught himself, and forced in better things: the thoughtfulness of his wife, for one, or his memory of her extended belly's taut warmth as he rubbed in ointments to relieve her anxiety over stretch-marks; the vision of his impossibly tiny son asleep in the bassinet he'd forged from an empty dresser drawer. Only thoughts like these were honestly useful, he believed, and he held to them as he exited the station to start another day. He had to be in the right state of mind for when the rest of the crew arrived (he made certain he was first to get there, always); it was important to be ready, for there was always so much work left to do. ❧

New England College

Creative Writing
Fiction | Poetry | Creative Nonfiction

MFA

Low Residency Program
Nationally Recognized & Published Faculty

New England College, Henniker, NH, USA
nec.edu/creative-writing-mfa | MFA@nec.edu

AMO, AMAS, AMAT AND MORE, Eugene Erlich

Jana Martin

Mea Culpa. Something e pluribum. *Pluribus?* Latin phrases, at times, have scuttled around my head like newspapers on the platform in the gust of an oncoming train. In my case, when my life suddenly changed, here barreled back that train of word-fascination, and with it, all these phrases I'd once loved were littering my boots: *Veni vidi* what?

Due to midcentury conservative elitists like William F. Buckley, Latin was relegated to unsexy status. Superficially, it seemed the language of irritable patriarchs in togas, quick to quip, scathe in damning generalities, lob cleverness like heartless rocks into the bloody floor of the Coliseum. It did not seem compassionate (ergo poor Russell Crowe and his gang) or sensitive; worse, it was terribly politically incorrect. Yet it stamped our lexicon with a kind of granite permanence, trademarking certain sentiments to the point where we use the phrase without remembering the source. And in truth, there are some amazingly wise phrases in there; Shakespeare took note.

As a mutt culture, we're good at that. And forgetting language worsens an already raging case of historical amnesia. We say *antebellum South* and think: hoop skirts, parasols, and okay, slavery. But *ante* is Latin for before; *bellum* is Latin for war. In the 1970s, when my grandmother insisted on calling her refrigerator a *Fridgidaire*, she was observing that same principle. I'd say, Grandma, it's *not* a Fridgidaire, it's a Hotpoint. She'd say (leftovers in hand as she kicked shut the streamlined door), "Well, that's what we always call them." The *royal* we, which meant the aproned populace. Americans, in general.

Thus we are a fallen people. We have tumbled out of the grand hopper of our own vocabulary like illiterate strays, considering the mixed-up assembly that is English—part German, and then, post Norman invasion, part Latin too. Latin also came from old scholarly trappings: until not too long ago, it was taught in high schools. But now, those hoppy-sounding words we blurt out—what *are* they? Once, copyediting, I wrote n.b., short for *nota bene*. "What is that, *Italian?*" the ever-irritable editor wanted to know. "We don't have time for *non sequiturs*."

True story. Employment *veritas*. I'm not a linguist; the way I treat words has more to do with abstract expressionism than scholarship: drunk on them, I fling. My ardent fascination for language was rekindled of late when my life turned dramatic—and seemed like a grander episode of history, requiring grander ways to describe its terrible anti-grandness. The reactive twitch of a man's arm sent an object on a perfect arc smack against my body; a fragile domestic peace was irretrievably shattered.

The die was cast. Weeks after, I and my ragtag battalion of dogs crossed the Ashokan—as in the reservoir, moving from a hamlet below it to a hamlet above it. Heading into an unknown fate, it did seem like I was crossing my own Rubicon, though I had to do some research to find out why. It was winter: I stood facing my new home, surrounded by the dogs, wrapped in a white blanket, railing with a raised fist at the ice on the front steps. Inside, once warm, I luxuriated in that old act of cracking open books, and found my reference, and was no longer lost. When Caesar crossed the Rubicon (a bold act with irreversible consequences), he apparently uttered a common Roman expression: *alea iacta est*—the die is cast. To link my new venture to that Caesarean tale was oddly elevating, like coming out of the woods and landing back in a library; and further, in the world of educated humans. True north is a black and white printed page.

What I am recommending here is part ephemeral, part material. To learn where those marvelous phrases come from, please get this book: *Amo, Amas, Amat and More*. It was written in the 1980s by Eugene Erlich, who, in his acknowledgments, quaintly thanks the person who taught him to use an "IBM Personal Computer." Yes, Buckley wrote the introduction, but forgive that fact. My paperback edition (I'll get to its source in a moment) has a simple cover: serif typeface (Garamond, I think) and the silhouetted head of Julius himself with a speech bubble. The book thus seems pitched as a kind of conversation-starter for young republicans trying to get laid. No matter. Yes, you can nearly hear Buckley's "I went to Yale and you didn't" flaunting sneer. "It is not plain to me why I was asked to write the introduction," he starts. But let's not let such prep-school piggishness ruin it for the rest of us anymore. Or we'd never have the joy of Sarah Palin Latin: "You *Betchus*!" (Maureen Dowd, *The New York Times*, 2008). The book is simply organized: a small pronunciation guide, a list of "personages" who apparently said the phrases first, like Ovid. The phrases are in alphabetical order, making it easy; the explanations are conversational, and it's good fun.

One fine day last summer, a visitor arrived at my new house. He'd made it a point to find me after some thirty-seven years. I'd once been infatuated with him, and spent a night in his teenage bedroom concocting a private mythology that shimmered all these years with a familiar but intangible light. And here he was: six feet and change unfolding from a car. Those same upslanted, unusually dark blue eyes, that quiet but ready smile. Decades had hewn him with a startling, pleasing symmetry. He had a book tucked under his arm. Old poems. *Ergo hunk*.

Soon I again strove for expressions that allowed for both time and astonishment, for sheer crazy luck and / or a larger intelligence: what marvelous fate brought him and took my breath away? Clearly, I needed a reference, though I thought I kept my conundrum well pocketed. Clearly not: a few weeks later, he gave me this book, a slightly hefty paperback, made the more accessible by its already used state. What's this? I said. For you, he said. *Carpe diem.* ๛

Doctor Tukes, Off the Clock

Andrew Morgan

But that's all blather. I can't even remember how old I was. Can't remember my teacher at the time, my closest friend, or whether that summer I played T-ball, "minor league" (where the coach pitches), "major league" (where I pitched, "hard" and under the pretense of "wild") or even later still when there was but rocks and glass and a gameless kind of running. I can't remember whether we'd yet crossed from printing to cursive, which I do remember took place in third grade which was the same year that Susan Crandle, prancing across the gymnasium as she was lunch-hour-prone to do, tripped—"it must've been her laces"—and broke her nose right there on the free-throw line and wailed a gurgled wail and dripped a splatter which even years later when me and Teddy Lagere snuck in after hours for some one-on-one, even then, and that must've been at least ninth grade 'cause Teddy didn't transfer back till I'd started shaving and that was on a rainy night at some point in the summer before high-school (having started not so much 'cause I needed to but 'cause I wanted to and why not I had just enough money for a razor and other needs for a razor and so what with birds and stones and whatnot there I tremored, determined, eye to mirrored eye beneath the single swinging light of the basement bathroom which hissed as its arc's apex occasionally synched with the random rain's drip making it down past what sealant there was between the trapdoored porch and the alcoved chunk of mirror Timor, my sitter's younger brother, and I snatched from his Auntie's when she was away at her praying; there, without cream which I *hadn't* the money for and without method which I hadn't the traditional intactness of family to provide, bringing a blade to bare not for the first time [but near the first time] with purpose) but even then, Teddy and I at least a year deep in friendship and not for the first time (or near the first time) sweating in the gymnasium's half-dark, tested our athleticism a little too vigorously, and limbs tangling, ended up both face down on the floor at that same line where even then, after who-knows-how-much sweeping and waxing, a shadowed hint of crimson haze still remained somehow clear-as-day apparent and I said "Look: it's Crandle's randle" and that took us funny and we laughed and clutched one another unsurely in what I remember thinking would've resembled, in collective contour and especially so from above, a more cursive styling than that of standard print. I can't remember if I'd yet to lose a tooth or already had those I grind while not remembering this or if this was somewhere in between the two when Allie Alters called me "notch face" and I swung at her all clumsy like 'cause she was pretty but she swung back, not one bit clumsy, and doubled the gap which had inspired the namecalling. I can't remember if my sister had yet begun her womanly or when that actually was as she at least twice prematurely claimed her adulthood 'cause her friends at least twice beat her to it. I can't remember my nose-ornament status or that of my nipple(s), my hairstyle or its color, my lunchbox, parent of custody, or even my handedness for sometime 'round then I switched dominance left to right as I was still but the beginning of a golfer and it was still, then, a righty and only the wealthiest of lefty's (and I was certainly not, not by far, the former of the later) sport. I can't remember if The Falcon's training wheels were on or yet off or even if this was before or after The Falcon was traded for a Mickey Mantle rookie card Bubba's daddy found in the wall when the plumbing blew out in the winter and he had to half-ash fix it himself because Little Lil was only two and was small and cold and sick and Bubba's ma was havin' none of that or so Bubba said when he handed me the sticky envelope with Mantle inside and I, clutching its stick and suddenly remorse-fearingly uncertain about my choice's wiseness, knee-jerk spun and kicked The Falcon over straight at Bubba's feet and stood silent as its handlebar gouged his shins and Bubba dropped and cried and said "mah mah mah" over and over like he said Lil did when she kicked off her covers and frostbited her toes 'cause of the blow out and it being winter and all. I can't remember if I loved Dora or Nina or Carl or Otto. Can't remember if it was before the glasses or after the glasses with the contacts or during the glasses just before the contacts when Rudy kept thieving my lenses for convexing the sun onto flies. I can't remember the decision, its ease; how it was void of malice, of cruelty, how there was even a taste of the generous. Can't remember the red gloss on the pavement, the reflection of the streetlight like a bubble-gum bubble somehow rippling as if notifying us all of an earthquake we had yet to register. Can't remember Willie—compelled against the nature of safety, compelled by the nature of fearing not fitting-in—sticking the tip of his left thumb first-knuckle-deep into the center of that bubble and then rigidly freezing, eyes focusless, as if he had instead inserted that thumb's filed-point-of-a-nail straight on into an electric outlet. I can't remember pushing Willie back, can't remember jumping into the midst of that gloss, can't remember sweeping my feet left and right like miniature snowplows gale-caught and hauled straight on across a thicker-than-water lake, can't remember the splatter along Willie's arm and along his shoulder and across his neck, thickening as it climbed until curling off with a clearly-cursive-not-print flourish to form a toothless clown smile just beneath the bobbing nose of his Adams apple which was itself bobbing beneath the I'll-never-smile-again clenched-in-horrorness of his lips. I can't remember Willie's eyes the instant his pupils exploded away any hint of the pulse-blue his mumma called her "cloudless frontier"; can't remember the drip of snot from his left nostril or how it revolted me that he wouldn't wipe it away, couldn't wipe it away; can't remember the woodpeckering tap that kept increasing in volume until there was a thunderclapping crack and a wail from Willie as he unfroze and thrusting both hands into his mouth removed what seemed to be fistfuls of shattered teeth. I can't remember my mother weeks later driving white-knuckled with her left hand at ten and the right ticking down to three and then to her lap and the sound of a bottle and up again to her mouth, toss toss gulp gulp, polly want a num num and then ticking back down to three and her for some reason not responding as I ask again and again why Willie don't want to come over and play. And I wish I could remember the day nearly a month after that when Willie showed up unexpected at the front door and still all just gums and bandages rang the bell with his red gauzed left stub of a thumb and I peeked from behind the curtain of the window beside the door and seeing it was Willie got very still and kinda lost focus with my vision and then with my body entire and felt all of a sudden like I was sitting in a bath and tasted the steam deep in my throat and heard the sound of fingers on doorknobs and the bobbing rubber of miniature animals afloat and the creak of hinges and the rippling water and its warmth on my thighs *but why only my thighs?* and with that hiccup of confusion coming back to myself at the door, so close to and yet separate from Willie and it feeling proper and like something expected and I began to (gently and then with a little more force) allow an inkling of hope to buzz deep behind my eye only to see it swiftly peter away startled bird-like as I realized the dampness as wholly real and bodily and wrong just wrong and I wailed and Willie ran and my mother turned up the volume on the radio either so she didn't hear me or so I didn't hear her practiced twitching and the gulp gulp of the pellets down her gullet and polly-want-a-numb-numb numbness for a long, long time. But that's what I'm saying. All blather from far and long ago and not very interesting at all to poor oubletted Dr. Walter Reinhold Pence, my colleague (and so much brighter than the others), whose interest, at the moment (but not for the first time), is bloodshot-and-non-blinking-eye lasered in on beggary and how its potential to elicit the ultimate of mercy might be somehow realized through force-forgetting the camouflage of why I'm making him repeat the polly numb numb thing and focusing instead on the singed fingers of the melting mannequin and why I painted its eyes in the endless tones of a cloudless frontier. ❧

Marie to Eleanor, Resenting Her Elasticness

Andrew Morgan

■ ■ ■ or like a flower on a footstool with a soft summer breeze coming in from the porch where your grandmother's casket is sitting half-opened in the sun and you're whistling to yourself some stage tune your sister had a record of because her post high schools dream-year boyfriend thought he was a singer and not a rock star singer but an on-the-stage-some-day-singing-and-dancing-in-a-rustic-costume-while-people-in-suits-that-cost-half-as-much-as-the-set-stare-down-the-dresses-of-their-dates/wives-and-wonder-why-art-has-to-be-so-boring-and-why-it-isn't-easier-to-stare-down-the-dresses-of-their-dates/wives singer and you wonder if your whistling would sound more inappropriate to your sister or to your grandmother but you know the answer to that because there was nothing that was ever fully appropriate in your grandmother's book and your sister could give a shit because that boyfriend did become a singer and when he did he gave your sister a son he found in the alley outside the off-broadway theatre that burned down after the third night's performance of his second play which, unlike the first, had some real moving parts and the role fit his voice if not like a sock does a foot than like a necklace does a neck and for once he felt positive about his choices and there was this son in the alley and he thought of your sister and how she played records and encouraged him and said to himself "I think she would be a good mom" and he took the child and gave it to her and the real parents, who apparently were just ripping a joint around the corner, were not happy to not find their child when returning and said some things to some people that were not quite true because they didn't want to give all the details about the joint and such because that would have been bad news for the dad who wasn't supposed to do that 'cause of his heart and the fact that he was just up for new life insurance and he needed that because he was planning to off himself in a way that was not able to be recognized as self-offing so that the mother and the child could live a life a little less cold and empty, that and the fact that they didn't want to be the parents who went around the corner to burn a joint and lost their child because no one really does and certainly not Claude and Marie who already had enough judgment upon them as both their parents had expected so much more of each and had told them so often and still did and would until one night Claude's mother looks at Marie's dad and says "I bet they lost that baby 'cause they went around the corner to smoke a joint" and Marie's dad doesn't respond right away but begins to think then and there that he'll take Claude's mother to a play sometime, just him and her, and during the play he will look down her dress and think about art and the grandchild it took from them and he'll whisper something about Monet or Mozart which he'll have researched beforehand and she'll stare at him and half-smile and he'd half-smile back and a little later their hands would brush gently against one another and they'd both wonder what-if and then they'd correct themselves, readjust their posture and soon after leave early because of something they both would agree to find pressing and on the cab ride home Marie's dad would tell a joke about when Marie was four and Claude's mom would find it crass and there would be an extended silence no one would be able to do anything about and it would be forever between them and in the end too much so for Claude and Marie and Claude's dad and Marie's mom to ever think it was not something a little more than it was and everyone would eventually pull back and think about how much this isn't what it should be and count the ways in which they were clearly the least at fault and so when he finally responds with "I bet you fuck non-Claude's dad men all the time, what's a fucking joint and a lost baby to you" it's not because of what she said but because of what she would have done to him had he done to her what he wanted to do to her and the irony would be that she would think that his saying of this was actually an attempt to open up an opportunity for him to accomplish the same thing he had wanted to do and she wasn't put out but tired by the whole thing and she half-smiled that response and Marie's dad half-smiled his own smile and they would be no more lonely and not alone than they were before this exchange and they would both in their mind's thank the other for that a little too often and a little too much until that thanks inevitably bent toward a resentment that would be forever between them and in the end too much so for Claude and Marie and Claude's dad and Marie's mom to ever think it was not something a little more than it was and everyone would eventually pull back and think about how much this isn't what it should be and count the ways in which they were clearly the least at fault and having assumed custodial duties of their son your sister was far too busy to hear whistling and if she did her inappropriate radar was so-to-a-different-frequency tuned that she jumped not like the moon in the fog, but more like the feeling of the moon in the fog, like a whisper you're chasing down a hallway in a nightmare you know to be nightmare, but not yet consciously enough to facilitate caution to an extent which eventually asks for everyone to just pull back a bit and think about how much this isn't what it should be . . . ☙

Elegy for a Cousin

Brad Geer

We shot sparks from our fingertips. I had to fall down. His were stronger, he said. Yeahbut, what about my sparks? Doesn't matter. Mine are stronger, he said. You have to die.

So I did. I died. I closed my eyes. I stuck out my tongue.

We amassed armies of mismatched action figures and mired them in savage combat. In the game of "Men," warriors attained glory in living room armageddons, coffee table campaigns, in sofa-back and sill-dust theaters. His were stronger, he said. Mine had to fall down. Yeahbut, this guy has a magic sword that shoots flames. Nobut, my guy has flameproof armor. Yeahbut, my guy has armor piercing lasers. Doesn't matter. Mine are stronger, he said. Yours have to die.

So they did. They died. They bounced and rolled and found rest on the green carpet battlefield, stiff limbs of rubber and plastic protruding from the ensnaring forest of shag.

Remember them?

We lay on tables and suffered from unnamed maladies, plagues so evil we could be saved by only the greatest doctors. Cures discovered at the eleventh hour, vaccinations rushed to bedside even as we winced and wheezed. You didn't make it, he said. You have to die. Yeahbut, my body held the cure. I came back, miraculously. Look, this stethoscope is on my heart, the shot's in my arm, the fists are pounding on my chest while the doctor-cousins, our sisters, cry, *"Don't you die on us! Not now! Stay with us!"* Nobut, doesn't matter. My body is stronger, he said. You have to die.

So I did. I died. I writhed and then lay lifeless on the operating table while the girls lowered their face masks and shook their heads sorrowfully.

We shared a bed during sleepovers. From older boys we heard dirty jokes. From older boys we heard dirty words. We tried to live the jokes, the words. We tried to understand what we could not understand, find meaning where there was no meaning. No punchline, no significance, no advancement in age. So we lay quietly in our sleepover bed and wondered what we'd done, wondered if it meant anything. We can't tell anyone, I said. This is a secret, he said. No yeahbuts, I said. The memory of this night has to die.

So it did. It died. Time and shame tamped it down, molded it into a shadow, a penumbral image of childhood innocence that neither of us spoke of to anyone, ever again.

Do you remember that? Did that even happen?

We grew up, slowly, in different places. We became conscious of our differences, and then suspicious of them. Of my education, of his dropping out, of my arrogance, of his arrogance over being able to identify my arrogance. I graduated from college, wore glasses with my button-down shirts, taught school somewhere, and bought a home in a town he'd never visit. He got fired from fast food joints, grew fat, became addicted to drugs on the far side of the gateway, and lived at home with his parents I never cared to see. Insurmountable differences like mountains at convergent plates. But what about our shared childhood, our memories, our secrets? They have to die, no one said. Childhood has to die. Yeahbut, we were going to marry a set of sisters we had crushes on so we'd be cousins but also kind of like brothers-in-law. Nobut, that was never going to happen. Those girls didn't like you. And you two have nothing in common. Not anymore. Yeahbut, we'd been co-buckled in the backseat of an Oldsmobile staring at the same interminable green landscape for immeasurable eternities during eons of youth. Doesn't matter. Childhood has to die.

So it did. It died. It now decays somewhere in a heap of junkyard scrap like the Oldsmobile, like the toy men, like the cheap syringe and stethoscope, like the plastic plates we ate our macaroni-and-hotdog lunches from, knife-scoured, edge-frayed, lying askance in the acres we hide outside of cities and dedicate to our castaways.

We spoke for the last time when our grandmother died. We shared memories (but not the dead one, not that memory). We recalled playing the roles of Disney characters, building castles in the yellow and orange cabinets of the spare room in her dingy second-floor apartment. Maybe we remembered our sisters as princesses and us as villains, or maybe we were heroes, or princes, or both. We were sad about Grandma. Yeahbut, we were happy playing pinochle. We followed suit, counted trump, laid cards on the table, and talked about her. She was timeless. And this was her game, her favorite. Nobut, doesn't matter. She had to die.

So she did. She died. Her weak body finally tired of fighting for air. They closed around her a simple casket and our mothers wept and held one another.

You remember her?

And maybe you cried, or not, and maybe I cried, or not, but there was no more "we," not after that.

Years passed, then, remember? Can you? Your mom, my aunt, our ... (there are no more "ours") was dying of cancer on her own bed. You came home from rehab that day and my mom was visiting. You ODed in the bathroom, remember? Yeahbut, you can't, can you. Can't remember lying there encased in your heavy body and forcing my mom, your aunt, our ... (there are no more "ours") to play *real* doctor, to put her face on your face to give you air, to push her weight against your huge chest to jump start your heart with her hands. You can't remember how she stared at your blue face with tired eyes while her dying sister yelled her name and yours from a bed in the other room. You can't even remember why you did that, why you died there, on that tile, between rehab visits, between jobs, between lunch and dinner, between 30 and 31, between weekends, between the twin glories of toilet and tub so that your own dying mother's final effort would be the arrangement of your funeral. Nobut, you can't remember that. It doesn't work that way. You had to die.

So you did. You died. And I didn't go to your funeral. And I didn't ask about it. And I didn't cry, either. I was too far away for that. Just too far away.

Now you can't remember the sparks from fingertips, the men in bellicose pose, the operating table. I had to fall down, you always said. I had to die, you always said. You were stronger. Yeahbut, doesn't matter. *You* had to die. Nobut, not me. Yeahbut, you. ॐ

NOON

A LITERARY ANNUAL

1324 LEXINGTON AVENUE   PMB 298   NEW YORK NY 10128

EDITION PRICE $12 DOMESTIC $17 FOREIGN

Bells

Remy Smidt

The sun fell on the town in patches around the clouds. The town was neither small nor large but it felt larger or smaller depending on the season. The air smelled of red and dirt and sweat and the ground was dark from the previous night's rain. Younger people, mostly girls, huddled like clumps of hair on the edge of town and quickly shut their mouths after each shared secret. Urbanites who saw the huddled bodies on their way out that day fiercely regretted leaving them behind and the comfort of the heavy burly trees that canopied the road.

Sara did not huddle with the other girls. She was lying on her bed waiting for Mary to call. But she didn't. Mary was a flame of a girl. The ends of her chartreuse hair jetted out into space. Sara thought of her when she saw a large barn owl, an owl that sinks into the night like mud. After they were done being together, Sara was never left with a swelling feeling in her stomach. From Mary she learned how to read stars, how to dance. She taught her how to find fun in a town riddled by the monotonous drone of balloons and deaths. She walked awkwardly, her hips too small to support her. "I swear," mother had said once to a friend, "Sara and Mary do everything together but have sex."

When the group of girls on the edge of town released a collection of balloons, Sara moved to the chair by the window. As sun leaked through the bottom portion of the glass, Sara trailed the pink and blue balloons across the sky. She liked the way the balloons wiggled and rocked back and forth like boats. She watched until the balloons offered themselves up as black pupils for the white of the clouds' eyes. Sara looked at the phone, at her book collection, at her shaking thigh, and then climbed down the ivy trellis beneath her window on the side of the grey house. As she descended, she fingered a couple of leaves, feeling for remnants of dew. She nearly smashed a yellow caterpillar. It moved seductively on the edge of a dying strip of vine. Sara paused long enough to watch the trail it left behind draw the speckles on the leaves together like Orion's belt. She thought of last February when in the middle of a thick snow Mary had forced her to lie on her back. "Look at them!" Mary had said, pointing to the wire-trap of stars.

"I am cold as shit," Sara replied, angrily balling up her fists.

"Look, there's Andromeda."

"I can't see it."

"Right there, follow my finger with your eyes."

"Oh, okay, maybe I do."

"You know right now we are looking out, not up."

"That's hard to think about."

"It's not so hard."

"Yes, it is."

"No, it isn't, just try."

After that, Sara went outside at night to try and see what Mary had. That was around the time when Sara had wished to be small enough to hide behind the ivy leaves. As Sara thought about the small of her palms, closing then opening then closing, a pathetic voice turned from dull echo to roar. It was her mother. Sara had a tunnel behind the eucalyptus tree. It was created out of necessity, a relic from a relationship with the olive oil colored boy down the street. Sara hopped off the trellis and burrowed.

Sara's mother was proud of her because she didn't know about this hole. Even so, this ignorance and Sara's bright caramel-green eyes did not incite a lasting feeling between them. They did not possess what others had. Sara later determined that this something was not necessarily unconditional love. She saw it as a body, a blob of light, standing at the opening of a garden. What in Sara's mind limited this welcoming was her hair that fell immutable and dark like fossils from her head. Ringlets and lightness never took hold, despite her mother's efforts. Her body was also, "vandalized," as her mother said. Her upper thighs were covered in angles. Sara connected her freckles together repetitively with permanent marker.

That afternoon, she was supposed to have met her mother to collect the yellow caterpillars that chewed pebble-sized holes through the tomato plant's leaves. Sara could never remember a damned thing. The teachers in school agreed with her mother. They said, "Sara you will never be anything." Each morning the teachers reminded the class to keep Sara in their prayers. What Sara resented most about school was not this public damnation but rather the sweat that collected under her thighs when her legs were properly crossed. To distract herself from the hellfire of the teachers, Sara thought about how large her tits were becoming and how splendid her funeral would be if she ever decided to off herself.

She compartmentalized the funeral attendees by their relationship to her. Authority figures inhabited one pew, a line of grey faces. Next came the boys, who were very vocal in their grieving. They lamented her death, but also, to the pride of Sara, the body they'd never get to press into. Sara, in moments of panic, briefly told herself she didn't really want to die. Then she accidently prayed. A short bout of an Our Father or a Hail Mary fell out of her, before a request. "God," Sara said, the word almost drooling out of her mouth, "Please, if I am to die tonight, make my funeral large and full like the moon."

The tunnel had made Sara's linen dress damp and smeared with brown. The wire fencing had scratched the back of her neck. She walked on the periphery of the road. It was good to be outside, the heavy air coated her skin. A deep, warm feeling resounded within her when her feet made contact with the damp earth. Once before the sanctuary, she paused. She wondered if Mary had called by now. The sanctuary was on a flat, dried piece of land next to a hill. Arsonists, of the teenage realm, had taken to burning things near the building. The hill was a victim, and nothing remained but the plague of burnt trees hanging around like cast-off cigarettes.

The sanctuary had been there, according to Mr. Charlie, since the beginning. The chatter that followed discussion of the beginning was tinged with contempt and authority. Sara, being a fan of neither, spoke little to Mr. Charlie. A sweet "Mhm," lolled out of Sara's mouth after his declarations. The task of pacifying him depended on this, but also on the sweetness of her caramel eyes, a slight opening of her pink mouth, and a full devotion to her chest beaming outward, welcomingly. Despite the complacency of Sara's deportment Mr. Charlie had managed to lecture her on many important things.

The whole of the town gathered to hear the bell ring, but no person was permitted to enter the chapel. Nobody was really sure why, but warnings were always bestowed with such meanness and paired with such a dramatic crinkling of the eyes that not even the arsonists dared to defy the common law. Only the clergy entered it. Because the priest slipped in and out of life, Sister Patricia was bestowed with the honor of ringing the bell. Mr. Charlie loved to discuss the sanctuary and the bell's clapper. He told Sara (and Sara had told Mary) "the position of the bell's clapper represents the bodies that used to hang from the gallows."

The "o" sound in "gallows" provided an opportunity for the extra saliva in his mouth to slosh audibly. Upon hearing such a claim, Mary responded, briefly, poetically, "that's fucking bullshit." Unlike the girls, most others agreed with Mr. Charlie's explanation. Mary blamed this on the folds in his face. As he galloped around Sara with his lashings of statements: devoid of poetry, imagination, and worth, she wondered about the time he spent in the bathroom. *Did he have to clean out his folds with q-tips?*

Sara liked to come to the sanctuary. When they were younger, depending on the solemnity or celebration of the occasion, Sara and Mary were dressed in either blue or black pinafores. It wasn't until last year that they had found a way to go inside. The decaying priest and sisters trusted too much in the fear of the town and they had started to leave the heavy, dark wooden door open.

Sara liked the cold stone. She liked how her nipples looked when erect. The high, arched ceiling felt to her like another night sky. Of the once ornate paintings, only the fading nose of St. Francis de Assisi was visible. A patch of the chapel was cracked to expose earth, and tufts of grass and dandelions were thriving in the cracks; there was mud in the pools of holy water. The pews were marked by the bottoms of centuries. Mary stood on the altar one day and pointed.

"Let's go up there," she said, hardening herself to the idea and its heat. Mary looked at Sara like Sara looked at older women. In her body language was an obvious yearning for a tenderness that would never come.

"What if they catch us, what will happen?" replied Sara, her eyes wandering.

"I don't know, but it doesn't much matter, I want to see the bell, the clapper."

"I do too, but, but still . . . It's a silly thing to commit to seeing, if we get caught who knows what will happen."

"All threats are empty," replied Mary.

They had imagined what it would look like. They had dreamt of it. They had drawn pictures and whispered in hushed voices, in the crevices of the green, moss-covered town. They'd had sat by the edge of the river, stacking stones, watching them teeter, whispering. In Sara's mind it was black and glossy, the tip of it as spherical as a moon. Mary challenged her. She was convinced it was deep blue in color, the tip of it like a drop of rain. They felt as if it was the only thing they had yet to see. They liked the idea of something housed under brass and age.

Whenever questions of the sanctuary, the bell, the bell's clapper, were brought up, parents shushed their children, their eyes favoring the upper corner of their sockets. Mr. Charlie owned most of the town.

The stairs were smooth and slippery in the center, as if someone had rigorously rubbed them down. Sara liked to be there and to be alone. But her tongue began to swell. Mary was supposed to have been there. She was happy she wasn't. The whole of Sara's body: the back of her neck, the edge of her collarbone, her kneecaps, were overwhelmed with a sense of roundness. Climbing the stairs indented with divots of use, she passed the baby blue stained glass that seemed to hang on the wall of the chapel, instead of being integrated into it; she went up and up and up. It was cooler in the winding staircase, and at points Sara felt her chest heave from the narrowness of the stone, windowless walls. Her nipples began to sting through her dress from the rubbing of the dirt and the wetness from the earth.

Sara knew a baby had been born last night because of the hysteria: the piling up of cars, the shooed children, the men sitting in circles with their eyes drooped downward. But she had not remembered. Unlike Sara, other people had remembered things that day. Jerry remembered that he left his knapsack at the café next to the small bridge that burned in a triumphant blaze years ago. Ms. Monroe remembered that she still hadn't bled. Jeremy remembered that his girlfriend left two hickies on the space that kissed the edge of his collarbone. Luckily, Sister also remembered that she forgot to say three Our Fathers before she ate her breakfast of poached eggs and smoked salmon, so as she repented, Sara had time to see the clapper in peace.

She made it to the top. She giggled at the stone arches that had been boarded up with wood, and at the exposed cracks, left open to allow the sound to escape. She followed the rope up to the clapper, which was neither dark blue like the crust of night or black like the middle of it, but bright orange like dusk. The clapper in shape was like a raindrop, except the end of it suddenly became cylindrical and straight.

The old of the brass was unlike the old of the sanctuary. Despite the light green washy color that tinged the outside of the bell, there seemed something more lasting about it. She could not imagine the earth reclaiming the bell as it did the sanctuary. The inside of the bell was shiny and reflected the cracks of light tendrils that snaked into the top tier of the sanctuary. Sara was filled with good feeling. It was a feeling that forced the edges of her hair up and prickled her skin. She decided to do it. She pulled on the rope, and the bell swung violently back and forth, like the balloons released that day, like meteors moving across the sky, like the people who remembered pacing in their rooms, like Sara's mother waiting for her in the garden, like the way Mary moves in times of heat.

It was on the eighth swing of the bell that Sara remembered what the ringing meant. The town was going to gather. She almost shit her pants. On her way down the steps she threw her body, banging into the narrow walls, clamoring to make her way out before people arrived. Sister Patricia was the first to see Sara, who was belched out by the building like a calf. Sister noticed that Sara wasn't wearing anything under her dress and tried to ignore the tightness she felt growing inside her. Sara looked at the clouds, then at the sanctuary, then at her feet, ignoring the first set of eyes that were touching her wet, dirty, lanky body. Their eyes, Sara noticed, were not filled with horror, but curiosity.

What a silly, silly, silly girl the small, green pupils of her community seemed to say. Sara's mother, however, was filled with absolute disdain. The word 'cunt' clung to her mother's breath. As the father brushed the dirt from his loafers, the mother bunched up the end of Sara's dress, and after several tugs managed to peel her away from her frozen position in the front of the crowd. "What the fuck," her mother screamed, "Sara, what is this?"

Sara shrugged.

"I'm sorry," she muttered, while trying to avoid the stinging eyes of mother.

And as her mother marched her home, the contact of her feet against the earth growing in intensity, Sara thought of Mary, her stars, and the clapper that was neither black nor round but bright orange like dusk. She smiled as she passed Mr. Charlie and his saliva-filled mouth. Once at home, she sat down and folded her hands gingerly in her lap like an infant. At night, Sara called up Mary. She told her, in hushed tones, that the position of a bell's clapper represents all that hangs between heaven and Earth. "I think," Sara, said quietly, "this establishes a relationship between them." ❧

Talking Faith with a Friend

Jennifer Wheelock

You can polish the silver
to death. Spit shine
the fine china and wax
the wood floors until
the dogs slip and bark
at their reflections.
You can dust up-top
the doorframes and frame
the photos you'd put away.
You can shave your legs
until your shins bleed.
You can spray some scent
like lavender on the linens.
You can wash the windows
inside/out as if the world
is some ancient coin
and you're scraping
off the caked-on mud
to discover the luster.

He still stomps in
dragging dirt, reeking
of communion. And you offer him
the children and a hot meal.
You splash around him
like he's a life raft
and you're caught
in a rip current. Every time
you close in on the save
a wave rises between you
and baptizes the boat.
You cook because you want him
full of something of you.

Halfway through the pre-heat
he'll get a call and whisper
with his back turned
and rush out. Shaking,
you spill things. Salt
falls around the eyes
of the stove.

You do this, you say,
because faith is all
you have left, and I listen
again, nod my head,
silently pray you
off your knees.

Regarding His Alzheimer's

Jennifer Wheelock

for my father

It's like he got to the end
of the road, and there was no way
forward, nothing left to do
but turn around and wander
back through the factory years
after the war to the drive-in
teens to the ten-year-old helping
Mom in the kitchen. Now, like a baby,
he sleeps through his days. He grabs
at mother's breasts. She leaves the room,
and he follows, clinging, inconsolable
at times, then quiet, floating
like a particle through his past.
Slurring as though his mouth is full
of river stones, he swims against
the current of the lexicon:
courting, rag top, schoolmarm, negro.
I loathe to say I love him more
this way, nostalgic, softening
at the edges, as if he and I
are looking in a mirror
and slowly backing away.

Letter to a Young Man in the Ground

Lincoln Michel

After Julio Cortázar

Words, I've always found, are hard to gather. When I spot the right ones, they hop away before I can trap them and put them in the needed order. I've always preferred a light touch on the shoulder or a well-timed smile. I've never been a poet, or read much poetry. I never even—can I confess it now that you are gone?—read your translations, Horacio. Don't be mad at me. I tried once, but the syntax was hard to swallow, getting caught on something on its way down to understanding.

I'm not mad at you. Still, it's unnerving to breakfast by the window your house sitter jumped out of. They say that ghosts haunt the place of their death, but does that mean the sidewalk you landed on or the balcony you jumped from? Are you leaping over and over, tumbling downward for eternity while I sip my tea? An invisible blur disturbing the order of the morning air?

You left the apartment in an acceptable state. I want you to know that. I'm not bothered by the little nibbles from the corners of the wallpaper or some old books—I never read them anyway. A bit of nibbling adds character, the nonchalance of a properly lived-in room. I have always been too neat, pretending that I could tidy up my life by rearranging furniture. Frederico always scolds my constant repositioning.

Did you really vomit each of those rabbits up? Is that why Sara, the housekeeper, said you looked so gaunt—nearly a ghost already—before your death?

By the time I returned, the city had cleaned every trace of you and your pet rabbits from the sidewalk. I know, because I looked. I ran my fingers through nooks and crannies of the pavement. I tilted my head at different angles to see if the sun caught a slick reflection. But there were only the usual oil stains and cigarette butts. No dried blood or bits of fur. Sara told me they used a hose attached to a van, and rerouted the school children to another block. (She also told me that an old widow sliced several of the hind feet and has been selling them as bad luck charms to the superstitious with enemies.)

I don't know if that would please you. I hardly knew you at all. We had only spoken a few times—conversations at parties about books I hadn't read—and I only lent you my apartment while I was away because Frederico said you were feeling down and needed a change.

Then again, can you ever know another person? I think that we are all strangers, especially to ourselves. No one knows what they have hidden inside that's trying to get out. I've known Frederico for nearly a decade, seen all his private parts, inside and out, and still could never have predicted that he would break down weeping on the patio when I returned.

Oh, I'm taking far too long to get to the meat of things! I'm burying the most interesting facts, and whoever might find this letter in the future will hardly even bother to get this far. This is why I have never been a writer. I'm too busy struggling to cough up my words to worry about what a reader will think! I vomit up these words on the page, but they are not nearly as pretty as your rabbits. I try to pet these words, love them, but they remain ugly, unlovable, pests.

Let me get right to it: you didn't toss all of your rabbits out the window. One was left behind.

Did you miscount? Was the horror of eleven actually a terror of twelve?

After I read your suicide note, I emptied my luggage and began frying up an afternoon snack—you will forgive me, I'm sure, for eating as I learned of your death. The return from Paris, like the end of all trips, was disorienting. (So many things are disorienting. Leaving, arriving, waking from a dream, walking out of a building to find the sun has set. Sometimes I feel like my body is a poorly made vase that is constantly being jostled and rattling on its base, never settling.)

The smell tickled his nose. He crawled out from beneath an old chair in the parlor. I squatted and gave him a slice of carrot. Dust bunnies clung to his ears.

He didn't look like you, the. I'm not sure why I thought he would. Perhaps it was how you described the process of pulling the rabbits out of your throat as a "birthing." I assumed he would share your DNA. Maybe he does. What do I know of throat rabbits?

I fed him a few more slices and named him Julio. He was white with a few spots of dark black, like little wells of sadness, on his brow.

"Since when do you keep pets?" Frederico asked when he came by to pick up your things.

"It's just a way to pass the time."

"Paris really changed you, Andrea. But I still love you, even with a bunny." He stood beside me, placing one hand in the small of my back and pressing down Julio's ears a little too hard with each pet.

I resented Frederico being there in that moment. He was holding a glass of wine in the casual manner of someone surveying his castle, even though I have not consented to have him move in. "After Paris, we'll talk," I had said, hoping, I think, that the situation would be forgotten by both of us. An impossibility, of course, but what do we have to hope for except the impossible?

You did not kill yourself for me. Men always feel the need to pretend the things they do are for women, but we both know that is a lie. If I'm being honest, it angers me that you hoisted this all on me. I don't mean little Julio. I mean the weight of your death and your confession. A confusing letter with dense prose. I read it seven times and only came away with a headache. You are more a stranger to me now than you were before you died in my apartment.

And yet, I would like to understand you if I could, because I would like to understand other people. I think if I understand them, I will understand myself. No, that's not it. I think that if I make the effort to understand other people they will be forced to make the effort in return and then perhaps I, too, will be understood?

Oh, who am I kidding? I would not have even written you, never even thought to bring a pen near paper, if Julio the rabbit had not started vomiting himself.

The first time was a week after I had returned. I was having tea with Frederico—"Andrea," he had told me, absurdly, "we must keep Horacio in our memories so that he never truly dies"—and feeding Julio pinches of clover. Then somehow we were fighting again. "You only think about how things will impact your life," he was saying, "as if I'm not a human being but a piece of furniture you don't know where to put!" When Frederico left, I decided to nap. Julio hopped onto my breast and made a sound halfway between a gag and a squeak. He made that noise again and again until I became very frightened. My heart was beating very fast, which was an odd sensation with Julio weighing it down.

When he was finished, there was a little naked man on my breast. He was damp and crawling on his hands and knees. He was the size of a salt shaker. Julio sniffed this homunculus, then hopped away with animal indifference.

This little man crawled onto my left breast, lying prostrate across my areola. He did not look me in the face. He was preoccupied with the mound—or, I suppose, mountain from his point of view—of flesh. I'm used to men looking at my bosom instead of my face. Frederico spent all of tea flipping up his eyes every time I turned back. And yet I didn't hold it against this little homunculus. He looked like a man, but wasn't. His sex was no bigger than a bee's stinger.

I had an old aquarium that my parents had bought me for an axolotl that had passed long ago. I placed him inside with some paperclips and a handful of blueberries. He seemed happy when I watched him from across the room, but whenever I walked by on my way to the bathroom, he ran and pressed his naked underbelly to the glass.

A philosophical question: is Julio the little man's mother? Is no one? Am I?

Sara was quite disturbed. When she came by, she gasped and clutched her breast. "Where did you get that filthy thing?"

She meant Julio, the rabbit. I tossed a sheet over Hernan's—as I named him—aquarium when she came by to clean.

"Keeping one after the . . . incident," she said, "is beyond morbid." She looked as if she thought the rabbit itself was a ghost.

Frederico was also distraught, thinking he was responsible for your death since the housesitting was his suggestion. I think he believed the apartment killed you. During our fights, he would look around nervously at the looming walls. And yet still he insisted that he must move in soon if we are to keep our relationship.

Can I confess to you that I was unsure? Frederico made me happy, I think, or at least as happy as I thought I could be. But this space was my space, it has been ordered in the way I ordered it, decorated with towels and cups of my choosing. I could tolerate guests, even those who kill themselves, but I am not sure I could tolerate another order intruding on mine.

And then I had little Julio and even littler Hernan to take care of. I will not deny that they opened a motherly instinct in me. I never thought I wanted children, not even when Frederico pointed out which corner of my apartment could hold a crib and which a playpen.

If you were still here, would you have taught me how to care for little Hernan? I gave him slices of all my food, but he only wanted raw meat and orange juice.

I would have given Julio to the butcher, at least to give Sara some peace of mind, and let Hernan loose in the woods, had Julio not vomited again. A week after Hernan, after devouring a little bowl of cabbage, he puked a second little pale man. I rinsed the man in the sink and placed him beside Hernan. The two of them pressed into the aquarium glass, watching me.

However, when I left to refill my wine, they ran at each other. I could hear a pained squeaking sound, and when I came back in Hernan was nursing a broken arm in the corner and the new homunculus was inert, face down in a pool of apple juice.

It is impossible to give mouth-to-mouth to a head that fits between your lips. I could not revive the man (I hadn't yet had time to name him). I looked at Hernan and he seemed to be smiling.

When the next man came sliding out of Julio's throat, I placed a divider in the aquarium so that they could not fight. When I stooped down to look at them, they stared back at me. When I left, they ran into the glass divider, pounding and making rude gestures at each other.

"So then we'll move to another apartment on another street," Frederico said, tossing his hands in the air, when I told him that I'm unsure that I can share this space.

"I need time to gather things, get my life in order, is all."

"Paris infected you," he said. "I knew it would. Your eyes are still dazzled by the city of lights. I'm just a burnt-out bulb."

I was trying to move him toward the kitchen, but Hernan and Mauro—the third vomited man—were banging on the glass divider. Julio hopped toward the aquarium, worried.

"What kind of dirty rodents do you have in this place anyway? It's filthy!" He stormed out while the righteousness lasted.

Did you feel that the rabbits were filthy, Horacio? Did you feel that you were filthy because they came, somehow, from inside of you? Frederico has that Catholic fear that his body is corrupt. He told me that as a child he could not help masturbating, but would cry each time he spurted. Was that how it felt to you each time a rabbit emerged from your throat, glistening and new?

Frederico said you were a fastidious friend, part of the reason I agreed to have you housesit, but I've begun to suspect that those of us who keep order on the outside are trying to hide the chaos inside.

I can't think of Julio as dirty. His fur is soft and I take him to the park bench and let him hop around my feet. (Sitting on the patio where you died was starting to bother me. Too many children walking by, pointing up and shouting.)

So there has been peace, for a time.

The little men, Hernan and Mauro and Tomas and Santiago—yes, like your rabbits before them, the little men kept popping out of Julio's throat—I'm not so sure about. Like dolls or babies, they contain the delicate features of anything small, and yet they piss and shit and, if I take two out to try and socialize them, cause one another to bleed. The only way I've found to calm them is to rest them on my chest, so that their attention is directed elsewhere.

There have never been any women, only little men. Perhaps if you had left another rabbit I could have started a whole new miniature human race to live and breed in the cracks in the walls.

But I come now to the part where I begin to understand you. Because four was one thing, but other numbers quite another. The men keep crawling out, covered in slime: five and six and seven and eight. Lucas, Brian, Hector, and Jorge. Their hair different colors, their skin new shades. When I rest, I take a different one out and let him stumble around my lap.

These men that I had not asked for have begun to feel like a responsibility, and all responsibilities are burdens. I told everyone I've been recovering from the trip, but really I'm running around trying to feed these unasked for men and make sure they don't beat each other's tiny brains out of their nutshell skulls.

Frederico came by calling yesterday. He told me that I was his world.

Then that I was a snake in his field that strikes without warning, sinking in its poison teeth. Then that Paris was the snake and I the poisoned. I tried to cry, for his sake, but couldn't. My many thoughts were pounding on different parts of my skull. He sighed, then went away.

I kept adding dividers to the aquarium, but how many divisions can there be?

Tired of math, I write this letter to you. The now ten little men, silent for so long, grunt and howl, bang their fists. The glass is stained with tiny smears of blood and waste.

Is this the way you have chosen to haunt me? Or are these men the result of the chaos you brought into my clean apartment in the calle Suipacha?

I know you will not answer this letter, but I feel the need to put my thoughts down in some order. It helps me feel as if I'm working towards a solution, towards the proper arrangement of thoughts, that might suddenly solve everything for me.

Frederico is not part of that equation anymore. I have to compartmentalize Frederico in my mind. Yes, we broke up. I knew it would end. I knew that Paris was an escape, a time to be by myself in another city and determine if I could share my room, my apartment, the rest of my life with this other person. Now, I take all of our memories—walking hand in hand to the market, his knuckles brushing across the breasts that the little men so adore, our morning meals of toast and tea—and put them in a box beside the other men that life has regurgitated in front of me: Thiago, Nicolas, Alejandro, Ossip, and the rest. Each one locked away in a room of memories in my head.

The line of full-sized men is as unending and overwhelming as the men that Julio can't help but spit up. Or the ceaseless series of choices that existence keeps asking of me: where to work, who to love, when or where to move, what to say at dinner, and so on and so forth. All of these little moments, every little moment of every day, offering new sets of choices and demands.

The little men, whatever else they are, are machines of demands. They want. They reach out to me with fingers as tiny as inchworms. Their eraser mouths asking always to be fed. I have been trying to answer their demands, and trying to control their desires. But I cannot.

I am not going to die. I've been coming closer to an understanding of you, but I am not you.

No, I will not die, but if Frederico is right, that my life is too ordered, that I try too hard to control, I think I have to embrace the chaos of these miniature Neanderthals.

I am going to take away the dividing panels, tip out the aquarium on the floor. I'll let their naked bodies tumble to the carpet. What will happen then? Will they run after me, demanding more and more, or will they turn their desires on each other and beat and destroy each other as only brothers can? Or, who can predict anything, perhaps they will come to terms, learn to talk and form a society of little men who come from a bunny who came from a man who needed a place to stay for a little while.

The way they bang on the glass and press their organs against it, I almost wonder if they know what I am thinking. There are eleven of them now, or twelve if you count the one that Hernan killed.

I am going to do it now, and then retire to my room. I'm feeling overwhelmed by the words here and need to rest. I will try to write you later, when the new order has settled.

Sincerely,
Andrea ❧

Selections from *The Week*

Joanna Ruocco

Meme

I bought my mother a small hospital with a decent operating budget and she picked out a rheumatologist, an oncologist, a cardiovascular surgeon, an orthopedist, and an anesthesiologist, and that used up the salary lines, but then she replaced the anesthesiologist with a nurse anesthetist and there was enough left over to add a phlebotomist and a Reiki practitioner. Architecturally, it was a very nice hospital, more like a mad house, with ivy on the walls, and expansive grounds and willow trees, and my mother, when she saw the willow trees, said, "Maybe I'll learn how to make aspirin," and I said, "Mother, I didn't buy you a hospital so you can learn how to make aspirin," and she said, "No, dear, of course not," and she said, "Does the lab here have a tablet press?" and I said, "Mother, it's a fully equipped lab," sharply, because I hadn't thought to inventory the lab and could that possible oversight point to additional oversights? And if so, what could they be? We walked inside the hospital, and I showed my mother her room. I'd arranged it so that it was nearly identical to her room in her former home. Instead of apple trees, she could see willow trees from her window and that wasn't a bad trade, an even trade I'd say. Also, there was a skylight at the end of her hall. Her former home had no such skylight. Beneath the skylight, I'd arranged a dozen massively potted aspidistras. I walked my mother to the end of the hall and she said, "This is lovely," and I said, "Thank you, Mother," and she admired the aspidistras ("These are lovely aspidistras.") and she said, "When your Uncle Billy came back . . ." and I said, "Poor Uncle Billy," and she said, ". . . he told me he felt very comfortable in Vietnam because the jungle was filled with houseplants," and I said, "Do you want an exercise bike?" and she said, "No, dear, the hallways are so long." We walked a lap around the whole first floor to get back to her room and then I said goodbye. Driving away, I felt wonderful about buying my mother the hospital. And since that first day, I've learned more about the hospital—that Al Jolson died there, and that Georgios Papanikolaou once came to give a talk—and I feel more confident than ever that I did not make a mistake, even though I failed to inventory the lab and, it turns out, check the elevator inspection notices and the generators. The lab is fine; the elevators are fine; the generators are good as new and never been used. My mother says everything is perfectly pleasant and I feel good about that. As tens, hundreds, thousands of adult children start buying hospitals for their mothers, I feel good that, by acting quickly, I managed to buy my own mother the most desirable hospital. It's in the best area for our purposes, a rural county neither too close nor too far. I used to get phone calls about it from would-be buyers, but for months now I've kept my phone turned off, and when the contract expires I will cancel the plan altogether.

Drone

My father goes to the pines. He checks on his hive. His hive is destroyed. The bear wrecked the hive. My father goes to his house. He paints his body with honey. He applies many coats. He goes to the pines. He goes to the wreck of his hive. He lies in wait for the bear on the wreck of his hive. He wears six coats of honey, six full-length coats. It smells like pines in the pines, and it smells like strong honey. Honey attracts. My father waits for the bear to attack, to come through the pines, to rush toward the honey-thick smell in the pines. Surprise! There's no hive in the pines. The hive is destroyed. Dead bees. Mangled boards. No hive. A decoy in pines. It's not a hive . . . it's a man! My father smiles. Silly old bear. My father will kill the bear with his hands. Every man wants to kill a bear with his hands. Every silly old man. My brother calls my father a silly old man. My father is old. He has no teeth, has no hair. He has very strong hands. The bear will rush through the pines. My father will smile. Surprise! He will put his hands on the bear. Even now he is preparing to choke out the bear. My brother has entered his prime. He's not a boy. He knows his own mind. He knows my father will fail. It's not hard to see: a silly old man, his old hands, and a bear. My brother proposes an alternate plan. He'll spread tacks. He'll plant mines. "Come back inside," he yells, but my father does not respond to commands. He won't surrender the field. He is lying in wait, his toothless head in his hands. It's not hard to see: my father will die. This is the plan. My brother throws a grenade at the pines. It rips through the bear, but my low-lying father, my father is spared. He comes through the pines. He comes through the smoke. He is covered in hair, all that honey covered over with all the bear's hair. On his head, on his cheeks and his chin, on his chest and his legs, on the backs of his hands and the tops of his feet. My father looks young, a dark, hairy young man. He holds up his hands. He says, "That bear destroyed his last hive." He's alive. That's the plan. He comes out young and alive. My brother pretends he was nowhere nearby. He trims his black hair. He builds his own house from the pines. He feels too alone then remembers that honey attracts. He paints his body with honey. He waits. Driving with the window rolled down, his future mate brakes. She smells pines. She smells something strong: warm caramel, red clover. She leaves the car on the side of the road. She walks to my brother's pine house where he's waiting outside. She sees ants thick on honey, but beneath the honey, she sees the shape of a man.

Bailout

Now that the son is grown and wants to move the parents into a smaller house, he needs to convince the parents—who are not incompetent, not in the legal sense of the word, just impractical, stubborn, dangerous, and very old—that a smaller house will be suited to their needs. They can manage and afford a smaller house, and they can't manage and afford the house they have now. The son might say this to the parents, but he knows saying it would not convince the parents that they should move into a smaller house. The parents have never felt that they need to be able to afford or manage anything in particular. When they can't afford something, they do without it. Not only do they do without it, they *disdain* it. Who needs that thing? It's amazing, isn't it, how many things are available today that people really don't need? When the parents can't manage something, it blows up or falls apart or gets away from them. It creates a bad situation that either disappears on its own or doesn't, gets better or worse or stays the same. And so? The parents have survived innumerable bad situations. They've survived far longer than the son, who thinks life is supposed to be easy, that situations don't arise. The son can show the parents where their roof is leaking, where the stovepipe from the basement furnace glows orange and flickers with the black shadows of flames. He can talk about the rising cost of gasoline, the distance between their house and a supermarket, their house and his house, their house and a hospital, their house and another house, any house, a house where they can find help, reach help when they need help in haste. But the parents don't need help. That's what the son doesn't understand. The parents don't need the son. They did without the son before and they can do without the son again. They don't need each other. They don't need themselves, not really. What selves do people think they're hanging on to anyway? Not their old bodies, their very old bodies? Who wants to hang on to a very old body, even your own? People remember being young and they think that's what they need, those selves, supple and strong, but they don't. They don't need them. Not really. Those selves are gone and people make do without them. Every day people have less of those selves, but they go on living. The parents do enjoy living. They enjoy puttering in the yard, feeding the birds, making late night pancakes, watching TV, and feeling warm inside the big, untidy, half-rotten house that the son can't convince them to leave. It's a death trap, a money pit, a pigsty, an eyesore, an outpost. It's more than the parents need. The parents need so little, though, it's unforgivable that the son would try to take that little bit away.

Real Value

A wealthy woman of my acquaintance was just deprived of her fortune. Never having had a fortune myself, I did not understand that a fortune, once possessed, is as essential to a person as a limb or organ. I had always thought of a fortune as something external, something that could, and even should, be expropriated from the wealthy in the service of the greater good. For example, I had judged my acquaintance negatively for buying shoes that cost more than two weeks of my salary when she might have bought herself more attractive and serviceable shoes for under $300 at a department store and sent the remaining money to earthquake survivors or given it as a startling, perhaps life-changing tip to a taxi driver. Once she paid my airfare to Italy so I could visit her and some mutual friends for a week at her home in Tuscany; that was, of course, very generous. When she showed up at my door asking to spend the night, she was no doubt calling in that very favor. However, I almost sent her away from my door, not out of malice. I didn't recognize her! Her lower jaw seemed longer, her facial skin was scabby and everywhere red-threaded with capillaries, and her clothing hung on her body in a way that suggested double mastectomies or drug addiction. I took her in the first instant for a stranger, someone who would tell me a story about the tank of gas or bus ticket she needed to get home to her children. I noticed, though, upon further inspection, the complexity and impracticality of her footwear. Her footwear was obviously hand-stitched; the design was one of a kind but also familiar. As soon as I noticed the footwear, I realized my acquaintance stood before me, a woman I knew fairly well but who was now changed in some essential way I didn't yet understand. I invited her to dinner and at dinner, she told me her story. I'd always heard that she'd inherited her fortune from an old uncle who lived, and died, in Johannesburg, but what my acquaintance told me that night was this: she had inherited her fortune from a young uncle who lived in Johannesburg and died in Malmö, Sweden, where his body, per his last wishes, had been kept ever since at low temperature in a private hospital. After two decades of failed attempts, the doctors were able to restart his heart. Her uncle was no longer dead, and so the fortune that she had come to depend on now reverted to him. Even in Sweden, the cost of reviving a dead person and maintaining him or her in this revived state is very high. Her uncle would need every penny of the fortune to maintain himself, and so when he died again there would be nothing left for re-inheritance. His new life and the fortune, explained my acquaintance, were coextensive. I found my acquaintance's story interesting, and I was impressed with her phrasing ("His new life and the fortune are coextensive"), although now I think it likely she was parroting her lawyer. At the time, I saw the situation as highly specific, singular really. I didn't find in my acquaintance's formulation a general principle about wealth. Our conversation for the rest of the night was confined to reminiscences. Several weeks later, I heard from our mutual friends that she had died. My acquaintance had died the second the funds in her final bank account were transferred to the uncle's bank account in Sweden. Our mutual friends knew many of the forensic and legal details surrounding my acquaintance's death, but no one knew what was going to happen, or had already happened, to her shoe collection. All I could ascertain was that she hadn't left it to any of them. She obviously hadn't left it to me, either. She was single, no siblings or children, so the whole thing was even more mysterious. Is it possible that the uncle's executor was petty enough to repossess my acquaintance's shoes? The shoes were worth quite a bit, so I suppose it is possible. Maybe the shoes ended up getting shipped to the private hospital and the female doctors divided them up amongst themselves. Once I had this idea—the female doctors working around the clock to keep the uncle newly alive while wearing my acquaintance's shoes—I couldn't get it out of my head. I knew it was the truth of the matter, even if it wasn't strictly speaking what came to pass. ❧

The Baby

Ethan Rutherford

The weather outside is feral, and snow-clotted. And when the doctor says hold the baby, they do.

They're in the emergency room. The baby had thrown a fever, and that's why they brought him in, through the Oregon winter, at this time of night. Now, everyone is worried.

Hold him so he sits up, the doctor says. She is on one side of the hospital bed, and they, Sean and Clare, are on the other. The baby is between them, crinkling the hospital paper.

Earlier he'd been lethargic, ashen. But now he seems fine. A male nurse had given him sugar water from a plastic capsule, which had perked him up. He is alert and chirping now, moving his arms straight up and down as if practicing a swim-stroke, or signaling a truck on the road.

He seems fine, Sean says.

This is just a precaution, the doctor says. We're worried about the things we can't see.

The baby is five weeks old and has almost no hair at all. Little boy, his little head a little melon his body can't quite support. He is so small. The room is curtained, and large impassive machines, pushed against the wall, bulk into the room like sleeping sentinels, powered down. He, Sean, assumes they are life-giving, used in emergency situations, but their screens are blank, so he doesn't really know.

Ready? the doctor says. She had warned them about the needle but still it is a surprise to see it. They nod.

They prop the baby up so his back is to the doctor, and coo to distract him. They see the pain flash across his face and it registers as their pain before he cries out. But the squall passes quickly, and as soon as the doctor's face relaxes they take him into their arms and bounce him around. He is their first, and hadn't come easily. And now that he is here, in this hospital, they think only of losing him.

Is that hard to do? Sean asks the doctor. He means threading a large needle into the back of a baby, and finding the fluid that would give them the information they required. He means using a needle as a divining stick. He means causing pain in order to possibly prevent more, and worse, pain.

Not really, the doctor says. But she is sweating. When she leaves, another young woman parts the curtains and stands at the foot of the bed. This is how the hospital works: doors open and shut with no sound. Curtains part. She's holding a clipboard.

Would you say the care you received today has been satisfactory, unsatisfactory, or exceptional? she asks.

Who are you? Clare says. She's holding the baby, threading his arms back into his pajamas. The woman disappears.

The baby falls asleep on Clare. They wait and wait for someone to tell them what will happen next. Eventually the male nurse from earlier comes in.

Angels when they sleep, he says.

Do you have kids? Sean asks.

Oh, no, the male nurse says. He tells them to grab their stuff, and follow him to the NICU.

What stuff? Clare says.

The male nurse seems confused. He looks around and sees no stuff. He checks his clipboard. Yup, his head seems to say. Well, he says, follow me anyway.

The new room has a television, a small crib, and more sleeping machines. On the walls there are comforting paintings, fat ships in calm seas. In one corner is a large chair. With a flourish, the male nurse shows them how it folds into a bed. Voila, he says, and leaves.

They tuck their baby, still sleeping, into the crib. They'd followed the male nurse through empty corridor after empty corridor. They'd turned: left, right, left again. An elevator dinged. Left, left, right, and then he'd swiped the door with a card and they'd followed.

Where is everyone? Clare asks, now that the three of them are alone in the new room. There are no clocks or windows in the room and therefore it feels like there is no time in the room. In their hurry, they'd left their phones at home in the kitchen.

We should sleep, Sean says.

Sleep! Clare says. The lighting in the room is industrial and humming a fluorescent tune. Neither of them can find a switch to turn it off, but the baby doesn't seem to mind. He's decided on sleep. He's powered down.

They know it's morning when a doctor opens the door and says Good Morning. This doctor is a young woman, though a different young woman than the doctor they saw before. She's holding a clipboard. The tests are going well, she informs them, but they are inconclusive. They will need to run more tests before discharge.

Why is the baby still sleeping? Clare says. Why isn't he hungry?

It's natural, the doctor says, and leaves.

More doctors come into the room, but no one will answer any questions about the baby. The only thing that anyone will say is that they will have to stay in the hospital for a little while longer while more tests are run. The baby sleeps through all of it. The male nurse walks in.

Whoops, he says. Wrong room.

Why won't anyone tell us what's wrong? Clare says.

Well, he says, these doctors? They're also scientists. They believe in certainty. They don't really like to guess at things.

How long have we been here? Clare asks.

The male nurse checks his wristwatch. Two days, he says.

It doesn't feel like it's been two days, Sean says.

I hear that a lot, the male nurse says, and leaves.

When they're alone, Clare cries. I'm going to wake him up, she says. She means their baby. I'm going to wake him up and we're going to leave.

I don't think that's a good idea, Sean says. We don't know anything.

No one knows anything, Clare says. She's not crying anymore. She picks the baby, who is still sleeping, up from the crib and puts him to her breast. His eyes flutter but he won't open his mouth.

Come on, Clare says. A small alarm goes off and suddenly there is a nurse with red hair in the room, looking at Clare disapprovingly.

We get signaled when the babies leave their cribs, she says. There are sensors in the mattress.

When does he eat? Clare says.

This is a hospital, the red-haired nurse says. She takes the baby from Clare and eases him back on the crib's mattress. The alarm stops. We'll take care of that, she says. You should try to relax.

Are you a mother? Clare says. Are you asking me to relax?

You're not here for nothing, the nurse says. If you need to hold a baby, we can get you a baby to hold. But this baby needs to stay on this mattress. She looks at Sean as if to say, this is your responsibility too, to keep the baby in the crib.

Sean nods as if to say, Roger that.

When the nurse leaves, they stand near the crib and watch the baby. He's sleeping with his arms over his head like he's stretching things out.

I don't like any of this, Clare says.

Maybe we should turn on the television, Sean says. But when he picks up the remote it doesn't work. He pushes all the buttons he sees but still nothing happens. Finally he finds a different remote and uses that. Christmas music comes faintly and tinnily through the ceiling speakers, but the television remains cold and off. Silver Bells, Sean says. He recognizes the song because he sung it in school when he was younger. He has a memory of his grandmother in the audience, listening to him sing with her eyes closed, and crying.

Please turn that off, Clare says. It's not even Thanksgiving.

The door opens and in walks four doctors. They are dressed exactly alike, as if they are in a movie called Doctors. One of them is the young woman they saw in the emergency room. An older doctor nudges her forward, and says, Go on.

I'm sorry, she says. But I need to use the needle again.

Why? Clare says.

I didn't do it right, the doctor says, and we need to be sure.

Well, Clare says, that's not happening. But Sean talks to her in one of the corners of the room, and then holds her as the older doctors instruct the younger doctor, who is holding a needle that looks different from the first needle. All four of the doctors are hunched over the baby's crib like crows looking at their own reflections in a puddle.

Oh, the younger doctor says. I get it now.

This is outrageous, Clare says.

I understand why you feel that way, the older doctor says. But she needs to learn.

Do something, Clare says to Sean. But by the time he turns to face the doctors they are gone. The baby is still asleep, though undressed. His face signals calm weather ahead. There are two small pricks of blood on his ribcage like punctuation marks. Clare threads his sleeping arms into his pajamas, checks his diaper (clean), threads his legs, then zips him up and sits down heavily on the chairbed.

Why is our baby sleeping so much? Sean asks the male nurse when he comes in again.

All babies sleep, the male nurse says. They have to. It's how they recharge to face a complicated world they know nothing of.

That's condescending, Clare says from the chairbed. She's lying down with a napkin over her face like she's trying to keep a headache from spreading.

The male nurse notes something on his clipboard and clicks his pen closed. You'll have to talk to a doctor, then, he says, and leaves.

I'm in pain, Clare says. She's holding her head. I'm having thoughts I'm not proud of.

I'll go get us some food, Sean says. When Clare says nothing back, he takes that to mean that food is a good idea.

The nurse at the large desk near the locked door is wearing blue scrubs that have the word Tuesday printed all over them. There are Christmas lights hung haphazardly on her computer. On the screen little toasters with wings flap around in diagonal patterns. Is there a cafeteria? Sean asks.

And good morning to you, she says without looking up.

Hallways give way to hallways give way to sucking doors that give way to elevators. Every wall is beige. All the doctors he passes look bored, and stand at computers like they are waiting for something. I'm definitely lost, Sean thinks. Just when he is about to give up hope he sees a McDonald's.

You look tired, the McDonald's guy says when he places his order.

Sean eats two cheeseburgers next to an enormous Christmas tree that sits atop a mountain of perfectly wrapped presents. Outside the snow is waist-level. The line for McDonald's is filled with blank-faced people who are getting their food in an orderly way. It seems to him that he's been here before. Or that they've been in the hospital for a very long time. Two doctors, one old and one young, sit down next to him.

And *that's* a conversation you never want to have, the older one says to the younger one. Sean strains to listen, but the doctors notice and clam up.

Where have you been? Clare says when he gets back. She is frantic, with the light of great knowledge in her eyes.

What'd I miss? Sean says. She gestures to the baby. He's hooked up to a large machine. A small tube is taped to his arm. One end of the tube is fixed to the machine, the other end goes into his armpit.

It's for food, Clare says. The baby is still sleeping like an angel. Sit down, she says to Sean. He sits and watches as she closes her eyes and then opens them, closes and opens them again.

What am I looking for? Sean says.

Just then a box of Kleenex lifts off the counter behind him and hovers slowly across the room. Are you doing that? Sean says, but Clare doesn't answer. The Kleenex box comes to a floating stop just in front of Sean's face. Then it drops from the air into his lap.

I've developed a power, Clare says.

I can see that, Sean says.

One of the paintings comes off the wall and glides gently around the room. Cabinets open and shut. The remote spins like a top on the side-table. Does it hurt to do that? Sean asks.

Yes, Clare says. No. It's too complicated to explain. I can tell you it's exhausting. She walks to where he is and sits down. She lays her head on his shoulder. It feels like a huge rock of some kind. He puts his arm around her and gives her back a small double-pat. They'll figure things out, he says.

I don't know about that, she says.

The machine connected to the baby beeps and comes to life. It purrs and hums and they watch as a heavy beige liquid is pushed through the coiled tube. The baby raises his arms and drops them. He's not smiling, but he's not frowning either. His small face is perfectly relaxed.

I had some food for you, Sean says, but I don't know where it is now.

Who can eat? Clare says.

The male nurse walks in with a young girl who could be his child. Who moved everything around in here? he asks when he opens the door.

The child is holding a clipboard. Would you say your stay here has been satisfactory, most satisfactory, or leaves something to be desired? she asks.

What a winter we're having, the male nurse says. He has a beard, now.

Where'd that beard come from? Sean asks.

I lost a bet, the male nurse says.

I imagine you did, Clare says.

When Sean sleeps, he dreams of a huge cathedral bell that has no tongue. He can see it perfectly. He knows in the dream that he's in Rio de Janeiro, and that the swinging bell will never sing because he has the tongue in one of the bags he's left at his hotel. Clare is in the dream too, but she won't turn to face him. They've been walking through mountains for months, and now here they are, at the top of this cathedral. Some monk in the lower level of the cathedral is tugging on the rope, confused. It's his job to ring this bell but no matter what he does he only hears the wooden joists creaking with the bell's movement, a sound that announces nothing to the city, whose people depend on the bell to tell them when to leave their houses and when to stay.

When he wakes up, a trashcan is hovering over his legs. There is also a new machine near the crib, but this one is connected to the baby's foot.

Sorry, Clare says, and the trashcan bobs gently back to its place under the sink. She's standing in front of one of the paintings, looking through it like a window. We're not supposed to touch him anymore, she says. Just so you know.

In the hallway outside their room there is a sudden commotion. It sounds like a drawer of forks being emptied on a marble countertop. Sean leaves the room to investigate. He's come to know this hospital very well. At the far end of the corridor near the nurse's station a large group has gathered. What's happening? he asks when he joins the group. The man next to him is dressed like Santa Claus. He points to a young doctor who has her hands over her flushed cheeks and is crying. It's the doctor they saw when they first came to the hospital with the baby.

She's getting married, the man says. Finally.

The doctor is hopping up and down with happiness. She is trying to address the gathered crowd but everyone is cheering and clapping too loudly for Sean to hear what she is saying.

She's not a very good doctor, Sean says.

The man dressed as Santa Claus gives him a hard look. Everyone is entitled to his opinion, he says, and continues clapping.

Sean looks around and sees that everyone's there. The older doctors, the younger doctors. The male nurse and the child with the clipboard, the guy who works at the McDonald's. Other parents with other babies. Some of these babies are grossly deformed. Some are hooked up to portable machines. All of these people! Every door on the hall is open.

How did you hear about this? Sean asks Santa.

It just sort of occurred, he says.

Then a strange thing happens. As Sean looks around, he discovers that above each person gathered he can see a floating green bar. He's seen these bars before. In video games, they tell you how much life your character has left. At the beginning, the bar is full and humming. As you progress, and take hits, the bar gradually goes down until your character dies and you have to start over.

Are you seeing these green bars too? he asks.

I think I'm done talking, the man says.

This is horrible knowledge to have, he thinks. But he can't make the bars go away. Most of the bars are at least half-full, but there are some that are very low. The male nurse has about a quarter full energy left. The young girl with the clipboard has a full bar and it pulses over her head with fluorescent benevolence. The joyous doctor who is getting married has only a sliver of blinking red hovering above her flushing face, which means that very soon she will be toast and will exist only in the minds of the people who loved her. Everywhere he looks are babies in tiny hospital gowns being held by their tired parents.

Turn off, he says. He hits his cheek with the palm of his hand. Restart, he says. Everyone is looking. Turn off! he yells, and hits his ear with his fist.

Sir, the male nurse says as he approaches with caution. He moves like he is testing his weight on young ice.

One more hit does the trick and shorts the circuit. The life bars are gone. Many happy returns, Sean says to the young doctor, who nods graciously.

Where have you been? Clare says when he returns to the room. I figured out the lights.

He is relieved to see no bars above Clare or above the baby. I don't know, he says. Is he still sleeping?

Yes, Clare says. They took away the machines.

He looks and sees that it's true. It's just the two of them now, and the crib. And, of course, the baby.

Is that a good thing or a bad thing? Sean asks.

They wouldn't tell me, Clare says. She's crying. I think it's better, she says. She takes his hand and leads him to the chair bed. She blinks her eyes and concentrates and the lights in the room dim. A blanket floats from one of the cabinets above the sink and covers the two of them. Watch this, she says.

The television flips on and on the screen comes the story of their life together.

I've seen this before, Sean says. He's joking, of course. He's never seen anything like this.

Shhh, Clare says.

On the screen, two actors with a passing resemblance to Sean and Clare meet at a supermarket. They go on a date. They fight and have misunderstandings and make up. They have sex and they laugh. They leave their families to move to a new state where they know no one at all. They take pictures of a growing belly and then they are at a hospital very much like the hospital where they are now.

We were good looking back then, Sean says.

Weren't we? Clare says.

On the screen Sean is feeding Clare ice chips in the hospital. She is bouncing on a large exercise ball and is in a great deal of pain. Then she is on her side and the baby is coming. The camera cuts to the waiting room, where two old people are pacing holes in the carpet.

Here we go, Clare says.

The baby appears like a gasping fish, and the two actors open their arms and welcome him to the world. They take turns holding him. A purple chord is cut, a car seat is fitted, a freshly painted nursery. There is blood in the shower and residual pain in the room. There are nights so long they feel like months. The baby holds a finger. The baby takes a breast. The baby pees in a perfect arc directly onto his own face. The actors do a marvelous job. There is the first walk into the neighborhood, the calls to the grandparents, the perfect happiness that comes only from feeling the weight of the baby falling asleep on your chest.

Sean feels Clare stiffen slightly beside him, but they keep watching. On the screen, the days fall from the calendar. The actors bundle for winter, take pictures in the snow. Then: a mild cough. Then: a waxen complexion. Then: a small fever. Then: a worrisome fever. The actors bundle the baby and rush him through a winter storm. At the hospital the young doctor is still alive, and tries her best with the needle. They follow a male nurse down beige hallways, and the baby is hooked up to machines. No one will give them the answers they want. The actors break character and address the camera. The old film begins to deteriorate, reverse, and play forward. The time stamp evaporates. There are no more exterior shots, no sweeping boom cranes, no tracking shots set to music. The doctors talk to one another in hushed tones and come to decisions. There is nothing but pity and love and suffering and hard facts delivered dispassionately, new machines and old machines, the sound of rubber soles on polished floors and gurney squeaks. They see souls enter the world and souls drift slowly away from the world. There are no windows in the building. The air is thick and clean-smelling. The actors squeeze together on a small chair that folds into a bed and watch on the television the movie of their life and then the television turns off.

The room goes fully dark. Someone is trying the door from the outside, but the door is locked. There's a tentative knock, the sound of a knob being twisted back and forth.

Should we watch it again? Sean says.

No, Clare says. I just want to stay like this.

There's a louder knock at the door, and muffled talking. The baby is sound asleep.

If you could take someone else's life, and give it to him, would you? Sean says. Clare says nothing. What would you trade? That's what I've been thinking about.

The dark in the room has taken on weight. The sounds at the door are getting louder.

I would murder everyone in sight, Clare finally says. Car crash upon car crash. There is nothing I wouldn't do.

Everyone in the hospital is outside now, trying to get in.

The male nurse. The young doctor, and the child with the clipboard. The two older doctors, ready now for the conversation they'd been putting off. It sounds, now, like someone is hammering at the door with a mallet. The hinges are starting to pull from the frame.

We don't have much time, Sean says.

I know, Clare says.

Across the room, the crib begins to shimmer, and glow. The baby floats up and away from the mattress until he is above the rail. He hovers briefly in space before bobbing slowly toward them to nestle in the crook they've made with their arms. When he settles down he is heavier than either could imagine. His breathing is regular. He's having the dream of dreams. He is thinking of fat ships on a placid sea. Hello? Hello? someone is shouting from the hallway. Don't wake him, Sean says. Boo, Clare says. And the baby opens his eyes. ❧

Carnality

Angela Woodward

1 Coffin

I used to keep my weekly cash money in a little coffin my friend Dave made. He had worked in a library, where he repaired books. When things were slow, he put together coffins out of the backing board they used. The coffin sits up on a shelf over my bed, where I can get to it, but when the kids were little they couldn't reach it. Not that I ever worried about them stealing from me. It just seemed like a good thing to keep safe from them. Under the money lay a rubber Halloween skeleton we called Boney Benny. The kids and I liked to play with that skeleton, so I'd get it out for them. But the coffin always stayed up too high for them. I don't know why. I liked the money being in a coffin, as if I were disturbing my grave whenever I took out a twenty.

Dave was a tech guy almost before there were tech guys. The library job where he made the coffins must have been an in between gig. He wrote a story once about a bialy that goes wild and makes outrageous demands. He wrote poems, too, and someone published an essay about his poems, though I don't know if Dave published his poems, and it seemed like there were only a handful of them. He didn't consider himself a poet, or didn't think he was good enough, in spite of the essay about him. He was so alluring. I visited him often in his New York apartment, though I lived in the Midwest in various states. Across the street from his place was a heroin outlet. It was called "Mad." When the coast was clear, the dealers came out in the street and called "Mad is open! Mad is open!" Despite my terror of his violent neighborhood, I stayed with him whenever I was visiting. Once I went to a movie on Waverly Place alone. I enjoyed the movie, though all through it ran an undertone of fear of my walk home by myself at close to midnight. It didn't occur to me to take a cab, or to get Dave or another friend to meet me. I walked back to Dave's place in the cold and dark, head down, quick steps. A man in a black leather coat swept up to me, arms outstretched, the coat billowing behind him. He yelled something at me. I ran out into the street and kept on going. Dave and his friends thought I was so cute, their little friend from Michigan. I kept my terror to myself. Once one of Dave's friends found my box of tampons in Dave's bathroom. He came out with it in his hands. "Look, Dave's got his period!" I had to confess it was mine, I was the guilty menstruator.

Dave did heroin. He seemed ashamed of himself for doing it, but it was also a big city bad boy thing that he seemed proud of. He was from dreadful suburban Texas. I only saw him do it once. It was at a party around the corner. After he shot up, his big boner shone through his tight pants. I couldn't stand it, and left. He slept until about three in the afternoon. Everyone loved him so much. His friends sat by his bed and talked to him when he couldn't get up. I sat there with Larry Odegard, Larry and I talking to each other about *The Prison House of Language* across Dave, Dave not saying much. We loved him. He had the best books. He had a tiny chapbook of some letters between a Dada poet and his friend. The Dada poet couldn't get out of France because of the Nazis. He wrote apologetically to his friend that he couldn't come visit. He wasn't writing much anymore. It was really hard to write poems these days. He was sorry even his letters weren't much. Not much happening here of note, he wrote. I mean, everything is terrible. Unimaginable. I wish I could come to England or New York and do those literary things you're inviting me to do, but I can't right now, because of the war. If you have any money you can get to me, that would be great. I can't see putting out the new edition. I don't have the time for it. It's not really very good anyway. Thanks for being so kind about it. Maybe later, when things are better.

2 Car

I read that a sign of low morale in a workplace is when the cars in the employee lot are backed into the slots. That means that when the workers drive in, they're already thinking about getting out. I used to never see this where I work, but now I see it every morning. The lot is really tight. It's hard to pull out in the afternoon, and often other cars are coming in at that time. It makes sense to back into the slot if you get there early enough. I won't do it, though.

Once I saw my friend Roberta sitting in her car talking on the phone well after eight A.M. She was probably talking to her daughter. Often the car next to me sits idling, and I wonder why the driver doesn't get out. They're waiting for their song to end. I do that, too. I can't bear to turn off the music. About the only place I listen to music is in the car. It's like my symphony hall. That car has four seats, and room in the back for the dog. But it's me by myself and the music, the beat coming up through the seat. It goes right up the spine that way, tantric. Music is much sexier in a car. I don't doubt that. Everyone must feel that way. Getting out of the car in the morning—turning the radio off and opening the door, taking out my bag and lunch, shutting the door, locking it with the clicker—is like shutting off my carnality. Gone for the day. Click. The lights flash, the horn beeps. The locks whump in. Very secure. Final. Getting back into the car at the end of the day is not like stepping back into carnality. It's the news, and traffic.

3 Doors

Dave and I made up a story once about doors. The doors had had enough of being flung aside and went on a one-day strike. Always difficult, temperamental, they groaned on their hinges, but we had ignored them over and over again. So they sank into the floor. They left only emptiness, open gaps. The scent of jasmine from the garden blew into my mother's house. Next door, the seven Zweifler kids rushed in and out through the blank portals. They made their own commotion even without the percussive slams and bangs. The oldest and most beautiful of the Zweifler girls, Tonya, ran out to meet her much older boyfriend. The car doors too had joined the communal action. "Let's go, let's go," she said to nasty Rick, all cigarettes and weed and stringy hair. He gunned it, but without that vicious thunk of steel sealing the chassis, her escape lacked conviction.

Evelyn in Room 308 at the Hyatt sat staring at her knees. She'd been planning this meeting with her lover for months. Even if he was late, yet again, like he always was, these couple hours would be worth it. Now it was ruined. They weren't going to get up to much without a door to close out the rest of the world. The dolled-up call girls in the Blue Lounge sighed into their gin and tonics. They wouldn't give up, though. It would all be okay. Stall the elevator between floors. Use the landings on the back stairwell. They preferred lean, anonymous condom sex. That's what they were paid for. Bending over the railing, stockings shredded around their thighs while he pounded it in from behind, quick, fierce, terrified of being seen—it had been years since sex thrilled them. They didn't want to get used to that.

Then what happened, Dave asked.

I didn't know. He had to do the rest of it.

The doors conferred. Did anyone even miss them? Everything ran right on time without them. The Jehovah's Witnesses walked directly into front hallways and plunked down their pamphlets. Mail carriers dumped the bills and shopper stoppers on the porch where there were no slots to stuff them through. Passengers leapt onto the bus and trickled their coins into the fare box.

We should have gotten the windows to come on strike with us, said the doors, Dave said. The walls should have joined us. Why aren't the floors sick of being trampled on? What good is it? No one notices if we're there or not there. We could lay down and die and they'd adjust in minutes.

4 Prayer

Dave made little things out of fruit. He put tangerines on the radiator, where they shriveled and dried. They developed gridded lines on their bottoms, where they pressed into the metal. Their sides collapsed into dimples and irregularities. The skin went from glowing with oil to brusquely leathery, and they weighed almost nothing once all the juice evaporated. He gave one to me, and I kept it for years in my kitchen. Once he took the stem from a bunch of bananas, set it up on its knob, and stuck razor blades through a couple of the ends. It held the blades up in its arms, like a blackened spider wielding weapons. It must have been quite a special bunch of bananas, that he could get the stems to stand up. He gave me this one too, but I didn't hang onto it. I might have thrown it away.

Dave had a friend who was also staying with him one time when I was visiting. "You're so sweet and mild, Dave's little friend," said this friend. He wanted me to come lie down with him in Dave's bed while Dave was out, and scratch him all over with bottle caps. He was sure I could make him bleed, and would revel in it. He seemed to see it in my eyes, that I would be game for this, if he asked me outright. The innocent way I carried myself, how I sat on the edge of Dave's bed reading, was what attracted him.

Later Dave apologized for his friend's behavior. "He told me," Dave said, "that he lay in the bedroom praying that you'd come in there." He laughed, like it was no big deal.

He didn't know I had been praying from under my blanket on Dave's couch that I wouldn't go in there. ❧

rediVider

a journal of new literature and art

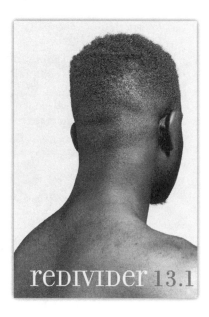

 redividerjournal.org

 facebook.com/redivider

 @redividermag

Jenny Offill's DEPT. OF SPECULATION

Angela Palm

It's difficult to cobble together the time needed to generate creative work when a full-time job or a child's preschool hours or both dictate your schedule. For me, that kind of scheduled creative writing time usually results in falling down Internet rabbit holes that produce a fat load of nothing. After finishing revisions to my essay collection this summer, I had planned to return to working on my novel-in-progress in small chunks of time when I wasn't working my other jobs or caring for kids. Not only did this plan work completely against the nature of creating art and novel writing in particular, but I'd also gotten so deeply wrapped up in the braided essay that I found it hard to abandon the malleability of that form in favor of a linear prose narrative that would force me to write within the confines of a three-act structure. In short: I was stuck and bored. I can't work on writing that doesn't excite me. I wasn't ready to let the braided essay go just yet, but I had exhausted all the essayistic material I had in me.

When I can't write, I read, an act that feels close enough to writing to count for something. It warms the engine when it's cold. So I began reading Jenny Offill's second novel, *Dept. of Speculation*, recommended to me by several essay writers, and I finished it in a single day. It obliterated my reluctance to attempt fiction again. Sometimes you encounter exactly the right book at exactly the right time, as if it has found you rather than you it. *Dept. of Speculation* restored my love of novels in the best way.

"Life equals structure plus activity," says the book's protagonist. So, too, does a novel, where characters do and say things within sequenced scenes in which actions rise, climax, and fall. But not in this book. *Dept. of Speculation* has no true scenes—only flashes of scene work separated by white space. There is a bit of quoted dialogue between characters, but it's relayed piecemeal and in retrospect rather than at length in a clearly described setting which the author has carefully constructed. This book is arranged, instead, as an extended braided essay that weaves together in short and occasionally disjointed paragraphs a domestic narrative told from the perspective of a young mother reflecting on the slow dissolution of her marriage and poetic asides that speculate on the nature of, well, everything. Including: whether animals other than humans experience loneliness, the nuts and bolts of consciousness, the innerworkings of the human brain, the existence of souls. My reaction: *Eureka! This is what a novel can be!*

But it was more than the book's structure that excited me. The protagonist's central problem is stated early on in the text: "My plan was never to get married. I was going to be an art monster instead." But she fell in love, got married, and had a baby. Well, a miscarriage and then a baby. A colicky baby. Having had a colicky baby myself, I was familiar with the sort of suspended love that cocoons such a child, the suspended life that his primary caregiver experiences, the strange loneliness that creeps in between the constant sense of failing at one of the most basic human roles and a relentless love. "The animal was ascendant," the mother states of her love for her new infant. Then, there was colic. This mother also soon discovers that she is the mother who is late to drop-off, the mother who forgets the plastic egg carton for preschool, the mother whose art stalls, the mother who was once and apparently still is lonely.

"There is still such a crookedness in my heart. I had thought loving two people so much would straighten it."

Here, I realize that the story this novel's unconventional structure houses is very similar to my own life. When I read *Dept. of Speculation*, my seventh wedding anniversary had just passed. I had two young sons and a husband who traveled frequently for work. I often dropped my kids off, just in time for school, in a state of semi-wakefulness—fresh out of bed hair, a combination of pajamas and street clothes that were already doused in coffee. I'd look around at the other parents: happy, well dressed, chipper, hair combed and styled. What was I doing wrong?

For a while, I'd thought I was just unhappy, or lonely maybe, despite being crowded by two boisterous children almost constantly. Then I realized that I wasn't unhappy, or lonely even, but maybe that part is a stretch—there is still a crookedness in my heart. I was very happy when I was writing or doing research for writing or reading in an attempt to start writing or going to hear readings given by other writers. I was happy when I was editing work for other writers. The problem was that being an art monster and a mother and a wife at the same time was challenging. Jenny Offill nails this in *Dept. of Speculation*; she aptly captures the precarious position of the art-monster-mother who is in a relationship with a non-art-monster as well as all the problems that follow.

In this predicament, the art monster must initiate an aversion of crisis or else enter a full-on crisis. I initiated mine by seeking a writing residency and eating a lot of popcorn. *Dept. of Speculation*'s narrator initiates hers by shifting from a first-person point of view to a third-person point of view. This allows her to consider her position as "the wife" and "the mother" from a more detached vantage. From this perspective, she is able to inspect her relationships differently: ". . . every marriage is jerry-rigged. Even the ones that look reasonable from the outside are held together with chewing gum and wire and string." They are structured to support activity. Here, the classic braided essay with its digressions and white space jerry-rig this novel's form perfectly. ❧

Eleanor

Joyce Ann Underwood

In 2012 the only thing I wanted for Christmas was the black garbage bag that held the diaries of my childhood neighbor, Eleanor. I don't know why I wanted it after all this time; for twelve years it had been left to rot in the storage building behind my mom's house. It sat in the corner of my living room for more than a week after Mom dropped the bag off at my house in Georgia on her way to Tennessee for Christmas. Eventually, my husband grew tired of tripping over it. Fearing that he would throw it out—or worse, begin looking through it—at 4 PM on Christmas Eve, after several days of frantic cooking, cleaning, crafting, and panicking about the upcoming holiday, I opened the bag to commune with the dead.

I had forgotten the ivy-like curls of her letters. I used to think it looked so graceful and elegant when I was a child. Now I could see that what I once found elegant was nothing more than mimicry. It was the writing of a child who had seen the beautiful script of some long dead relative in a family album and attempted their own scribblings in the same fashion. Each letter was meticulously written and re-written over and over until each word was boldly etched into the paper that still smelled like her.

The woman, her home, and now so many years later, these papers held a particular sweet and acrid odor. My whole life, I had known that scent and while it might sting the nose of anyone else, it held for me a strange yet comfortable familiarity. Everyone has a unique and personal odor. This is neither bad nor good—it simply is. A person's home will take on their odor, but sometimes the house is the source of scent instead.

Eleanor had not lived in a house at all—but then again, no one I knew did at the time. At least, not anyone I was close to. Single-wides, double-wides, modified trailers, and RVs; these were the status quo. She was the only person I have ever known to live in an Airstream trailer. A great silver bullet glistening in the sun, it had always been there, just to the right of my life. I assumed it would be there forever.

Widowed with no children, no driver's license, and no telephone, Eleanor relied on the assistance of my parents who saw her as both an obligation and a burden. If they didn't look after her, who would? She hadn't had a driver's license since I was a very small child; the cars in her yard had been sitting, gathering rust for as long as I could remember. When I was in the second grade the county decided that we had to clean up our yard which was littered with appliances in various stages of assembly. My dad was a handy-man by trade and he made a decent living off of repairing washers, dryers, refrigerators, and air conditioners. One of my favorite toys as a child was a washer drum which I could hide inside, roll on top of, or roll down the hill toward the swamp and chase. I saw our yard as an ever-changing playground, but the county saw it as an eyesore and made us clean up or face what was sure to be a crippling fine. Eleanor's derelict cars were included in the order but later removed when the county realized that she wasn't going to clean up her yard no matter what they threatened. Meanwhile, my dad had a heart attack in the process of cleaning up ours.

She would only come out at night, and then, only around the time her widow's pension from Social Security check came in the mail. All month I watched her door from my bedroom window with rapt attention for signs of her eminent emergence. Rarely did anything of interest happen in my drama-deprived childhood. It was a good day when the cows escaped from the pasture at the end of the dirt road and made a break for the paved county road. They never made it; cows are slow and the dirt road was half a mile or more. For a small child though, there's nothing more exciting than to find your yard host to a dozen head of cattle who at any moment may have decided to charge at your home. The red house we lived in until I was six was built by hand from a pole barn and salvaged materials my dad was able to cobble together into a livable construction. I'm not sure that it could have withstood the barrage of a disgruntled bull. Sadly, cattle escapes were even more infrequent than the visits from our neighbor.

When I was in the first grade we upgraded to a double-wide mobile home that was closer to her property than the red house had been. I would often walk over to her Airstream and talk to her through the door. As far as I was concerned, her yard was my yard. There were no fences, and Eleanor had no problem with me playing around the semi-trailer and derelict cars that littered her un-mowed lawn. Anytime I was in her yard, I could hear the multitude of doves she kept as pets cooing from inside her trailer.

My parents were usually less than thrilled with me whenever they caught me over there; this was Florida and rattlesnakes were a realistic fear. When they told her they would cut her grass: "I like my jungle!" she would say. My mom and dad didn't want her snakes inevitably migrating into our yard; when out of desperation they mowed it anyway she would insist on giving them some money for their efforts.

Eleanor didn't seem to have any problems with snakes, or any form of life for that matter. They were all God's creations as far as she was concerned. Once, a tiny scrub pine began to grow right next to the window of the Airstream's back bedroom. My parents offered to cut it down as it would eventually cause structural damage to the trailer. Eleanor wouldn't hear of it: "It's my lonesome pine. It's like me. I love it." Maybe she felt that her life was worth less than that of the snakes, trees, and grass. Or, maybe she didn't anticipate being around long enough for the nature she let grow up around her to cause her any real problems.

I found Eleanor more interesting than most of the kids at school. Through the door of the Airstream, we would talk about *Unsolved Mysteries*, space aliens, and science fiction movies. She was the only person I knew (aside from my best friend Heather, another *Unsolved Mysteries* fan) who thought there might actually be aliens and ghosts. I loved hearing all the old science fiction movies she's seen and couldn't wait to see them myself. *The Day the Earth Stood Still* was each of our favorites.

As I got older I told her about the boys I liked, although she would often get their names confused.

"I saw your boyfriend, Brady, at Miller's last night."

"No," I would laugh. "He's not my boyfriend. He's just a friend in the high school band. He's too old for me to date. I want to date William."

"Oh yes, William, George's friend?"

"Yeah. If we were together, we could double with George and Heather."

Eleanor seemed to be interested in what I was saying and she didn't have any compunction about the fact that I was twelve years old and talking about going on double dates with boys in the tenth grade. Her husband had been thirty-seven years older than her. In her eyes, William and I were practically the same age, and in my childhood, this view of age differences was the norm. My dad was twenty-nine years older than my mom. I never considered that there was anything unusual about setting my sights on high school boys while I was in the sixth grade. Just not Brady; he was a senior, after all.

"It's kind of funny, George plays the trombone and Heather plays the clarinet, so they are in different sections: brass and woodwinds. I play the trumpet and William plays the saxophone, so I'm brass and he's woodwinds. It would make more sense for me to date George and for Heather to date William, but Heather and George are in love and I love William whether he likes me or not. He's got the most beautiful eyes."

Such is the logic of a sixth grade girl, and Eleanor never questioned it.

When Eleanor wanted to go to town she would come over late the night before to ask if my mom would drive her the following day. Eleanor would always emerge from the Airstream after dark; she considered herself a night owl, mostly because it was cooler at night. She slept during the heat of the day with tinfoil and black garbage bags blocking out any light from the outside—an effort to keep the interior of the Airstream cool.

Conversely, my parents were the type of people who didn't leave the house after dark. If I needed something from town, I had better tell my mom about it before 5 o'clock or I could forget about it until the next day. I used to be very on top of school projects. I'd buy all my poster board and supplies the same day a project was assigned to avoid needing something at 8 PM the night before it was due. As an adult I have learned that my parents' stance on leaving the house after dark was not the norm. My husband's mother had been known to take his sister to Wal-Mart at all hours of the night for that one "must have" item for a project due the next day. My mom would have let me fail.

The only time my mom could be found in town after dinner time was on nights she had taken Eleanor to the store. They would leave the house at a reasonable enough hour, usually after I got out of school. Once or twice Eleanor was with my mom when she picked me up from the bus stop.

"Hey Joyce, is that your grandma?"

"No, that's my neighbor."

If I'm being honest, I wished she was my grandma even though she wasn't much older than my mom. There was something about her that struck me as youthful. She was as good a candidate for grandparent as any, though. I didn't have any. My Pa-Pa died when I was three and the rest of my grandparents had been dead since long before I was an accident waiting to happen.

On the nights she came over to ask for a ride to town, my parents would often leave me to deal with her while they went inside to get ready for bed. Her visits could be at any time between 7 and 10 PM and I was the only person in the house who didn't seem to care. I liked when she came over. I liked talking to her, and I liked how adult I felt when my mom and dad foisted her off on me.

Mom and Dad can't handle her, but *I* can.

She would stand and talk to me under the glow of the porch light about anything from alien theories to the morning show on the radio. If it was a week night, I would have to go to bed around ten, but if it was a weekend, we could talk for hours.

"Don't you need to go to bed, Joyce Ann?" The way she said my name sounded so different in her Baltimore accent, which to my North Floridian ears was nearly alien.

"No, it's Saturday. I'm staying up for *Tales from the Crypt* at 12:30."

"When I was a little girl," Eleanor would tell me, "I used to sneak out of bed and watch scary movies after my parents had gone to bed. I used to have terrible nightmares from that. Don't you ever get nightmares?"

"No, not really," I'd reply. "I like scary stuff."

On the nights my mother took her to the store, she would keep the supermarket open for hours after closing time. The management dreaded seeing her come in, but they were always very polite to her. Everyone at Miller's called her "Rainbow Brite" after the rainbow colored clips she wore in her jet black hair and her brightly colored attire. I always liked the way she dressed, even if it was dated and a bit garish. One of her dresses was beige with great big floral arrangements all over it. It looked like it might have had another life as a couch.

When my mom would finally pick her up from Miller's, close to midnight, Eleanor would have two carts full of food. She shopped for the entire month all at once and she would always buy more than she could accommodate in her tiny home. The mornings after Eleanor went shopping were like Christmas for me. She would send home all sorts of things my mom never bought, like *real* Pop Tarts, Basic 4 cereal, and Breyer's Natural Cherry Ice Cream. She was the type of person to have given away everything she had to help someone in need. God would have wanted it. The trouble was, we weren't in need. My mom and dad would try every way in the world to get her to keep the groceries she forced on them, but she would insist that they take several bags in return for helping her.

When we took her grocery shopping it was easy to see that the refuse on the floor of the Airstream was at least knee deep throughout the entire place. More came into the tiny structure than ever came out of it. She slept in the living room because the bedroom was too full of trash. Conditions had deteriorated gradually over the years. By May of 1998, the septic line was backing up and exposed. She no longer had running water. The electrical system was faulty, only supplying enough power for an oscillating fan and a small portable television which itself eventually gave up the ghost.

As summer approached, there was a drought and wildfires raged throughout the state. The temperatures reached record highs nearly every day. One by one, the doves she kept were dying in the heat, their little tongues hanging out of their beaks desperate for water and cool, fresh air. She told us all of this, weeping, through the door on nights when my mother would beg her to come out and accept some help. Despite the heat and the inadequate living conditions, Eleanor chose to remain sealed up inside that aluminum sarcophagus, all alone except for the birds. My mother sought to have her involuntarily institutionalized via the "Baker Act" but this course of action failed. The Sherriff declared that she was neither mentally ill nor a harm to herself or someone else in the eyes of the State of Florida. She was a grown woman and free to remain in her own home if that was her choice.

Never mind the fact that she had blocked out all light and air with a combination of black garbage bags, newspaper, and tinfoil over all the windows. We worried that the wildfires would reach our neck of the swamp and she would refuse to leave even as the flames threatened to engulf her entirely. For weeks, we pleaded with her to at least come sit with us in our trailer for a little while—to enjoy the air and a nice shower. Even as the temperature rose, each day she politely and steadfastly refused.

Eventually, my mother gave up. No one was concerned about the situation, least of all the woman herself, so what more could my mother do? She stopped walking over to talk to Eleanor through the door. Throwing her hands up in despair, Mom took to her chair to silently worry while chewing on the remnants of her nails.

The tension in the house was palpable. I lived for Tuesday and Thursday mornings when marching band practice provided me with my only means of escaping the house. I was twelve years old; it's not like I could drive. On those afternoons I did my best to use up the rest of my day in the company of my best friend Heather. At her house I could escape the scene that had grown unmanageable. At my house, I felt safe in her shadow.

June 18, 1998 was a Thursday. Heather had come home with me. I thought I was safe. We were doing what middle school girls did in Crescent City—chatting about high school boys and listening to Usher. That day, in addition to what I can only assume was yet another discussion of boys, Heather was teaching me some new techniques for making friendship bracelets. She had been making them for years, her graceful fingers deftly weaving differently colored silk threads into flat, geometric patterns. Works in progress were always pinned to her purse for easy access, leaving the unwoven threads to trail behind her as she walked. I could not seem to learn the technique that Heather was trying to teach me. That afternoon, as the seventh grade loomed before me, my greatest concern was that I only knew how to create a rudimentary style with a rib running in a spiral up the side of the rounded chord.

At some point we foolishly decided that we might venture out of my bedroom into the living room. I can't imagine why. Maybe we heard my mom and dad talking about Eleanor and our emergence was an attempt to diffuse what was sure to become a tense situation. Even if that was not the reason—it became the subject when my dad asked us to run next door to check on her. We gladly accepted.

While I was intensely uncomfortable with the climate the Eleanor situation had wrought under my roof, I was still intrigued by the situation itself. I had no idea how serious it really was. Eleanor would be fine. She had always been there. Eventually someone would get her to come out. Why shouldn't it be me and Heather? We would be heroes.

The afternoon was hot, but cooler than the morning had been. The sky was overcast, threatening to deliver much needed rain. The air was wet and thick with smoke from the fires. We bounded over to the Airstream with light hearts. If nothing else, it would be fun to talk to Eleanor for a moment, and I felt some sort of pleasure in performing a job from which my mother had informally resigned. We leaned our heads into the hot metal and I knocked on the door.

Silence.

I knocked again. "Eleanor? Are you okay?"

Silence.

Heather and I looked at one another. Fear began to creep upon us. I knocked louder. "Eleanor, it's Joyce and Heather. You remember Heather? Her boyfriend is George?"

Silence.

I pounded on the door and waited, holding my breath. I heard a faint cough. I waited. Speech was usually precluded by these faint coughs. She was like a bird in that way, cooing before she spoke. I looked at Heather. She looked at me. Then we heard a crash.

We hauled ass back to the house, swearing panicky oaths under our breath.

The rest is a blur. 911 was called. A first responder arrived. I remember being there, just outside the door, when he found only a small piece of twine holding it closed. That fact alone would be enough to haunt my mother for the rest of her life. I remember seeing him cut it with a pair of medical scissors.

This memory of being there conflicts with my memory of the ambulance. Maybe after the first responder found her on top of the trash, my mother sent Heather and I back to the house? I almost remember being told to leave—why don't I remember being made to stay at the house in the first place? Was I really there, or is this a creation of my overactive imagination? My mother is the only person who could say for sure, and we don't talk about this day.

By the time the ambulance arrived, the yard was chaos. When you call 911, you get police, paramedics, first responders, and firefighters. They all bring their own service vehicles. A rainbow of flashing lights littered the scene as I watched. It was like a silent movie. A tableaux projected onto the silver screen of the afternoon sky, her naked body the only bit of black and white in this colorized presentation. The stretcher was a litter carrying her to her chariot, her jet black hair the only bit of darkness on her pale grey body.

The chaos departed as quickly as it had descended, and soon I found myself alone with Usher and my own multi-colored silk thread. I had a safety pin attached to a pillow on my bed and I was knotting the colors into a chord with rib spiraling up one side. My head was down, my jaw was set. My actions belied my anxiety, but my brain was set on convincing the rest of me that it was all going to be alright.

My mind raced. "Her sister, Dolores, will come down from Baltimore. While Eleanor's recovering, we'll get her house fixed. Eleanor will finally let us come in her house after this. We'll watch science fiction movies and I'll tell her all about all the boys I like. She'll finally get to hear me play my trumpet. It's all going to be okay. It's all going to be okay. It's all going to be okay..." All the while, making tiny and precise knots out of colored string like her life depended on it. However, campfire crafts do not save lives.

She died in the ambulance.

When the paramedics took her temperature on the way to the hospital, it was 108 degrees. The health department was concerned about meningitis. The trailer went under quarantine until the autopsy proved that her death was caused by nothing more than heat stroke, brought about by the June sun beating down on a metal oven with no ventilation.

Somehow, two of the doves outlived her. We found the others, the dead, during the expedition to save those that remained and to unearth long forgotten papers—titles and wills and all those things that are only important when someone has ceased to be.

When my mother breached the threshold of the Airstream called home, I thought I was there just because I didn't want to miss anything. I wanted to be part of the story. I couldn't have known at the time that I was trying to make sense of Eleanor's story. I was so excited when my mother pulled out that blue tub full of tenderly wrapped parcels. In my experience, treasures were wrapped and stored in that way. Porcelain knick knacks or glass trinkets. Christmas ornaments. Fine china. Family heirlooms. I looked on expectantly. What was dear to her? Birds. Dead birds—individually wound in death shrouds made of toilet paper in the way that I wrapped my favorite fragile things.

Other than dead things, garbage, and the legal papers that spurred our intrusion in the first place, there was nothing left of this woman except some books, her notebooks and papers, and the flag from her husband's casket. These are the things that I pulled from the black garbage bag on Christmas Eve 2012. I suddenly needed some answers as to why. This bag that had been occupying my floor space and perfuming my home with the smell of decay contained the last remaining pieces of her consciousness—of her life—yet I could not find the words to explain why this thing that looked like garbage was so important to me. Maybe I thought if I could find one piece of paper that made some sense I could say "Look! There was a reason!"

If you have ever handled something that has sat derelict for a time, you are familiar with the particular odor that paper acquires. Musty books are famous for this—handling them leaves your hands feeling chalky and unclean, as my hands did when I looked through what was left of Eleanor's life. I waited more than half my life to find the courage for this moment. I thought I might find some insights on her offbeat interests, some reflections on her relationship with my family, or some vaguely logical reason for her dying the way she did. I needed a reason why she stayed in that gleaming metal tube long after the electricity and plumbing had stopped working. Why she stayed even as smoke hung heavy in the air from the fires that threatened to consume us all.

I pulled out a notebook and began to read and in that beautiful, delicate hand there were pages and pages of the same things.

Over.

And over.

And over.

"A woman on Star Trek – not ever part of me."
"The Jews are behind the AIDS virus."
"To live this way, one must have faith in God."

There were around twenty or thirty thoughts or variations on those thoughts. They were written repeatedly, frantically, obsessively on page after page of tablets, notebooks, and various sundry scraps of paper. I dug through the bag, searching for some coherent thought. Some idea as to why she chose to live the way she did. There was none.

There were thoughts on faith, rants on esoteric religious orders, and musings on new age philosophy. There was little to no variation in the sentences; the same sentence written in 1979 would appear in a notebook dated 1991. One sentence would repeat until it filled an entire page, or several pages. Letters were written and re-written, and written again, with almost no variation. I had seen this in movies, but I thought it was exaggeration. Artistic license. Cinematic hyperbole. This cannot be real.

But there it was.

I dug through and began to scrutinize everything I found that said "1998." Maybe there was something. There had to be. In April or May she apparently ran out of paper and took to writing notes on a 1998 calendar. There was very little at this point, and as time went on the writing deteriorated in both substance and style. What was once merely mental illness had, through the heat and living conditions, deteriorated into something else—dementia? My name was a footnote across the twelve years I had existed. L. Ron Hubbard's *Dianetics* (a copy of which I found in the bag with her writings) got more mention in her notes than I did. My name appeared once.

Throughout the years I must have thought that when I finally found the courage to look through the bag I would find some sort of justifiable reason for her actions. Maybe it was a religious thing, like the Christian Scientists. She put her faith in God, but she forgot that He only helps those who help themselves. I thought that in solving the mystery of her life and death, I might have some closure, and that I might also learn something about myself.

Conceited though it may be, I wanted to see myself through her eyes. I was the only person who did not shy away from her—the only person who genuinely enjoyed and even sought out her company, and I barely warranted a mention in her delirious compositions.

I sat on the floor for hours that night, moving paper, reading, leafing, searching, and soon I was surrounded by the remnants of her tragic, lonely life. All that was left of her were words and the smell; these remain with me. I was surrounded by words, and yet I could find none to express what this all meant to me and what it should mean to anyone else. She listened to me when I spoke, and I listened to her—but in sitting among her thoughts, I realized that perhaps we had both listened without understanding. I thought I knew her best and I found that I knew nothing. ❧

Ann Patchett

Kim Ablon Whitney

"What's your dream job, Mom?" My nine-year-old son asked the other day.

I had to think about it for a while, wondering if I should have taken another path than the one I did. Then I concluded, "Writer."

"So you *have* your dream job?" he said.

"Sort of," I replied. "I guess in my dream world I'd see people on the T reading my books. I'd be a much more popular writer."

"Like Rick Riordan?" he asked.

"Yeah, like Rick Riordan."

"So in your dream world, you'd be Rick Riordan." This was a statement, not a question. Even at nine, my son appreciates the difference between still-need-a-day-job author and *New York Times* Bestselling author.

As for me, I could definitely imagine being Rick Riordan. He's written many commercially popular books for kids, thereby keeping kids reading (especially the ever difficult boys) and made a good living along the way. That all sounds pretty appealing to me.

This got me thinking, though. If I could *actually* be any writer, who would I be?

I'm not talking have their life exactly, but write their books. Sorry Rick, I think you're great, but it wouldn't be you.

I'd choose Ann Patchett.

The first book I read of Ann Patchett's was *Bel Canto*. I wasn't dying to read it because I knew it was about opera, which didn't appeal to me at all. But someone passed along a copy to me and I knew it had gotten really great reviews and won awards so I turned to the first page.

I started it and was blown away. It was about opera, but it made opera interesting to me. And it wasn't only about opera, of course. It was simply a great story.

After *Bel Canto*, I read every book Ann wrote. Turns out they're all great, from the *Patron Saint of Liars* to *State of Wonder*. Some writers tend to write similar stories and that's not the worst thing. But I think it's entirely cool that each of Ann's books explores a completely different world. I'd like to know how she gets the ideas for these books and how, for that matter, she brings those worlds to life. How does she pull off opera, a home for unwed mothers, and medical innovation in the Amazon rainforest?

She seems to have mastered one of the hardest things in the world of books—she writes beautifully and at the same time has books with plots that move and keep the reader turning each page. She bridges the widening gap between what people call fiction and literature. She rightfully wins literary awards and probably makes a living off her sales to boot.

Turns out she also does non-fiction amazingly well. I devoured *Truth and Beauty*, about her friendship with Lucy Grealy, *This is a Story of a Happy Marriage* about her family and marriage, and her slimmer ebook *The Getaway Car* with advice on writing.

After all this, I found out that Ann even started her own bookstore in Nashville. Wait, maybe I want her whole life after all. ❧

Mafiosa

Suzanne Roszak

The seventh time they laugh about
my homicidal male relatives, I recall

the back of my father's truck plastered over

for peace. *Free Leonard Peltier*, the bumper
commands as we crest the hill, each of us

longhaired and flying a limb out

the open window like a cheerful flag of
surrender. This is what I recall

while they delight in the glistening

outlines of my father's imaginary
violence, to be realized in the manner

of a village clan with tanned faces

avenging something: maybe the town's guts
emptied out, figures passing through

stone houses, down the hill, into the sea.

Elegy for the Quiet House

Suzanne Roszak

It is a story for telling and not telling. A story
for floating, for tying down

with weights. A story for braiding
and re-braiding into forms

that can be stilled.

Imagine a hundred bright faces
at work. Hanging over the pottery wheel, the cutting

board, the pock-marked rhododendron.
Imagine them as a kaleidoscope

of impossibility: all the shining
repeated permutations

of want.

Move backward. Call up the faded intervals
after noon: kitchen radio static

between maracas and evangelical
tripe. Call up the terrifying force

of sweat. Raw nerves radiate
a pain that insinuates itself

into everything.

Mark it: the boundary
between spectacle and the quiet

house, hearth-fire curled around
the razor elbows of

our future.

Lydia Davis's "Happiest Moment" and the Convoluted Temporalities of Very Short Fiction

Ezra Dan Feldman

When *Sudden Fiction* came out in 1986, collecting short stories from one to five pages long by a host of American authors, the editors, Robert Shapard and James Thomas, wondered what to call the volume and the genre. They settled on *Sudden Fiction* after abandoning the working title *Blasters*, which some of their contacts loved but others reviled. Of the name *Sudden Fiction*, Shapard writes in the introduction that "[a]lmost everyone liked it, not only for the sound of it, but for its representation of the form."[1] Given the title's invocation of the temporal, it is perhaps ironic that the introduction is mostly about space—about the capacity of the short-short to "confer form on small corners of chaos."[2] Since the primary consideration of the very short story from a publisher's perspective seems to be the space it takes up on the page, this is understandable, and in *Flash Fiction* (1992), Thomas gives some thought to the experience of fiction that may be apprehended "all at once," that is, without turning a page.[3]

Nonetheless, the choice of *Sudden Fiction* as the title for the 1986 collection and as label for the form invites the considerations of time which Robert Coover takes up properly in "A Sudden Story," but which Shapard only invokes rather mystically at the end of his introduction. "If [short short stories] can stop time and make it timeless," Shapard suggests, "they are here for you, above all, as living voices."[4] One can even detect Shapard turning *away* from time as soon as the issue comes up. Explaining the editors' satisfaction with the title, originally suggested in a letter from Robert Kelly, Shapard writes, "So, for the present—at least for the present book—the debate ends."[5] Having speculated on the meaning of the short form's new, perhaps sudden, prominence on the American literary scene, Shapard drops the focus on the literary-historical moment, the present time of "for the present," in favor of the present object, "the present book." Nearly thirty years have passed since the publication of *Sudden Fiction*. The editors have stuck with the name-scheme,

---

1 Sudden Fiction: American Short-Short Stories. *Shapard, Robert, and James Thomas, eds. Salt Lake City: G.M. Smith, 1986. p. xvi.*

2 *Ibid.*

3 *Thomas, James. "Introduction," in* Flash Fiction: Very Short Stories. *Thomas, James, Denise Thomas, and Tom Hazuka, eds. New York: Norton, 1992. p. 12.*

4 Sudden Fiction. *p. xvi.*

5 *Ibid.*

publishing *Sudden Fiction International* (1989), *Sudden Fiction Continued* (1996), *New Sudden Fiction* (2007), and *Sudden Fiction Latino* (2010). But it is not clear that anyone else is using the term, even though short short stories remain cool. This may indeed be because of the conceptual difficulty in treating very short fiction as a unified genre.

The diverse notes on the form that appear as a kind of appendix to the original *Sudden Fiction* make a good starting place for thinking through the form's potential. Kelly's very brief essay, "Sudden Fiction: Notes on Fiction That Knows Its Proper Space," seems to suggest an acceleration of life and narrative made possible by television and movies: "People who grew up, ourselves, with movies and television had less and less *need* for descriptive exposition, though at the same time a sustained hunger for instantaneous entrainment of place, mood, scene, atmosphere. The coup d'oeil that movies gave us is what short fiction has learned to enact."[6] Today, however, we are more likely to think of short short fiction in the context of sound bites, tweets, texts, and Facebook status updates, snippets of text that often vanish almost instantaneously but can also go viral, taking on a significance that lets them persist in our media and our culture. Short short fiction can treat its own material in much the same way, either turning over and reproducing a phrase until it carries the weight of a life, or else passing instantaneously on. If the ultra-short form holds together as a set of spatially constrained texts, it can nonetheless be temporally capacious in surprising ways. In what follows I explore three temporalities of very short fiction: the *instantaneous present*, in which time nearly stops; the *capacious present*, in which a lifetime can appear and occur and be comprehended all at once; and the *speculative present*, the convoluted temporality of my title, which can dip with ease into the past and future, but always lingers as a set of open questions or open possibilities for character and reader alike.

The instantaneous present is legible in a story like Dan O'Brien's "Crossing Spider Creek." The protagonist, a man with a broken and bleeding leg, is trying to get his horse to cross a cold creek, and if he cannot get the horse to cross, he will die. He has tried twice, and twice the horse has turned back. He imagines that if the horse turns this last time (the last attempt for which the man has the energy), he will try to pull his rifle from its scabbard and shoot the horse, too, so that they can die together. This fiction offers enough backstory that we know a bit about the man and a bit about Carol, whose favorite horse he is riding and who "has never understood his desire to be alone."[7] But the story opens and closes in a single instant: "Here is a seriously injured man on a frightened

---

6 Sudden Fiction. *p. 240.*

7 Flash Fiction. *p. 29.*

horse" it begins.[8] And it ends: "Here is a seriously injured man on a frightened horse. They are standing at the edge of Spider Creek, the horse's trembling front feet in the water and the man's spurs held an inch from the horse's flanks."[9] The story offers repetition *without* difference. It gives a still scene, explains the scene, and gives it to us a second time. We may think of the image (both opening and final) as a painting, a snapshot, or a still from a movie. It essentially lacks duration, and since it spells out quite clearly the consequences of both success and failure, the story does not leave us to ponder the significance of what we see. If we are to wonder, we really have only two options: "Will he make it across the creek?" is of course one question, but neither an answerable nor a very interesting one. The other slightly more satisfying question has more than one formulation, but I take the following to be exemplary: "How can it or could it be—why is it permissible in the universe—for so much to depend upon something as small as a colt's shyness or fortitude in crossing some very cold water?" The scope of this question, too, lies beyond the story itself, certainly outside its time.

An instant, frozen and made visual. That the very short story can render this seems natural rather than surprising. More surprisingly, however, the short short story can also dispense almost entirely with the visual on the way to encapsulating an entire life or a whole assembly of similar lives in the space of a very few lines. Robert Coover's "frontistory" in *Sudden Fiction*, called "A Sudden Story," exemplifies the creation of a capacious present despite being set, ostensibly, in the past. "Once upon a time," it begins traditionally enough. Or no: "Once upon a time, suddenly, while it still could, the story began."[10] The formulation insists that the whole story will actually be the beginning of "the story" (whether this very story or another is not known). Coover's metafiction manages both to tell of the hero's encounter with the stupid, forgetful dragon and to insist that suddenness belongs to the dragon's perspective, or to the reader's, but never in fact to the hero's: "For the hero, setting forth, there was of course nothing sudden about it, neither about the setting forth, which he'd spent his entire lifetime anticipating, nor about any conceivable endings, which seemed, like the horizon, to be always somewhere else."[11] Clearly the story might have developed from here as a critique of so-called suddenness. It could have been a rejection of the capacious and forgetful narrative present in favor of full attention to

---

8 Flash Fiction. *p. 30*

9 *Ibid.*

10 Sudden Fiction. *p. vii.*

11 *Ibid.*

concrete history. As for the hero, "he'd been trekking for years through enchanted forests, endless deserts, cities carbonized by dragon breath."[12] But this past is parenthetical, and this particular hero, in his moment of almost-heroism, "found himself envying, as he drew his sword [. . .], the dragon's tenseless freedom."[13]

In this story, the reader, like the dragon, is a devourer, and the reader and the dragon get their meal: "Freedom? the dragon might have asked, had he not been so stupid, chewing over meanwhile the sudden familiar sourness . . ."[14] The hero gets consumed, the hero's perspective erased, when the covers of a book like a dragon's jaws snap shut. So the story affirms the confinement of a long fictional life to the reading present in which we typically encounter it. Long though the fictional life may be, it's all present and only *ever* present in the reading. Although "A Sudden Story" to some degree satirizes reading-as-consuming (after all, the dragon is "stupid") its closing parenthetical—"(Forgotten.)"—also concedes the inevitability of that reading practice. Its capacious present underlines what Kelly calls the "time of the experience of the text" at the cost of underlining the hero's lifeline, as perhaps always happens when a long life is pressed into a very short form.[15] But if such a compression is necessarily metafictional, the resulting self-consciousness isn't alone sufficient to transform the temporality of the narrative from one that winks out when the story is over into one that blossoms and changes on the page and in the mind.

Lydia Davis, unlike Coover, approaches the very short form anti-heroically. It is not, for her, a form that allows forgetting, but rather "a nervous form of story. You don't have time to get used to it (forget it) as you read. It keeps itself more separate from you than a longer story, maybe because it is more recently begun, and so it is more demanding of your attention."[16] This notion that a story can remain, as it goes along, "more recently begun" than another story, is typical of Davis's acute delineation of time.[17] Her prose and her characters bring their pasts along with them, folding past into present into possibility. (They would never be caught tenseless, like Coover's dragon and the hero it chews up.) Davis's stories tend to demand a speculative attention—maybe because her subject

---

12 *Ibid.*

13 *Ibid.*

14 *Ibid.*

15 Sudden Fiction. *p. 240.*

16 Sudden Fiction. *p. 260.*

17 *Ibid.*

matter is so often a feeling of unease, maybe because of her regularly discomfiting syntax. "The Sock," her *Sudden Fiction* contribution, begins by declaring, "My husband is married to a different woman now, shorter than I am, about five feet tall, solidly built, and of course he looks taller than he used to and narrower, and his head looks smaller."[18] The husband in this story is not a bigamist, of course. It's just that the narrator continues to possess him, in memory and in language. The narrator thus economically introduces multiple modalities of time. There is an ongoing present, unmarked so far by events, in which characters have certain legal relationships to one another that elbow out the past: the (ex)husband is married again; the woman has a particular body; the narrator perceives the man who used to be her husband as having changed. Of course he *would* have changed—in real life. But while he might be narrower (thinner) than in the past, he wouldn't be taller and his head wouldn't be smaller in actuality. So besides the ongoing present, the sentence also initializes a running commentary that contravenes the narration. And of course the past is present here, in the phrase "my husband."

Quite a lot of rich detail comes through in Davis's "The Sock," which runs to two-and-a-half pages. We learn about the husband's typical behavior in the past; we learn how his mother's fear of being upstairs in a building has developed over time; and we learn of the narrator's habituation to a new normal. But at the core of the story lies a meditation on the eponymous sock, a focus of the narrator's speculations that catch her out of time:

> It was a small thing, but later I couldn't forget the sock, because here was this one sock in his back pocket in a strange neighborhood way out in the eastern part of the city in a Vietnamese ghetto, by the massage parlors, and none of us really knew this city but we were all here together and it was odd, because I still felt as though he and I were partners, we had been partners a long time, and I couldn't help thinking of all the other socks of his I had picked up, stiff with his sweat and threadbare on the sole, in all our life together from place to place, and then of his feet in those socks, how the skin shone through at the ball of the foot and the heel where the weave was worn down; how he would lie reading on his back on the bed with his feet crossed at the ankles so that his toes pointed at different corners of the room; how he would then turn on his side with his feet together like two halves of a fruit; how, still reading, he would reach down and pull off his socks and drop them in little balls on the floor and reach down again and pick at his toes while he read; sometimes he shared with me what he was reading and thinking, and sometimes he didn't know whether I was there in the room or somewhere else.

---

18 *Sudden Fiction. p. 177.*

I couldn't forget it later, even though after they were gone I found a few other things they had left, or rather his wife had left in the pocket of a jacket of mine – a red comb, a red lipstick, and a bottle of pills.[19]

The sock resists forgetting not by persisting in time, but by drawing the narrator into a speculative mode, a speculative present. This isn't just reminiscence, but a folding over of events that include the recent past ("here was this one sock in his back pocket in a strange neighborhood"), the more distant past ("we had been partners a long time"), and the present of the narration ("I still felt as though he and I were partners"). There is also, embedded in the habitual past of the husband's reading in bed, the bisection of time into two possibilities: "sometimes he shared with me what he was reading and thinking, and sometimes he didn't know whether I was there in the room or somewhere else." The unforgettable sock somehow transports the narrator to the two possibilities equally, and not in the frozen mode of O'Brien's man and horse poised before the rushing water. These possibilities are ongoing, even though they are both past. They hang with the narrator, as with the reader, "later." We can infer that they persist even outside and beyond the time of the narration. Like O'Brien, Davis brings her narrative around to repeating a defining phrase. But while O'Brien's repetition begins verbatim ("Here is a seriously injured man on a frightened horse."), Davis's twists in the mouth and under the eye: "later I couldn't forget the sock, *because* [...]" becomes "I couldn't forget it later, *even though* [...]" This revision, however, doesn't get marked as progress of any kind. The two statements do not have unique places in the plot, but supervene on one another, versions of a single idea that derives its force *both* from its cause and from the resistance it overcomes.

Davis's speculative present is most exquisitely at work in "Happiest Moment," from her 2001 collection, *Samuel Johnson is Indignant*. It reads, in its entirety:

If you ask her what is a favorite story she has written, she will hesitate for a long time and then say it may be this story that she read in a book once: an English-language teacher in China asked his Chinese student to say what was the happiest moment in his life. The student hesitated for a long time. At last he smiled with embarrassment and said that his wife had once gone to Beijing and eaten duck there, and she often told him about it, and he would have to say the happiest moment of his life was her trip, and the eating of the duck.[20]

---

19 Sudden Fiction. *p. 178-179.*

20 *Davis, Lydia.* The Collected Stories of Lydia Davis. *New York: Farrar, Straus and Giroux, 2009. p. 359.*

The story conveys the conjectures and meditations of no fewer than five personae. From the inside out, we can identify, first, the Chinese student's wife, who "often told him" about her trip to Beijing and her eating the duck. Then there is the Chinese student himself, who "would have to say the happiest moment of *his* life was *her* trip" (and how strange is that?). Third is not the English-language teacher, who doesn't report anything, but the author of the book in which the English-language teacher appears. Fourth is the woman, herself an author, who may be asked "what is a favorite story she has written," and finally there is the narrator, whose if-then proposition ought to contain, but fails to encompass, whatever else is told.

All this, of course, leaves out the "you" who may do the asking and with whom the reader may most closely identify. What makes the temporality of "Happiest Moment" so peculiar is that the inner circles of the narrative are more concrete than the outer ones. In a sense, we have a reversal of the usual phenomenon of narratorial unreliability: We are accustomed to thinking of an unreliable narrator as the central object of our investigation, the persona about whom we will certainly learn *something* even if we cannot believe a word she says. Here, however, "the eating of the duck"—divorced syntactically from the person doing it— appears as the story's most concrete core. Around this action, however, we have a set of people who attach value unreliably to that event. The Chinese student presents as the happiest moment of his life something that never happened *to him.* Is this evidence of the depth of his connection to his wife, or does it mean that he can only live vicariously? Why is he embarrassed? Maybe he has misunderstood his teacher's questions.

The same difficulties attach to the unnamed woman author, who is not asked for a "happiest moment" but for "a favorite story she has written." Presumably she hasn't written the story with which she replies. Is she dodging the question? Is she claiming that all reading is writing? Or does her hesitation, like the Chinese student's, imply either a misunderstanding or some kind of interruption to her train of thought?

"Happiest Moment," as a title, contributes to this operation of turning the story inside-out. It conveys the reader's attention past the outer layers of narration, directly to the story's temporal core. The happiest moment, the title says, matters more than the questions that elicit its narration. Nonetheless, the eating of the duck, with which the reader is left as the story's essence, can never serve the reader as a meal, but only as a spur to thought. Without explicitly asking the reader to identify either a favorite story or a happiest moment, these reported questions may lure the reader away from the narrative's most puzzling features.

In the introduction to *Sudden Fiction*, Shapard speculates that "the modern short story was an adaptation of many older story techniques, including those of short-short forms, to the overwhelming popularity of realism and its expansive embodiment, the novel."[21] Though Davis's convoluted temporalities and layered narratives might indicate some resistance to realism, her note at the end of the volume gives a reading of realist short short fiction that is compatible with her own stories:

> People write parables about a world that has nothing to do with the modern world, or parables that do partake of this modern world, or more realistic very brief stories, and these last often begin and end in the middle of things and present us with unheroic characters, reflecting our willingness, now, not to aggrandize our lives, in which if something happens it always begins and ends in the middle of something else and in which there are also, or maybe only, conjunctions of the ridiculous and less ridiculous over and over again.[22]

The style of this note should be familiar already: Davis extends and deepens her list of what people write in a voice that invokes a collective disposition towards diminishment. Like Coover's "A Sudden Story," Davis's work leaves no room in the end for a hero, but she doesn't resort to a dragon to kill the hero off. Her "conjunctions of the ridiculous and less ridiculous over and over again" return her characters and her readers to multiple versions of the thoughts and scenes around which her narratives are carefully woven if sometimes frayed at the edges. We can't pin down the present, and that's her gift: a favorite story and a happiest moment may meld with the eating of a duck, even if someone else is doing the eating. ॐ

---

21 Sudden Fiction. *p. xiv.*

22 Sudden Fiction. *p. 230.*

Paul Beatty's THE SELLOUT

Wendy Rawlings

In 1963, Governor George Wallace stood in the entrance of Foster Auditorium at the University of Alabama and declared, "Segregation now, segregation tomorrow, segregation forever." Fast forward fifty-two years: a five minute walk from Foster Auditorium, I'm getting ready to teach Paul Beatty's novel, *The Sellout*. This is an undergraduate course focused on writing comedy, a class I've taught before. But I've never taught *this* book. In the novel's opening paragraph, the black narrator, by way of establishing his ethos, announces that he has never "boarded a crowded bus or subway car, sat in a seat reserved for the elderly, pulled out my gigantic penis and masturbated to satisfaction with a perverted, yet somehow crestfallen, look on my face." Okay. Deep breath.

I've never taught a comic novel about race written by a black writer before, and this first one is a doozy. Of twelve students in my class, one is an African-American woman. Another is the son of first generation Cuban immigrants. Everyone else is white, including me. They're a smart group, but the novel is linguistically challenging and dense with allusions to American history, particularly our country's lamentable racial history. After the narrator's slave, Hominy Jenkins (yes, this black narrator owns a slave, in the 21st century), begs to be whipped by his master and then attempts suicide when said master refuses, the narrator, nicknamed Bonbon, remarks, "Believe me when I tell you human bondage is an especially frustrating undertaking." The novel proceeds from there with propositions so outrageous—among them, re-segregating a high school in southern California—that the net result of reading this book is feeling as if Paul Beatty has given the middle finger to anyone claiming that America is a post-racial society.

Our class discusses the book's title: what it means in African-American culture to "sell out" others of one's own race. I show a brief Youtube video that features a voiceover discussing the implications of "selling out" as images depicting African-Americans in stereotypical roles flicker by, a painful four minutes of Stepin Fetchits shucking and jiving and cartoon Mammies singing spirituals. The stereotypical representations of African-Americans lead one student to notice that the book jacket of *The Sellout* features a pattern of tiny black lawn jockeys holding lanterns. "What's that all about?" the student asks. I explain that they're statues people—usually white people—used to place in their front yards. "My grandparents had a white one," a student says.

We reflect on why some of us automatically perceive lawn jockeys to be racist symbols. "Someone should Google it," I say, and Rachel, the African-American student, takes out her phone and reads from Wikipedia, "It is said that the lawn jockey had its origins in one Jocko Graves, an African American youth who served with General George Washington at the time he crossed the Delaware to carry out his attack on the British.'" She goes on to tell us that the General thought the boy was too young to take on such a dangerous mission, so he left the boy to wait for him on the shore. The story goes that the boy, "faithful to the post and his orders, froze to death while waiting for his master to return, the lantern still in his hand." Rachel pauses for breath as the rest of us gasp. "The general was so moved by the boy's devotion to his duty that he had a statue made and installed at Mount Vernon. He called the sculpture 'The Faithful Groomsman.'" We sit in silence for a moment, picturing the faithful, frozen kid with his arm extended.

A few weeks earlier, after using the expression, "That'll be a cakewalk," I decided to look up the etymology of that word. It turns out that some historians claim the term originated in the practice of slaves on plantations dressing up and dancing for the entertainment of their masters, with a cake as the prize to the winning couple. While the masters were enjoying the spectacle of their slaves performing, the slaves were mocking the mannerisms of their masters. I ask my students about the meaning of "cakewalk." Everyone knows the colloquial expression that refers to something easy to perform or achieve. Several who grew up in the Deep South remember county fairs where they walked around tables laden with cakes. When an adult called out for them to stop, each child claimed the cake nearest. "No one wanted carrot," one student recalls.

My description of the slave cakewalks fascinates and upsets the students. They're now caught in the conundrum of knowing that customs and iconography they previously perceived to be benign, are anything but. "I wish I could go back to being ignorant," says the student with the bright red dyed streak in her hair.

"No, you don't," says the Cuban student.

The Sellout addresses the knottiest, most perverse aspect of American history—that we allowed some human beings to own other human beings—in the most logical way it can: with the knottiest, most perverse narrative imaginable. While we're laughing, we get sucker punched: this book reveals the ugly, still-beating heart of racism on campus, here in Alabama and at every crossroads in America.

As Bonbon says, human bondage is an especially frustrating undertaking. ❧

Perishables

Becky Hagenston

Dean and Gina from across the street are the first to arrive in the grassy island in the middle of the cul-de-sac. Gina is hauling two folding chairs and Dean pushes a portable grill that looks like a robot trying to fly. I watch from my living room window as they stake their territory. Dean used to be a history professor. He would take students to European battlefields every summer and then submit fraudulent receipts to the study abroad office. I know this because I used to be the study abroad director, and when I asked about the receipts he said something about an affair with a woman in Normandy. Something about never doing it again, even though he did it again. They seem cheerful, Gina and Dean—well-adapted to off-line life. "Ignorance is bliss," Dean actually said to me the other day, and I said, "Until we're rounded up and shot," and he scowled.

"Dad." My daughter Lorna is standing in the middle of the room wearing the pink shorts and halter top her mother bought for her fifteenth birthday. This is apparently a "fun outfit," so I've refrained from saying she looks ridiculous. "I'm not eating a dead deer." She puts her fingers on the window, leaving smudges; in the other hand she's clutching her iPhone, which hasn't worked in months. Outside, Tom Reardon is pulling a deer carcass on a red wagon, his shotgun slung over one shoulder. "Plus, all we have to bring is canned shit like *beans*. God damn it. Where can we get corn chips?"

I don't bother scolding her for language, or remind her how lucky we are that we still have so much canned shit. "First," I say, "build a time machine." This is our joke, whenever we realize we're out of something we never realized we loved so much: *Entertainment Weeklys*, Gatorade, contact lens fluid, Altoids, toilet paper, corn chips. There are other things, I know, that Lorna misses and doesn't tell me about. And there actually had been corn chips until a week ago, when I scavenged them from the back of the cabinet in the middle of the night. I went outside and ate the entire bag myself, staring up at the amazing sky. Electricity is sporadic now, maybe two hours a day. The stars are so bright, and there are so many of them. I stared into the Milky Way as I selfishly crunched, feeling like a terrible person for denying my daughter her corn chips, yet unable to stop. Then I threw the empty bag over the fence to where the Morgans used to live, before—according to rumor—they left for the Alabama border. All four of them: first the teenage boy and girl, then the parents.

"What if we already did build a time machine, and this is where we ended up anyway?" Lorna asks. She looks worried, as if this is an actual possibility.

"Look on the bright side," I say. "This will go down in history as the most disastrous block party of all time."

"In all of human history," Lorna agrees.

"I'll tweet about how awful it is. As if summer in Mississippi doesn't already suck, now it sucks even more."

"I'll post on Facebook how much it sucks."

"I'll post Instantgrams—was that it? I'm starting to forget."

Lorna shrugs. She stares down at the dead phone.

I try again: "I'll text you if I get stuck in any awkward conversations."

"Okay." She looks up. Her hair is too long and hangs in her eyes and makes her look like her mother did at her age. "I'll come to the rescue, I guess."

"And then Mittens will show up, and we'll be like, wait . . . this isn't *so* bad."

Lorna stares at her phone again. "Let's not talk about Mittens."

"No," I say. "Let's not."

It was Joe and Martha Dwyers' idea to have the block party. They live two houses down, an African-American couple of early middle age with grown children who used to arrive for summer visits in Subarus with California license plates. Joe is tall and bald, a former cop, and when I saw him standing on my doorstep last week, I thought: *Shit, he knows about the notes.* But he was smiling in a way that suggested he didn't, so I pulled open the door.

"Why, hey there, Matt," he said. "How goes things?"

I told him things go fine, considering, and he nodded as if this was profound information. "You got your girl here, still?"

"Lorna," I said. "Yeah, she's here. Her mother's still in Boston."

He opened his mouth and then seemed to decide against whatever he was going to say. I considered asking after his own probably-dead family in California, but instead I said, "What's up, Joe?"

And he told me he and Martha were organizing a party for Saturday, for everybody who was left on our block. "Just a time to relax and fellowship with each other. Grill up some veggies, eat some perishables before they go to waste. Tom Reardon's going to shoot that deer keeps eating his greens."

I don't like it when people use *fellowship* as a verb. But I said, "Sounds good, Joe. Thanks for the invite. We'll be there on Saturday." It was a moment later that I realized I didn't know what day it was, and hadn't known for weeks.

These are the people left on our block: Dean and Gina, Joe and Martha, Wayne Jenkins and his son Josh, and Tom Reardon—who is about my age, but as different from me as it's possible to be. Beard, big white pickup truck with NRA and Confederate bumper stickers. We occasionally exchange tense words about whose turn it is to mow the island. His wife—according to Wayne Jenkins—left him a few years back. "Can you blame her?" Wayne said, and we both chuckled. This was before Wayne's son Josh broke my daughter's heart. Josh is seventeen, moon-faced, both thin and soft. A boy who wears visors inside. A boy who, last year, put a big sign in the island inviting one of the Morgan girls to the junior prom. She accepted, apparently: I remember seeing the two of them walking hand in hand a few times. According to Lorna, Melissa Morgan is (was?) a slut and a psycho, and Josh never loved her and only dated her because he felt sorry for her. When she and her family left for the Alabama border, he was glad.

"Okay, that's interesting," was all I could think to say.

MM would rather die than date Josh Jenkins!! Maybe she'll get her wish!!!

That was the note I wrote, folded into a neat football-triangle, and launched across the street, into the yard of a 70-year-old man named Bill who had a Prayer is America's Only Hope sign in his yard. Earlier, I'd written this note—*If Prayer is America's only hope, we are fucked*—and launched it into the Jenkins' yard.

I found this immensely satisfying, almost as satisfying as posting anonymous comments on blogs and right-wing websites. Almost as satisfying as being awake at one, two, three in the morning, engaging in word warfare on my computer while my wife Renee slept in the other room. But then, of course, she walked in on me while I was telling some complete stranger that he (or she) was too stupid to live, *so go ahead and throw yourself in front of a train, you goddamn piece of shit.*

"What are you *doing*?" Renee murmured behind me. "Good God. Who do you hate so much?"

"I have no idea," I admitted, and she started to cry.

"That smells good," Martha is saying, when I make my way out to the island with my bowl of cold baked beans. She's referring either to the yellow squash on the grill or to the smoldering venison in a make-shift fire pit. I put the beans on a card table next to a pile of tomatoes and cucumbers. Tom Reardon is relaxed cross-legged in a folding chair, his shotgun atop his lap, flanked by citronella tiki torches. He looks like a hillbilly on a front porch, with his self-righteous smile. *Fellowshipping.* His smile dims a little when he sees me, the Yankee with the Obama bumper sticker.

"Looks like somebody didn't get around to mowing, am I right?" he says, and pulls a cigarette from his front pocket.

"Well, I guess I was thinking it was Bill's turn," I lie. Bill disappeared a couple of weeks ago. So, oddly enough, did his Prayer sign. He left his house unlocked, a note on the kitchen table: *Please take everything. God Bless.* But—as I saw for myself—there was nothing really to take. No bottled water, no canned goods. Just a useless TV, a cat-clawed sofa.

"Bill's turn is over," says Tom, and something about the way he says it makes me wonder if he's the one who took all the canned goods.

"Good to see you, Tom," I say, as if this is just a regular block party and he's just a regular asshole, and I turn toward the sound of Wayne and Josh's jubilant voices carrying over the lawns, along with what sounds like eighties pop music.

"Anybody call for entertainment?" Wayne says, and this is apparently Josh's cue to heft a battery-powered boom box above his head, like a love-sick kid in a teen movie. I don't think either Josh or Lorna has seen this movie, but I see him turn to look at her shadow in the living room window; I can feel the weight of her eyes as she stares out. Then she's gone, a ghost vanishing. I see Josh's face flush, and Paula Abdul—for this is the cassette blaring from the boom box—is begging *straight up now, tell me*, which now seems less like a frothy pop song than a challenge, or a dare, or a command.

Lorna hasn't left the house in weeks. "There's gunshots outside," she told me, and I told her she was wrong. "Or yes, there's gunshots," I amended. "But it's people hunting rabbits and squirrels. It's not Mittens."

"Shut up about stupid fucking Mittens," she said.

I tell myself I'm being a very good parent, in light of the circumstances. In Boston, Lorna was starting to get in with what Renee called "a bad crowd," meaning kids who skipped school and drank. I reminded Renee that *we* were the bad crowd, once upon a time. I reminded her of those nights I drove us around drunk in my mom's Rabbit, the time we drove stoned to Foxborough in a snowstorm to see INXS.

I didn't remind her of what I have come to think of as my "rotten years," after my ten-year-old brother died. I was twelve. She didn't know me then, when I punched a kid for saying Timothy killed himself. She didn't know me when I put rotten eggs in mailboxes, sent death threats to classmates. A day on Lake Winnipesaukee, Tim and I set out in a rowboat. A storm swept in. I saved myself but couldn't save my brother. So I was the kid who sent threatening letters to the principal, signed with the names of other students, kids who used to be my friends. I was the boy whose family had to move from New Hampshire to Massachusetts, to get away from the rumors and from my own dark heart.

Renee and I split up three years ago. We congratulated ourselves on our impressive run—almost thirty years as a couple—and then I applied for jobs and ended up here. I went to Boston every Christmas, and Lorna came to visit me for a month every summer. I thought of dating again, then thought better of it. And at some point, Lorna and Josh started "hanging out," as she called it. I'm not sure what happened between the two of them, but it happened—whatever it was—when I was still biking to the university to try to pretend everything was normal. Even though summer school was cancelled; even though the internet was out, and the IT team—who I feel extremely sorry for—had abandoned their offices. "Did he hurt you?" I asked, when I found her crying at the kitchen table, writing FUCK YOU, JOSH over and over on a piece of notebook paper. "Did he *kiss* you?" And she got up from the table and slammed into her room.

That's when I began to feel the itch and burn again. I hadn't trolled for almost a year, but now I wanted to tell the entire world to fuck off—starting with Josh and with Bill and his prayer sign. When I'd told Bill what I did for a living, he'd said, "I would not care to go abroad. Too many *Moslems*."

So I launched the note meant for Bill into the Jenkins' yard, and the note meant for them into his. It seemed safer that way. But I had too much to say, so I started filling a cardboard box with notes, folded in tiny squares, and hid the box in my closet. Mostly, the notes I write are just plain immature. *God is an Ass Clown. You are all religious nut-jobs. You're too stupid to know how stupid you are.* Really dumb stuff. *Get back in your redneck pickup truck and drive off a cliff, you moron.*

Statistics show that most guns are used on their owners. Here's hoping.

I am not this person, I tell myself in the middle of the night, as I write *Are you too stupid to know your husband is fucking a woman in Normandy, or are you too smart to care?*

My heart pounds. *One more,* I think. *One more.* The box is almost full. I used to crave the thrill of someone writing back, horrified, calling me an evil, vile human being. Now, nobody writes back, and the box gets fuller. I have suggested that children are better off now that they won't have to go to school. I have said that Christians are fools, that southerners are ignorant. But I'm a good person, I tell myself. This isn't hurting anyone.

Tom Reardon is staring at the boom box like he wants to shoot it. I have some old Johnny Cash tapes somewhere. The thought briefly occurs to me that I could get them and put an end to Paula Abdul, but I decide against it. Gina and Dean have started grooving next to the grill. Somehow, there's beer, and Wayne hands me a bottle of warm Michelob.

"Here's to good friends," I say. "Tonight is kind of special."

"That's so true," he says, seriously.

"Or was that Lowenbrau."

Lorna has appeared in the yard, holding her phone in both hands. She seems stunned to find herself outside, blinking like a sleepwalker. I see Josh swivel in her direction.

"Hey, there," I call to her, but she doesn't answer, just heads around the side of the house, probably to pick some wild strawberries. Josh watches her go.

Wayne has started talking about the rumors. Gina sidles up, chewing on a carrot. Then Joe and Martha. Tom, Dean. We're all standing in a circle on the grassy island as if it's a life raft about to sink.

We'll be completely out of water by next week, Wayne says. Electricity—which we have sporadically now—will be gone. And has everyone noticed the way the animals keep disappearing? The dogs have run off. Even the squirrels: aren't there fewer of those? There have been explosions near Columbus, Mississippi. An entire eleventh grade class was seen marching down highway 82, waving black flags. Or were they American flags? The university burned. Churches are locking people out—or in. Which is it?

Before the internet blackout, we watched footage of helicopters burning, troops marching—but whose helicopters and whose troops? There used to be a news reporter who came around on horseback. He was blonde and wore a pink tie. This is how we found out about Mittens at the Alabama border. Or was it the Tennessee border? Or was it our own government, come to rescue us? Then came the looting. The sound of gunshots in the night. Fliers appeared in mailboxes, a simple message in black and red: YOU CAN MAKE A DIFFERENCE IF YOU JOIN US! And people began to disappear.

"Damn," says Dean. "I never thought I'd say this, but I wish I had a gun." Dean: at least he's studied battlefields. Even without a gun, he knows more than I do about how to stay alive in a war. Strategy. What can I offer? I can show you Oscar Wilde's grave at Père Lachaise; I can tell you the entry fee to the British Museum. I can tell you about my honeymoon in Venice with my twenty-year-old wife, how we dared each other to jump in the canal. How it all seemed so dangerous.

When I first moved here, I was braced for everything I'd heard about Mississippi: the racists, the ignoramuses, the disregard for common sense and healthy eating habits. I fended off a few offers to attend church, and maybe a few people smirked at my Prius. When I told Bill across the street—after about three inquiries about my "home church" and my marital status—that I was a divorced atheist, he didn't gasp and scream hellfire; he just patted my arm and said, very sadly, "I will pray for you."

Even Tom Reardon helped me tear down a rotten dog house in the back yard when I first moved in. Gina and Dean had me over for drinks, and we talked about the best bars in Brussels. My colleagues at the university welcomed me. Everyone has been kind, in their way. Which is why I feel even more awful about the things I think and feel and write on tiny pieces of paper.

Lately, I've directed some comments to myself: *What is wrong with you?*

You are a terrible father.

How can you protect your child, when you don't believe in any of the things you need to believe in?

"We're safest if we stay put," Joe is saying.

You are vile, a bad person, bad bad bad.

"I've got a shotgun you can have," Tom tells Dean. He nods in my direction. "You, too."

I don't bother telling him I've never fired a gun in my life. I say, "Thank you," because I am grateful.

"We could pray every day, make our own church," says Gina. Nodding heads.

Really, the only person I hate right now is Josh, with his goofy smile and his backwards baseball cap. This is a terrible thing to admit, but I wish he would just leave. Disappear. He pops out Paula Abdul, pops in Wham!. These cassettes must be his father's. Or his mother's. What happened to his mother? I realize I never knew.

"Anybody want another grilled squash?" Dean says. The fire pit is dying down. The baked beans are gone. Wayne is eating from a box of stale Wheaties. I discovered the other day that I have wild wheat growing in my yard. Could I make bread? Yes, I decide. We can survive this, until some switch flips the world back on again.

I think of over-hearing Lorna a few weeks ago, talking in her room. "Yes," she was saying. "He's fine. He's very nice." Long pause. "No, of course not! Geez." A longer pause. "He says it's all in the Bible anyway, nothing to be afraid of."

I rapped on her bedroom door.

"What!" she shouted.

"Who are you talking to, honey? Who are you talking to about the Bible?"

She opened the door, held up her dead phone. Her eyes were bright. "I'm talking to Mom," she said. "Are you happy?" And then she slammed the door in my face.

Fine, I thought. *Do what you have to do.* If she wants to believe in an imaginary person looking out for her, that's fine. Maybe it's good.

"We can boil the water from that pond behind the development," Martha is saying.

"My generator'll work for a few months," says Wayne.

The cassette tape clicks itself off mid-song, and no one flips it. The cicadas and the crickets are a riot of sound; everywhere is the rustle of shadow creatures: rabbits, squirrels in their nests. The sun is gone; the street is dark, and the mosquitos are out in full force, despite the citronella torches. I can see the whirl of galaxies above, a small fire far away. A bonfire, perhaps. Another block party. Or something else.

"Let's not call them invaders or beheaders," I suggested a couple of months ago to Lorna.

"What then?"

"Something less scary. The least scary thing you can think of."

"Like Mittens?" She laughed. We once had a cat named Mittens, a white rollie-poly kitten who grew fat and lazy. She'd curl up at your neck while you slept.

"That's it. There's no reason to be afraid of Mittens."

She laughed again, then grew sober. "Mittens got hit by a car."

"Let's bow our heads," says Joe now.

I bow my head, close my eyes, and try not to think of the study abroad students who were in the air when whatever happened happened. I try not to think of the students deep in the Paris metro when everything stopped. "Have faith," is what people say. Believe in what you can't know for sure.

The fire in the pit is flittering out, everyone fading to shadow. The two beers—my first in months—have made me feel calm, benevolent, even hopeful. Inspired.

"I'll be right back," I say, and I dash into the house, into my dark bedroom, and pull the box of notes from the closet. I'll burn them, burn the whole box. *See?* I will say. *I have something to offer after all.*

"Kindling!" I call, as I carry the box out to the island, to the sputtering fire. The dark sky is growing darker; there is a smell of rain in the air.

Joe is still standing in the middle of the island, tiki torches burning around him like in that TV show Renee and I used to watch. "Whatever our differences, wherever we come from." Joe looks at me. "We have the greatest chance of survival if we're in this together." Yes—*Survivor*. That was it. I feel myself grinning, even though I know nothing is funny. "We can't have any more of our people, especially our young people, running off to the border."

Josh and Lorna are shadows in the bushes, but I can tell they're holding hands.

It's them, I realize, and my heart feels like a grenade, the pin in Lorna's hand as she moves away, into the darkness. They're the young people planning to run off. And here I was worried about him kissing her and breaking her heart. Now I remember something else I heard her saying on the phone to her imaginary Mom: *It's all going to be okay if we stay on the right path. We can make a difference!*

She never fucking talked like that before.

The fire is almost out. I squat next to the fire pit with the box, scoop a handful of paper into the dying flames. There's a spark, a flicker of new flame. A gunshot in the distance. I add more paper, create more light, stand and scan the yard for my daughter. "Lorna!"

I feel a sudden gust of wind, and then the notes are in the air, some still folded, some on fire, some falling like sparks, some rising like snow.

"Fortune cookies!" says Martha, chasing a piece of paper into the street.

"Lorna?" I call, and I head across my lawn, but even in the firelight I can't see where she's gone. Another gust of wind whiffles the shrubs; a piece of paper drifts by my face.

First, I think, *build a time machine.*

Everyone is laughing, even Tom, as the notes fly and burn and flutter, as if I've brought them party favors, a reason to celebrate. I make my way around the house, past the sweet-smelling jasmine bushes and wild strawberries, all the way back to the island and its torches and fire. "Lorna!" I shout. But she doesn't answer. The stars wheel above me, and the laughter of my neighbors trails into silence as they catch hold of those falling scraps of paper—no one's fortune but mine—and unfold them, and begin to read. ❧

superstition [review]
an online literary magazine

[art, fiction, interviews, nonfiction, poetry]

recently featuring...

Aimee Bender
David Kirby
Susan Steinberg
Lee Martin
Kamilah Aisha Moon
Adam Johnson
Alix Ohlin
Ira Sukrungruang

"I would recommend Superstition Review to
anyone who wants good, honest writing."

The Review Review

 Superstition Review @SuperstitionRev  superstition.review@gmail.com

  @SuperstitionRev Superstition Review  superstitionreview.com

THE STORIES OF BREECE D'J PANCAKE

Jason Ockert

Not long ago a friend asked, "If a new book was discovered by a dead writer, which writer would you want to have written that book?" My first instinct was to say Flannery O'Connor. I cut my literary teeth on her and would trade a pair of incisors to read some resurrected manuscript she'd penned. Still, though, we've got three of her books and lots of notes and letters. There's an army of O'Connor scholars to boot. So, I thought twice and answered, Breece Pancake, a writer I've only recently discovered.

Pancake's one and only book, a collection entitled, *The Stories of Breece D'J Pancake*, was published posthumously in 1983. It was nominated for a Pulitzer and he was lauded by a pantheon of notable writers including Joyce Carol Oates, Andre Dubus III, and Kurt Vonnegut. There's no reason why I shouldn't have read him sooner. My hunch is that it's because the book is rather quiet. It's introspective and unassuming. It reads like it doesn't really need you.

It's difficult to put your finger on what makes a great writer great or a moving book moving. Hard to say why one book is esteemed while others equally great are not. The authors I like best are mystery-keepers. They write stories that offer clues to a riddle I didn't quite know I was puzzling through. I'm drawn to stories that unsettle. Ones that leave me—that I leave—a bit mystified. Sometimes the best books are the hardest to explain; each time you try, you omit something, and in frustration, thrust the book into a friend's hands and say, "Just read it." (Flannery O'Connor had it right when she said: "A story is a way to say something that can't be said any other way, and it takes every word in the story to say what the meaning is.")

On the cover of my copy of *The Stories of Breece D'J Pancake* there's a black-and-white sketch of a fox head accompanied by its shadow. (I'm curious what overhead light is creating that shadow. Maybe some cold sun in an unseen sky.) The fox's eyes are fixed on something we can't see (maybe a rabbit; maybe its own demise). For certain, it's not looking at us. Inside the book you'll find stories that are set in rural West Virginia populated by rugged, downtrodden, grizzled folks. While you'll find plenty of violence woven into the stories, stark and raw, the key that tripped the lock for me was the role that animals play in the book.

Like good writers, animals are secretive, too. We observe them and draw conclusions about patterns of behavior. Scientists follow methods and make claims. There are books and magazines about all kinds of creatures. You could fill a library with texts about dogs. I suspect that people are fascinated by animals because they are not us. They are not burdened by our hopes and dreams, our anxieties, trepidations, and vanities. Animals remind us what it's like to be wild.

Most of the protagonists in Pancake's stories are outcasts. They're awkward in the company of others and more at home on the fringe where a bevy of critters live. On one hand, there are the animals that are killed in the stories: "turkles" (turtles) in "Trilobites," dogs in "Hollow," a rabbit in "The Mark," and squirrels in "First Day of Winter." The narrator in "The Scrapper" recollects grouse-hunting and ". . . the funny human noises the birds made before they flew, and how their necks were always broken when you picked them up."

On the other hand, there are a number of animals that survive. The closing perspective of "Hollow" is given to a bobcat as he watches and waits for the protagonist to leave. "Fox Hunters" opens from the point of view of an opossum. The fox, in the same story, escapes when the protagonist, Bo, decides to protect it. When asked, Bo explains in a drunken slur, "I's sorry, but I's tryin' to save foxie." The widower in "Time and Again" refuses to slaughter his hogs and comments, "Hogs die hard. I seen people die in the war easier than a hog at a butchering."

The animals are more than simply a part of the landscape; they are entwined with the lifestyle of the people. The sentiments of the characters are transposed onto the creatures. There's a second fox that appears in the collection which, in a "fit of meanness," the character tries to shoot. He misses. That same story, "First Day of Winter," my favorite, ends this way: "The sun was blackened with snow, and the valley closed in quietly with humming, quietly as an hour of prayer."

The strength of this book is in that palpable silence and the sad hope that somewhere somebody is bearing witness to folks who are struggling and unnoticed. That's how I try to write: unabashedly and with a modicum of faith. Pancake's home was rural West Virginia but the breadth of his sweeping empathy knew no bounds.

Perhaps the writer understood that within the primitive is mystery. Through all the rabid violence and feral desperation from a collection of disparate men, it's the moments of calm that resonate. It's a little like cupping your hands into a stream after you've been chased by a bear. Only after your heart stops pounding do you realize how thirsty you are. That's what this book is in your hands. I recommend you sip, not gulp, because it's all you get. ❧

Index

The following is a listing in alphabetical order by author's last name of works published in *Post Road*. An asterisk indicates subject rather than contributor.